BRITISH TRAMWAY ACCIDENTS

BY

FRANK E WILSON

MCIT, FPWI

EDITED BY

G B CLAYDON

CB, LLB, CMILT, MInstTA

PUBLISHED BY

ADAM GORDON

2 0 0 6

ISBN: 1-874422-58-3 (978-1-874422-58-7)

Publication no. 60

Published in 2006 by Adam Gordon, Kintradwell Farm, Brora, Sutherland KW9 6LU

Tel: 01408 622660

E-mail: adam@adamgordon.freewire.co.uk

Printed by: Launton Digital Press Ltd, Fritwell, Oxfordshire

CONTENTS

Page

THE AUTHOR — 4

EDITORIAL NOTE — 6

BRITISH TRAMWAY ACCIDENTS

    PART I   – Administrative and Legal Background by G B Claydon — 9
    PART II – Tramway Accidents Reviewed by Frank E Wilson — 19

APPENDIX A:
Accidents listed by location, with operators, dates and fatalities — 195

APPENDIX B:
Details of certain Railway Inspectorate inquiries culled from trade journals — 198

APPENDIX C:
Review by J D Markham of the Mossley accident of 20 October 1911 — 200

APPENDIX D:
Commentary by J D Markham on the report of the Rawtenstall accident
of 11 November 1911 — 205

APPENDIX E:
Instructions to conductors by Tynemouth & District Electric Traction
Company following the Tynemouth accident of 27 September 1919 — 207

APPENDIX F:
Facsimile copies of Railway Inspectorate reports of significant tramway
accidents in Dover, Rawtenstall and Mossley — 208

APPENDIX G:
Miscellaneous photographs of tramway accidents not the subject of
Railway Inspectorate reports appearing in the text — 221

THE AUTHOR

FRANK EDWARD WILSON was born in Clapham, London, on 10 August 1905, within sight of the Wandsworth Road horse tramway. He was the second of three children and his father served as a bandsman with the Scots Guards and later was a trombonist with the Sadler's Wells Opera Company. After attending local schools, Frank became an undergraduate at the Battersea Polytechnic, where he studied under A T Dover, the authority on electric traction, and where, so he claimed, one of his fellow students was William Joyce, later to become the Nazi collaborator "Lord Haw-Haw" ("he didn't like trams!"). Frank's interest in transport led to a career in the railway industry, beginning with his joining the London & North Eastern Railway Company in 1924. Later he was to play a major part in organising the operation and maintenance of loco-motives and rolling stock, duties especially vital during World War II, when he was Chief Running Foreman at Stratford, East London, with responsibility for a workforce of 1,700. At the time of his retirement, he was Chief Safety Officer for the Eastern Region of British Railways.

He exhibited an early interest in tramways: even at the age of four he showed an inordi-nate interest in the sound of tramcar wheels passing over points and crossings. He soon formed a deep attachment to the tramways of the London County Council (LCC), espe-cially its conduit operations, as is demonstrated in the pages that follow. He was also fortunate that a favourable distribution of aunts and family friends allowed him to visit, even before he was eleven, the tramway systems of Torquay, Bournemouth, Peterborough, Sheffield, Rotherham, Llandudno, the MET, the LUT, Southmet, Thanet, Hastings, Croydon and Yarmouth.

During the General Strike of 1926, he volunteered to assist in keeping London's trams running, spending five adventurous days at New Cross depot, training as a conductor and driver, and taking the road through hostile crowds. He became an outstanding tramway modeller, working to a scale of ¾ inch to the foot, even constructing a working conduit layout. His tramcar models, not surprisingly, were representatives of LCC tramway classes and (for reasons which will shortly become apparent) also various types of Guernsey cars. Interest in models drew him to the Tramway & Light Railway Society, and he was its chairman for many years, before becoming a vice-president and ultimately its president. Each year, in his memory, the society runs a competition which awards the Frank Wilson trophy for the best tramcar model. As to his own models, certain of them were on display at the Science Museum, South Kensington, but all his LCC models are now held by the Tramway and Light Railway Society and the Guernsey models are in the custody of a Guernsey museum, save for one on display at the National Tramway Museum, Crich.

In 1961, he produced an informative technical work, its scope aptly summed up by its title *The British Tram*. Then in 1970 he delivered the inaugural Walter Gratwicke memo-rial lecture, significantly taking as his subject *Permanent Way with Special Reference to the LCC Tramways*. He was a Fellow of the Permanent Way Institute and an active member of the Chartered Institute of Transport.

Frank had been a visitor to the Channel Islands from 1923, and in 1933 he married a Guernsey girl, Lily Maud Bewey. They had a daughter, Jancis, who now resides in the Isle of Wight. With the passing years, he developed an ever-closer affinity with Guernsey and went to live there after his retirement in 1968. His interest in the islands led to his becoming president in 1972 of the Guernsey branch of the Channel Islands Occupation Society. He also carried out researches into the former Guernsey tramway and railway, culminating in his publishing *Railways in Guernsey*, which was described as a book "which only a railwayman could have produced". He was engaged in other projects, including this work, at the time of his death from leukaemia on 7 November 1975. So saw the passing of a strong-minded, but kindly and engaging personality: one of whom it could verily be said that he was "the salt of the earth". It is hoped that this publication will serve as a fitting testimony to his memory.

EDITORIAL NOTE

WHEN FRANK WILSON died in November 1975, he was part-way through writing a book on British tramway accidents, based on the reports of such accidents that had been prepared over the years by officers of the Railway Inspectorate as a result of the inquiries held by them. It was a work which I had encouraged him to write and over which he had consulted me, as a colleague and friend. His death was therefore both a sad event in itself and the loss of a contribution to tramway history and technology.

After his death, I was therefore moved to take over the incomplete manuscript from his widow, Lily, with the intention of completing the work and seeing it through to publication. I was at that time heavily-engaged in the Government Legal Service and made it clear that I would not be able to undertake the task until my retirement from work. In the event, my formal retirement was deferred until 1995, engaged, as I was, in overhauling tramway and railway legislation then on the statute book and little changed from the 19th century. Then, even in so-called retirement, I found that I was still helping both Government and professional bodies in monitoring and advising on such legislation. In truth, retirement (as such) has never come about. It is therefore only recently that I have been able to honour my long-outstanding pledge.

So far as the manuscript itself is concerned, the first task was to identify the parts which had not been completed. These were mainly accounts of accident reports of which Frank Wilson did not have copies and so was unable to incorporate in his text. Chasing copies of these missing reports has not been an easy task, and I extend particular thanks to Major John Poyntz, formerly of HM Railway Inspectorate, for his kindness and cooperation in making those available from the archives of the Inspectorate. Even such parts of the manuscript that were extant were not in straightforward form. Much of the text was clearly in a preliminary stage of writing; text which had originally been type-written was often overwritten or interlineated in ink; some parts were solely in the author's hand, which was not always easy to decipher. At other points, Frank Wilson would append riders by means of pins, and sometimes there would be scribbled instructions in the margins. So the task of converting the text to computer-based form has been a mammoth effort and I am profoundly grateful to my publisher, Adam Gordon, for undertaking this gruelling exercise.

Frank Wilson had, of course, an engineering background and he commented from an engineering point of view. Because the manuscript was both in preliminary form and incomplete, I felt it highly desirable to have any adjustments and supplements made to it checked by an engineer. Here, too, I have been fortunate in engaging the services of someone sympathetic to the project, namely John Markham, who is an engineer with widespread electric traction experience and, before his retirement, was a member of the Railway Inspectorate.

Many others have assisted in the compilation of this work. This assistance is for the most part acknowledged on an individual basis in footnotes and acknowledgments at relevant points in the text. But at this juncture I also offer general thanks to Glynn Wilton, Curator of the National Tramway Museum, Chris Gent, David Frodsham and Frank Palmer of the Tramway Museum Society, John Prentice, the Chairman of the Tramway and Light Rail Society, David Voice, the Archivist of that body, Ian Stewart of the Scottish Tramway and Transport Society, and Alan Brotchie. My warmest thanks also go to my publisher, Adam Gordon, and his colleague, Trevor Preece, for their generous acceptance of my somewhat demanding typographical and layout requirements, often at variance with their own house style.

Frank Wilson's style tends to be somewhat discursive, but it seemed right to retain his often lengthy digressions. Apart from being a notable characteristic of his writings, the digressions often offer illuminating vignettes of issues rarely recorded elsewhere. For like reasons, it has been thought appropriate to retain his robust swipes at what he perceived to be the follies and shortcomings of his day. It needs also to be borne in mind that at the time he was writing he supposed tramways in this country to be largely a phenomenon of the past, so that much of his work adopts the past tense. It was not until a decade after his death that the first stirrings of the British tramway renaissance became evident. Nor was he in a position to anticipate the subsequent growth of heritage tramways in this country.

So as not to commit too much violence to the text, many of the editorial adjustments have taken the form of footnotes. Frank Wilson himself contemplated the use of footnotes, and some of them are his, but most have been contributed by either John Markham or myself. Given the former's command of the subject, and knowledge of the ways of the Railway Inspectorate, I have thought it useful to readers to include some associated contributions from him in Appendices. It has also been thought appropriate to retain references to measurements in imperial units since these are the units employed in the reports. For the same reason, references to pre-decimal currency have been retained.

Frank Wilson left virtually nothing in the way of illustrations, although it was clear that he intended to include both technical drawings and photographs. I have therefore drawn heavily on the photographic archives of the John Price Memorial Library, at the National Tramway Museum, Crich, Derbyshire, and also the resources of my publisher, Adam Gordon. Other illustrations have kindly been provided by tramway colleagues. The line drawings have come from the pages of Dover's *Electric Traction* (both the 1917 and 1929 editions) and the I.C.S. Reference Library. The opportunity has also been taken to reproduce in facsimile some of the Railway Inspectorate's accident reports.

Part I, which follows, deals with the administrative and organisational aspects governing the Railway Inspectorate's operations. Frank Wilson touched on some of these, but the references were dispersed amongst the text and they have largely been overtaken by recent events. So I have contributed Part I and taken the opportunity to bring the story together and up-to-date in view of recent radical changes.

In Part II, the accidents are considered in chronological order. To assist readers who may wish to check on a particular accident, the date of which is uncertain to them, the accidents have also been listed in alphabetical order according to location in Appendix A, along with other information.

A word or two on the title of this work. It may be objected that *British Tramway*

Accidents, is not strictly correct since one accident considered relates to Dublin tramways. However, as this is the only reference in Part II to an Irish tramway accident (an indication perhaps of the island's excellent safety record), it would surely have been misleading to have widened the title to "British and Irish Tramway Accidents" and I trust therefore that readers, particularly Irish readers, will find this explanation acceptable. By the same token, trolleybuses: the text contains two accounts of trolleybus accidents, but again it seemed inappropriate to add a mention of these in the title given this minimal coverage.

Perhaps in writing about tramway accidents, I should, like Wilson, admit to having had personal experience of them. My most dramatic encounter occurred in April 1977 when, while travelling on a tram in Lisbon, it was violently struck in the rear by a runaway car of older and more robust design, which overrode and demolished the back platform of the car in which I was travelling. Although the sudden impact brought my head into sharp contact with an adjacent draughtscreen, more memorable for me was the sight of the runaway tram embedded into my tram to such an extent that the fender and cab of the former had come to rest against the rear saloon bulkhead of the latter. Combined with this vision was an ear-splitting hiss, as compressed air from ruptured air piping escaped, causing passengers to be showered in dust and dirt. No one was severely injured. Two colleagues who had been standing on the back platform of my car fortunately saw the runaway racing towards them and leaped quickly back into the saloon moments before the impact!

Returning to the chronicle of this publication, I have to report that Lily Wilson, alas, has also died, and so it is to their daughter, Jancis, that I offer my most profound apologies for the long delay in the publication of this work. I trust that she and other readers will find it not only an informative and interesting contribution to tramway history, but also a work that may offer some lessons and guidance for both modern light rail systems and for the dozen or so heritage lines now established in this country. Most of the latter are still using traditional equipments, of the kind described in the accompanying text, so what has been written may well have particular relevance for them. And, in any event, while both modern and heritage enterprises have good safety records, some of the elements of past failures, such as human frailty, are likely to be forever with us.

Finally, may I ask readers to bear in mind that wherever the first person singular is used in the pages which follow (except where otherwise attributed, such as in quotations), it will be the voice of Frank Wilson that will be speaking?

G. B. Claydon

London and Duffield
August 2006

BRITISH TRAMWAY ACCIDENTS

PART I

ADMINISTRATIVE AND LEGAL BACKGROUND

by G B Claydon

The roles of Parliament and Government

THE RAILWAY AGE, as we know it, began with the opening of the Liverpool and Manchester Railway in 1830. This new mode of travel soon attracted the patronage of the upper and middle classes. From the opening day when, as many will recall, a former President of the Board of Trade, William Huskisson, was killed, accidents occurred on the railways and, given the nature of the patronage, Parliament and Government soon took a keen interest in such matters, with early legislation designed to reduce the liability for accidents. At the same time, the Board of Trade was designated the Government department with responsibility for overseeing railway operations.

With the passing of the Tramways Act in 1870, tramways were recognised as a mode of transport separate from railways, but they still followed in the wake of railways and they too came under the overall supervision of the Board of Trade. When the further mode of light railway later emerged, responsibility for this form of transport was conferred on Light Railway Commissioners by the Light Railways Act 1896. Then in 1919 the Ministry of Transport Act of that year established the Ministry of that name "for the purpose of improving the means of, and the facilities for, locomotion and transport". At the same time, all the powers and duties of other government departments, including those of the Board of Trade, in relation to railways, tramways and light railways, and trolleybuses, were transferred to the Minister of Transport, although the Light Railway Commissioners survived until 1921, when their residual functions were merged with those of the Minister of Transport.

Over the years, the title of Minister of Transport changed: for example to "War Transport" during World War II and to "Transport and Civil Aviation" from 1953 until 1959. In 1970, the Ministry of Transport was dissolved (although the term "MoT test" for motor vehicles lives on from those days[1]) and the functions of the Minister were transferred to the Secretary of State for the Environment. After several more metamorphoses, general responsibility for railways, light railways and tramways, together with trolleybuses and certain other guided transport systems, has now come to reside with the Secretary of State for Transport, heading a department styled the Department for Transport.

---

[1] *Cf* compulsory "Board of Trade" stops on tramways.

More recently, responsibility for the investigation of railway and tramway accidents passed to the Health & Safety Executive and, even more recently, to the Rail Accident Investigation Branch of the Department for Transport. More is said on this below.

Safety

Of particular relevance for the purposes of this publication is the manner in which issues of tramway safety have been dealt with. Although the Tramways Act 1870 required any new section of tramway not to "be opened for public traffic until the same has been inspected and certified to be fit for such traffic", the Act was silent on the subject of investigation of accidents. However, following the recommendations of a House of Commons' select committee which reported in 1870, the following year saw the passage of the Regulation of Railways Act. This applied to tramways as well as to railways and provided for:

(1)   the reporting of railway and tramway accidents to the Board of Trade;

(2)   the Board to appoint inspectors to make inquiries into the cause of any railway or tramway accident;

(3)   powers to be conferred on such inspectors in performance of their duties –

(a) to enter any property;
(b) to require the attendance for examination of any person concerned with the railway or tramway and require that person to answer any questions put to him by an inspector; and
(c) to require the production of any relevant documentation;

(4)   the Board to direct the setting up of formal inquiries with equivalent powers to those of a court of law;

(5)   the Board to be able to appoint inspectors to act as assessors to assist coroners in the holding of inquests into railway or tramway accidents.

Section 7(4) of the Act was of special relevance in the context of this work. It provided:

> *An inspector making an inquiry into any accident . . . shall make a report to the Board of Trade stating the causes of the accident and all the circumstances attending the same, and any observations thereon or on the evidence or on any matters arising out of the investigation which* [he thinks] *right to make to the Board of Trade, and the Board of Trade shall cause every such report to be made public in such manner as they think expedient.*

It should be noted that the 1871 Act was limited in its application to railways and tramways authorised by statute[2] and was primarily concerned with safety of the public, whether as passengers or as members of the public otherwise caught up in rail accidents. Safety of the workforce received lesser emphasis and it was not until the passing of the Railway Employment (Prevention of Accidents) Act 1900 that attention also focused on "railway servants" and with them the appointment of Railway Employment Inspectors.

These powers, vested in the Board of Trade (BoT), followed the same progression of transfers as those outlined above in relation to the general issues, ultimately coming to rest with the Secretary of State for Transport. But with the passing of the Railways Act 1993 and certain Regulations in 1997, responsibility for safety matters relating to railways and tramways, other guided transport systems and trolleybuses, was handed over to the Health & Safety Executive (HSE) and put under the more general powers of the Health and Safety at Work etc Act 1974, including powers regarding the appointment of inspectors, their own powers and the holding of inquiries. The 1871 Act was thereupon repealed.

Contrary to the emphasis on public safety adopted by the earlier railway legislation, for the Health and Safety at Work etc Act the emphasis was on safety of the workforce (as the Act's title demonstrates). It is, of course, towards public safety that the accident reports, the subject of this work, were principally directed. This change of emphasis has manifested itself in a number of ways. For example, there is no longer an obligation for the reports of accidents to be published, as we have seen a strong feature of the 1871 Act[3], although the practice (begun in 1870) of producing each year a report to Government on the safety record of the country's railways and tramways has been continued. Recently, in the light of a report by Lord Cullen into the Ladbroke Grove railway accident of 5 October 1999[4], certain safety responsibilities have been repatriated to the Secretary of State for Transport pursuant to the Railways and Transport Safety Act 2003. In particular, a Rail Accident Investigation Branch has now been established within the Department for Transport, charged with the task of investigating significant railway and tramway accidents[5].

HM Railway Inspectorate

Having briefly noted the legislative structure, we now need to examine the personnel engaged in the task of carrying out the requisite inspections and investigations, in

---

[2] The Act referred to "a railway or tramway . . which has been authorised by any special Act of Parliament". This was bad drafting since it overlooked the fact that tramways sanctioned by provisional order under the Tramways Act 1870 were not authorised by special Act and so were excluded. So far as the Editor is aware, this point was never taken in any proceedings. Apart from the original G F Train lines and pier tramways, non-statutory tramways were rare: notable examples were Alexandra Park, Cruden Bay, Pwllheli, Shipley Glen and Warrenpoint & Rostrevor. The advent of heritage tramways produced further instances: Black Country Living Museum (Dudley), East Anglia Transport Museum (Carlton Colville), Heaton Park (Manchester), National Tramway Museum (Crich), North of England Open Air Museum (Beamish) and Summerlee Heritage Museum (Coatbridge). Non-statutory tramways were brought within scope of the investigation process by the Transport and Works Act 1992.

[3] Note in this context that the report of the collision that occurred on the Great Orme Tramway on 30 April 2000 has never been published by HSE. Nonetheless, for sake of completeness, an account of this accident has been included in this work (as the last item in Part II *infra*). This has been compiled by J D Markham, who chanced to be the Inspector who investigated the accident.

[4] This was not an inquiry conducted by the Railway Inspectorate: it was a public inquiry directed to be held by the Health & Safety Commission, with the consent of the Deputy Prime Minister, pursuant to section 14 of the Health and Safety at Work etc Act 1974.

[5] The new legislation contains a number of arcane limitations: the Act does not apply to tramways in Scotland (s 14(2)) although it applies to railways there; whereas there is an obligation to investigate serious railway accidents, this is not so in the case of serious tramway accidents (s 7(1) and (2)); and the Regulations made under the Act apply only to railways and tramways that are crossed by a public carriageway (reg 3).

Catherine Slack, Queensbury, on 3 December 1920, with tramcars 98 and 50 of Halifax Corporation overturned by wind pressure. *Courtesy: National Tramway Museum*

generally enforcing the legislation and in advising Government on these and allied matters. These various activities have fallen to be undertaken by the Railway Inspectorate. This body came into existence in 1840, with the enactment of the Regulation of Railways Act in that year. That Act authorised the BoT to call for returns of traffic on the railways, as well as of all accidents attended with personal injury, and sanctioned the appointment of inspectors under the Board. The first person to hold such a position, with the title of Inspector General of Railways, was Lt-Colonel Sir Frederic Smith. He and his successors until recent times were drawn from officers of the Corps of Royal Engineers.

The choice of sapper officers for the important duties involved was motivated by the desire to secure a wide engineering knowledge, combined with broad general judgement and freedom from bias with regard to railway (and later tramway) managements, their employees, or any interfering interest, so as to secure impartial treatment of the frequently grave issues involved in assessing the causes and full consequences of an accident, or other matter calling for an expression of opinion and the tendering of advice to government. Their army background conferred on them a natural authority and sense of order: further useful attributes in conducting an investigation. The system accordingly provided an adequate degree of government supervision, exercised with the minimum of statutory powers and with an economy of staff unequalled in any other country. The effectiveness of this approach was clearly demonstrated over the years, not least by the high standards of safety achieved for both railways and tramways.

As already explained, the need to place the investigation of accidents on a proper footing was recognised by the passing of the Regulation of Railways Act 1871. Initially, the possibility of major tramway accidents occurring was not in contemplation given that at that time the well-nigh universal mode of traction for trams was limited to the horse[6].

All this changed, of course, with the advent of steam, cable and electric traction for tramways, although the first accident recorded in Part II was actually a product of gravity operation.

But it has to be recognised that any tramway may be at the mercy of forces outside its control: wind pressure resulting in an overturning is an obvious example. Perhaps the classic example of this phenomenon took place in the remote surroundings of Catherine Slack, Queensbury, West Riding, on 3 December 1920, when cars nos. 50 and 98 of Halifax Corporation were successively toppled by gales. A bizarre example of a different kind occurred in Dublin on 28 November 1921, when a ship struck Victoria Bridge, which carried the Sandymount tramway over the Grand Canal Dock, causing its bowsprit to soar over the parapet and penetrate the window of Dublin United tramcar no. 233, which chanced to be passing over the bridge at the time. Luckily, passengers and crew escaped injury[7]. An unusual recent example, selected for its horse tramway context, given what has been said above, occurred in Douglas, Isle of Man, which happily still has a horse tramway system. On the afternoon of 10 September 1999, as covered crossbench car no. 35 of Douglas Corporation was proceeding along Loch Promenade, a large crane working on an adjacent building site swung round in such a manner that its counterweight struck the car, crushing its rear half and bringing down the roof. There were only two passengers on board, two elderly ladies, one of whom was as a consequence detained in hospital with head and back injuries. Fortunately, the conductor was with the driver on the front platform of the car, and both they, and the horse, escaped injury. The car was later rebuilt[8].

In the first few years after the passing of the 1871 Act, the Inspectorate's major concern with tramways was with their inspection and certification prior to opening. In this role was usually to be found that most celebrated of Railway Inspectors, C S Hutchinson, who, it has been calculated, made 6,500 railway and tramway inspections and travelled on duty 1,250,000 miles. He is also said to have conducted 1,100 inquiries into accidents[9]. Charles Scrope Hutchinson (1826-1912) joined the Inspectorate in 1867 as an Inspecting Officer, when he was a Lt-Colonel. Later promoted to full Colonel, he retired from the army in 1877 with the honorary rank of Major-General. He served as Chief Inspecting Officer of Railways from 1892 until his retirement in 1895. During the period 1876 to 1879, he was heavily engaged in providing advice to the several select committees of the House of Commons and the House of Lords set up to consider the application of steam power to street tramways, travelling for this purpose to several Continental cities which already had steam-operated tramways.

---

[6] The occasional serious accident did occur on horse tramways as an innate feature of their operation. For example, on the incline in Leith Street, Edinburgh, on 24 September 1873, a heavily-loaded tramcar overcame its brakes and horses and careered down the hill until it collided with a car in front, resulting in a number of casualties: see *Edinburgh's Transport*, by D L G Hunter, published by The Advertiser Press, Huddersfield, 1964, at p 23.

[7] Even more bizarre, this was one of three encounters that the ship, a schooner named the *Cymric*, had with this particular bridge. Fortunately the other collisions did not involve tramcars. The Editor is indebted to R Clifton Flewitt for providing the information concerning these incidents.

[8] The Editor is indebted to Paul H Abell for providing information on which the account of this accident is based.

[9] These statistics are taken from *Railway Detectives: The 150-year Saga of the Railway Inspectorate* by Stanley Hall, published by Ian Allan, London, 1990, at p 30.

Car 35 of Douglas Corporation at Loch Promenade, Douglas, on 10 September 1999.   The car is seen severely damaged after coming into contact with the crane in the background.

D Lloyd-Jones

However, General Hutchinson's principal duties were concerned with railways and it was he who inspected the recently-constructed Tay Bridge in February 1878 and declared it fit for railway traffic.   As we all know, the bridge collapsed in a storm barely 18 months later and much criticism was accordingly levelled at him in that connection.   This led the then President of the Board of Trade, Joseph Chamberlain, on 15 July 1880, to issue a memorable statement, extracts from which are set out below.

> *My Lords desire, in the first place, to state that they have always placed entire confidence in Major-General Hutchinson.   No more competent, conscientious and intelligent officer could be found to whom to entrust the inspection of the structure in question, and they are of opinion that his conduct of that inspection has not been such as to forfeit their confidence . . .*
>
> *The Board of Trade are unwilling to conclude this minute without some general remarks on the policy of the legislation to which they have adverted.   It may appear to some that the present state of things is one which cannot be logically defended and that the Board of Trade ought to be entrusted with further powers. The experience of a great number of years has, however, shown that the present*

system does not work unsatisfactorily, and a little consideration will show that the public safety and confidence would not be promoted by such a change.

In the first place, if the Board of Trade were to be held responsible for the designs of railway structures and for the supervision of their execution, they must employ a staff as experienced, as numerous, and probably as highly remunerated, as the civil engineers by and under whom these structures are now designed and executed . . . If any public department were entrusted with the power and duty of correcting and guaranteeing the designs of those engineers who are responsible for railway structures, the result would be to check and control the enterprise which has done so much for this country, and to substitute for the real responsibility which rests on the railway engineer the unreal and delusive responsibility of a public office . . . To say nothing of the necessary evils of double management, any Government department exercising such control would, if slack in their supervision, appear to guarantee methods of working which might be really faulty and insufficient, and would, if the supervision were more stringent, interfere with railway management to such an extent as to alienate from it the public confidence and destroy with it its moral influence and its capacity for usefulness.

This approach is in marked contrast to that adopted for the motor vehicle industry, where Government determines standards of vehicles by means of the very detailed and prescriptive Construction and Use Regulations. But the approach has received strong reinforcement recently with the HSE planning to discontinue even the approvals procedure instituted by the Tramways Act for new or altered works (it was of course in respect of the equivalent inspection requirements for railways over which Hutchinson was taken to task). Instead, it is proposed that this task should in future be performed by a "competent person" selected by the undertaking concerned (the "duty holder").

Changes have come to the Inspectorate too. In 1990, to commemorate the Inspectorate's 150th anniversary, the Queen was pleased to bestow the title *Her Majesty's* Railway Inspectorate on that body. Other changes have been less felicitous. The link with the Royal Engineers was broken and, after having formed part of the Government department concerned with transport since its inception, the Inspectorate was transferred in 1989 to the HSE to become one of several inspectorates under that body's command. Apart from thus losing its separate identity and special character (it may be noted, for example, that apart from Sir Frederic Smith, no fewer than nine other inspectors received knighthoods[10]), inspectors became more like ordinary civil servants, sometimes to be switched around from inspectorate to inspectorate. The egalitarian nature of the new regime ensured that the title of "Officer" was dropped, so that, for example, the Chief Inspecting Officer of Railways became the Chief Inspector of Railways (later metamorphosed into the Director of the Rail Inspectorate)[11].

A crowning irony was that the Inspectorate was judged to be dealing with a "hazardous" industry and it was accordingly "brigaded" with the inspectorates dealing with chemical

---

[10] Sir Charles Pasley, Sir Lintorn Simmons, Sir Robert Laffan, Sir Douglas Galton, Sir Henry Tyler, Sir Francis Marindin, Sir Arthur Yorke, Sir John Pringle and Sir Alan Mount.

[11] The title "Chief Inspector" has returned to favour, with both the Rail Accident Investigation Branch and the Office of Rail Regulation adopting this designation. The current holders of both posts are women.

15

plants and nuclear and offshore oil and gas installations (a decision which had most unfortunate repercussions for railways and tramways seeking to secure or maintain insurance cover). However, the effect on the Inspectorate of its relationship with the HSE had not gone unperceived. This was made clear in a government White Paper that was published in July 2004 and which proposed that the Inspectorate should be removed from the HSE and placed with the Office of Rail Regulation. This proposal was translated into law with the passing of the Railways Act 2005 and the Health and Safety (Enforcing Authority for Railways and Other Guided Transport Systems) Regulations 2006. The Inspectorate remains responsible for the investigation of tramway accidents that are not covered by the Rail Accident Investigation Branch mentioned in the preceding section.

The Inspectorate at work

As mentioned earlier, the initial work on tramways engaging the Inspectorate's attention mainly concerned the approval of new lines, which task they combined with their equivalent duties in respect of railways. Since at that time both tramways and railways were in their expansionist mode, Inspectors were kept pretty busy, travelling from one undertaking to another and in many instances having to write their reports in hotel rooms during the course of their peregrinations.

On the other hand, by their very nature, accident investigations could not be anticipated, whereas when they had to be undertaken, this needed to be done as quickly as possible. Under the Regulation of Railways Act 1871, when a report of an accident was received by the BoT, in appropriate cases a senior administrator would appoint a named Inspector and instruct him to undertake the task of investigating its cause and the attendant circumstances. This instruction was often issued within hours of the accident and the Inspector would soon be on his way to the scene, almost invariably having to employ the often infrequent and comparatively slow railway services of the time. The need to be there while the scent was still fresh is obvious: to ensure that the wreckage could be examined before it had been disturbed and to tap witnesses' recollections before they faded.

Preservation of evidence was, of course, a crucial element in the investigation process. In the circumstances, it would be virtually impossible to preserve what is called "perishable evidence", such as the temperature of a brake block or the reading of a pressure gauge. But even other evidence might be lost. The culture of the time assumed the need to get things back to normal as soon as possible. Also, there was a natural aversion on the part of management to leaving to the public gaze the wreckage of an accident, with its psychological effect on potential passengers and road users, particularly if this implied possible shortcomings on the part of the undertaking. So the debris were likely to get pushed aside or be quickly taken to the works of the tramway undertaking: the current concept of "scene of crime", devised by the British Transport Police, in which everything over a large area has to be left untouched and vehicles and equipment are liable to be impounded for weeks, if not months, did not exist.

Compounding the desire to "get the wheels turning" as soon as possible, other factors present were the paucity of research and testing facilities, where equipment or materials might be sent for examination, and the unlikelihood of any follow-up litigation in a far less litigious age. But, apart from this practice leading to the possible loss of evidence, it also afforded opportunities to tamper with the evidence by persons who perhaps had things to hide. However, given their background, the Inspectors were not easily diverted or confused by such activities[12].

The inquiry itself would normally be held at a local venue, such as a town hall or courtroom, the cost of providing which would usually be borne by the operator. Evidence was not taken on oath; nor would the Inspector be bound by strict rules of evidence. Trade unions would be advised so that their representatives might attend. The admission of the public and the press would be at the discretion of the Inspector, but where there was the possibility of a prosecution, publication would be deferred until after the result of any legal proceedings. Given the technical nature of the inquiry, there was the possibility of separate independent proceedings before a coroner or magistrates (in Scotland, the procurator fiscal) which might take place before or after it. As mentioned above, the 1871 Act permitted Inspectors to act as assessors to assist coroners in conducting inquests and often the evidence provided for the purposes of one proceeding could be drawn upon for the purposes of the other.

Once the inquiry was over, the Inspector would draw up his report. Given all the circumstances, it is startling to observe, judged by present-day standards, how quickly Inspectors were able to write their reports: in some cases this might be only two or three days after the accident. Nor was anything skimped in the compilation of the reports: the salient factors would be set out in meticulous detail, couched in impeccable prose. Diagrams or drawings might be attached to assist understanding. The guiding considerations were the need to establish as quickly as possible the cause of the accidents, to determine whether any lessons were to be learned from them and (where appropriate) to offer recommendations. As a result, any modifications to equipment or practices could be put in hand with a minimum of delay.

The reports were originally written out in long hand and then sent to a copy clerk in the BoT, whose task it was to write out further copies. This practice had its problems if, as in the case of General Hutchinson, the Inspector had poor handwriting and the clerk was not versed in the technical expressions employed, sometimes leading to the copies having to be withdrawn and a corrected version issued in their stead. In later days resort was had to the typewriter. Copies would be sent to the railway or tramway undertaking concerned and to all other interested parties, including the press. Reports of all but the least significant accidents were sent for printing and copies would be available for purchase from HM Stationery Office.

It is the content of these reports that forms the basis for the accounts of tramway accidents which follow in Part II. But it is to be understood that not all accidents warranted an inquiry: the cause may have been plain to see, the remedy obvious and with nothing to be learned, so that reports would not have been issued in such cases. In other instances, no report has been traced even if it was likely that one was produced: a notable example being the runaway of MET 318 ("Bluebell") down Barnet Hill, London, on 17 June 1927[13]. With their constant moves, the Inspectorate's archives have not always

[12] For a graphic illustration of a possible case of such tampering, see Appendix C *infra*.

[13] The Editor is indebted to C S Smeeton, author of the definitive *The Metropolitan Electric Tramways*, published by the Light Rail Transit Association and the Tramway & Light Railway Society, Broxbourne, vol 1 1984 and vol 2 1986, for confirmation that, notwithstanding sustained research on his part in compiling the work, no copy of the Inspectorate's report into this accident could be traced.

survived intact, and despite diligent search of other sources, such as the Public Record Office, it has not proved possible to bring many further reports to light. There is clear evidence that other reports have existed: reference to the trade press over the years has elicited details of the existence of other tramway inquiries conducted by the Railway Inspectorate and particulars of the more noteworthy of these are to be found in Appendix B. The Editor is greatly indebted to the researches of Roger Benton for identifying these references: his source has been the extensive archives of the National Tramway Museum, Crich.

In conclusion, it perhaps needs to be emphasised that this work does not purport to provide an account of every serious accident that has occurred on British tramways. It was Frank Wilson's purpose to offer informed comment and analysis only on those tramway accidents that were the subject of reports issued by the Railway Inspectorate. This objective has been maintained in the editorial process, and this has allowed Inspectorate reports that have since come to light to be incorporated in the text. But it has also meant that some notable gaps in the coverage of serious tramway accidents have been left. To have proceeded otherwise would have been alien to Frank Wilson's approach and so the Editor has felt constrained to adopt the same *modus operandi*.

BRITISH TRAMWAY ACCIDENTS

PART II

TRAMWAY ACCIDENTS REVIEWED

by Frank E Wilson

Introduction

THE OLD ADAGE about accidents happening in the best-regulated families applied to the well-regulated tramway family, which is on the whole a fair description of the municipal- and company-owned tramway undertakings that existed in Great Britain. But, as in all spheres of human activity, some were better than others. Although they were nothing like so spectacular or so sensational as serious railway accidents, some tramway accidents did result in heavy lists of people killed and injured – passengers, staff and bystanders or passers-by. In fact, the accidents mentioned in this book, which is not by a long way a complete list, resulted in the deaths of 123[14] people and injury in greater or lesser degree to almost ten times that number.

I had a near miss when tram-spotting in my youth: I was in the direct path of a car which suddenly came off the rails at a tangent to the curve it was rounding, and made straight for the pavement where I was standing. I got quickly out of its way, and the car stopped with its driver and leading platform inside the saloon bar of the public house which stood in its path. No doubt the driver could have done with a drink after a shock of that sort! The car was resplendent with glistening varnish and paint fresh from a major overhaul – why, I wondered, could this not have happened to one of the dowdy, down-at-heel ones, apparently overdue for renovation?

Damage to rolling-stock and property was naturally less in quantity and cost than in railway accidents, and the results more parochial, but most tram accidents were newsworthy to the local papers, and some reached the national press. In the latter category was the case of a tramcar, somewhere in the provinces, which started inexplicably. Spiders got the blame! It was advanced as a possibility that these arachnida had been busy while the car had stood idle in its depot for several weeks before it went out on this particularly damp morning. The theory was that wetted cobwebs created a false circuit which energised the motors!

In compiling this account, the word "accident" has been used in a sense which conforms to the definitions given in dictionaries where it is translated as a "chance or unforeseen

---

[14] Details of the fatalities are set out in Appendices A and B *infra*. It should be noted that the total includes eight passengers in a bus who were killed when it collided with a tramcar: see the accident at Enfield on 11 December 1929.

or unexpected event". However, a few moments' thought will serve to testify that so-called accidents resulting from failures of men or materials are seldom either chance or unforeseen – except for the victims. It may be chance which produces the accident at a particular instant of time, but its seeds are generally sown beforehand by somebody's laziness, impatience, mismanagement, inexperience or outright breach of regulations. This review proves the point several times that "accidents" are generally attributable to the failings of human beings.

In one report, the Inspector observed that most serious tram accidents were those in which the car ran down a hill out of control, and derailed or turned over on a curve at the bottom. But apart from runaways resulting from trams getting the better of their brakes on the way down a hill, there were cars stalling on the way up and drivers being unable to prevent them from running back. In front of me, as I type these sentences, are accounts of no fewer than 60 such incidents over the years between 1874 and 1959. The list is by no means complete: I know of others, *e.g.* at Babbacombe, and I saw a derailed car only a few minutes after it had run away in Battersea, killing a woman. The list would probably have been longer despite the advance in design and practice, but for the gradual disappearance of the trams themselves. As might be expected, there is a measure of sameness in the accidents, but as many of them throw some light on one facet, or of further tramway design, management or operation, perhaps I may be forgiven for quoting them.

The material for this review has been drawn largely from the reports into tramway accidents investigated by Inspecting Officers of Railways. The reports have been considered in chronological order, although this has necessarily meant that some are dealt with out of context. I have however endeavoured to provide a link between some of the features common to more than one accident, where these occur.

Operator: **Glyn Valley Tramway Company**
Location: **Ceirieg River crossing, Glyn Ceirieg**
Date: **19 December 1874**

Our story begins with water and ends with fire: the first in Wales and the last in Scotland. But of course most of the accidents took place in England and, as already explained, most were runaways. It seems that the first tramway accident which the Railway Inspectorate was called upon to investigate occurred in 1874, although the report by the Inspector, Lt-Colonel Hutchinson, is dated 10 April 1875 since the tramway company did not report the accident and the inquiry took place as the result of a complaint from a passenger who had been involved.

The undertaking concerned was the Glyn Valley Tramway, which operated a roadside line between Chirk and Glyn Ceiriog in Denbighshire (now Clywd) on the curious gauge of 2ft 4¼in[15]. Passenger cars and open trucks to carry slate were at that time in the undertaking's history hauled in the upward direction by horses, but in the other direction they were allowed to run by gravity, controlled by brakesmen. On the occasion of the accident, "the 3 or 4 aggrieved passengers" had hired a car for the descent but none being to hand, two trucks were provided – one for the passengers, the other for their luggage and the brakesman.

On the way down, the brakesman was "remonstrated with" frequently about the speed, apparently without effect, and he was thought to be the worse for liquor. The speed was too high approaching the bend on to the bridge over the River Ceirieg, and the truck carrying the passengers left the rails, throwing all the occupants into the water, seriously injuring two of them. The company was blamed for being in breach of section 69 of their enabling Act, which stipulated that all carriages used on the tramway should be moved by animal power only. And they had also failed to report the accident, contrary to the requirements of the Regulation of Railways Act.

The Inspector, who wrote from his office in the BoT Railway Department, which surely had the grandest possible address for a government department – 1, Whitehall, London, SW – took what seems to have been a strange view of complaints about speeds on the line from local inhabitants, when he said the remedy was in their own hands – to sue for breach of the Act. One would have thought this to be the job of the police or the Local Authority, or indeed of the Inspectorate itself[16].

Operator: Huddersfield Corporation
Location: Westgate/Railway Street, Huddersfield
Date: 3 July 1883

The next accident of significance happened in Huddersfield, which had a tramway system doubly of note. It had the distinction of being the first municipally-operated system in the British Isles, and it had the very unusual track gauge of 4ft 7¾in – a peculiarity shared with the Portsmouth and Glasgow tramway complexes[17].

At the outset, the lines were worked by steam, with engines from the works of William Wilkinson at Wigan. Within barely a month of the opening of the Lindley route, a four-wheel double-deck open-top trailer hauled by one of these engines (no. 2) was involved in a disaster. This happened when the unit was coming in from Lindley and approaching the town centre. It attained too great a speed to negotiate the curve from Westgate into Railway Street, and the car turned over. The initial cause of the driver getting into difficulties was the breakage of a piston, but if the governor had been able to do its job, the brake would have applied automatically when the speed rose, bringing the tram to a harmless standstill.

It should be explained that under the Regulations then in force, tramway engines were not allowed to exceed a speed of 8mph and that each engine had to be equipped with a governor which operated so as to prevent the speed of the engine from exceeding that figure. On this occasion, the driver had closed the valve which prevented the action of

---

[15] Apparently chosen because it was precisely half standard gauge: see *The Glyn Valley Tramway*, by W J Milner, published by Oxford Publishing Co, Poole, 1984, at p 17.

[16] In fairness to the Inspector, neither he nor the BoT had power under the Regulation of Railways Act 1871 to institute or conduct prosecutions.

[17] This gauge was adopted so as to permit standard gauge railway locomotives and wagons to operate over the tramway concerned. The reduction in gauge was required since when grooved tramway rail is employed the wheels of railway vehicles run on their flanges (which are deeper than tramway flanges) on the bottom of the groove. Advantage was taken of this facility in Glasgow and at Gosport in the Portsmouth area, but not in Huddersfield. A similar arrangement prevailed in Cork, where the tramways adopted a gauge of 2ft 11½in to permit the operation of 3ft gauge railway vehicles over their metals: an option never utilised.

the governor from opening the steam cylinder, so that a speed of 11 or 12mph had been attained.

Preventing the driver from tampering with the governor had been a main aim of the Regulations. So far, so good – this was all very well, but there was still no means of preventing a driver, as in this case, defeating the object by the simple act of closing the cocks which supplied steam to the cylinder of the automatic brake. Over many years, I have come across this sort of thing time and time again – men will cut out or ignore features provided for protection or safety if they find them a nuisance or they make a little more work. Quite often they get away with it, but now and then they "come unstuck" – the price is paid in life or limb – with this Huddersfield tram the price was seven dead and 28 injured.

The Inspector in this case was Major-General Hutchinson and, in the light of the accident, he recommended changes to equipment and operating practices, including the following:

(1)   the fitting of a hand-screw brake to apply a block to each of the four wheels;
(2)   the discontinuance of the practice of allowing short fixed-wheelbase cars with roof passengers on systems having severe gradients and sharp curves;
(3)   the putting in place of arrangements to prevent drivers from tampering with the operation of the governor; and
(4)   the requirement that conductors were never to leave the brake handle on the trailer car whilst ascending or descending steep grades, or a special brakesman was to be employed for this purpose.

Operator: Wigan Tramways Company
Location: Union Bank, Pemberton
Date: 29 December 1883

We move from the county of the white rose to that of the red – to Wigan. This town had a company-owned tramway, one section of which ran for almost two-and-a-half miles to Pemberton. The Inspector was the ubiquitous Major-General Hutchinson, who recorded that the line of 3ft 6in gauge was opened in 1880, that a licence to use steam power had been granted in February 1882, and that he had reissued the licence for a further year when he re-examined the engines in February 1883. It was under the original stringent conditions that William Wilkinson, a Wigan engineer, built steam engines in his foundry for the local tramway[18]. One of them was involved in this accident in which, rather ironically, the local coroner was killed. (Is this what poets call "pathetic fallacy"?[19])

What happened? On the day of the accident, the coroner was a passenger in a car drawn by another Wilkinson engine which was waiting in a passing loop for a car to pass in the opposite direction when, seeing a runaway engine approaching from behind, he was alighting to get away from the impending collision only to be caught and crushed between the engine and the car, and carried along in that position until the runaway was brought to a stand 190 yards further on.

In order to simplify the construction of his engines, Wilkinson made them to be driven normally in one direction only, and in consequence a "run-round" triangle was laid at both ends of the line. Engine no. 4 had arrived at the Pemberton terminus with double-deck four-wheel trailer car no. 12, and the two had been uncoupled. Leaving the conductor with the trailer, the driver took the engine "round the triangle" (which sounds like a paradox) and when nearing the points at the Wigan apex, at about 4mph, said the driver:

> *I saw a young child about three years old walking towards the rails on which the engine was running. I reversed the engine and put steam full on; but it was not stopped and seeing this I shut off steam with my left hand, held up the reversing lever with my right hand, opened the engine door, jumped down, seized the child (who was to my right hand), with its left side towards me, by the back of its clothes and put it clear of the rails. The child was about three feet from the engine when I stepped off. As I was lifting the child, the right-hand corner of the engine caught me on the right hip and threw me down. I recovered immediately, but by this time the engine was going through the points at increased speed. I ran after it, and tried to get in, by the back, but missed my hold.*

The Inspector tried it for himself and found it quite easy to catch up with the other engine when he re-enacted the scene.

It is a point worth noting that the reversing lever on these engines would only stay in the "backward" position if held there, it being intended, as mentioned earlier, that they should work normally in one direction only. So steam had not been shut off when the driver let go the lever, and the engine ran away under power on a continuously falling gradient.

As is so often the case with accidents, this one was caused by a combination of wrong or negligent actions. The driver, the conductor and the company were all at fault. The driver should not have left his engine: he ought to have seen the child in time to stop short of it, but it was obvious to the Inspector that he intended to get down in any case to turn the points and remount the engine while it was still moving – the arrival of the child was a fortuitous complication. The conductor should have been in attendance at the points[20]. Had he been there he could have seen to the child.

The company was to blame for the fact that the governor on the engine was not working, a matter to which the General justifiably took strong exception. He had personally renewed the licence on condition that these appliances were kept in working order, yet only ten months afterwards they had been allowed to fall into disuse and disrepair. Quite plainly he had no doubt that, if the governor had been working, it would have stopped the engine, even if driverless, before it could have caused the accident. He said in effect that it was no good laying down rules if there were no means of seeing that they were observed. (The words may alter, but the music doesn't change – today we are still up

---

[18] The engines were unusual in several respects, compared with conventional steam tram engines, including their adoption of vertical boilers. An example of such an engine, built in 1885 under licence by Beyer Peacock, is on display at the National Tramway Museum, Crich, Derbyshire.

[19] The author of the expression quoted was the writer, artist and social reformer John Ruskin (1819-1900). He wrote in vol iii of *Modern Painters*, published in 1888: "All violent feelings . . . produce in us a falseness in all our impressions of external things, which I would generally characterise as the 'Pathetic Fallacy'".

[20] Given the way in which the triangle was operated, it is perhaps surprising that the points were not sprung.

against the same problem; we have a plethora of laws and regulations which are defied or ignored with impunity: depositing litter and emitting black smoke from diesel engines may be cited as examples.)

On the general question of governors, it was not only a difficult matter to keep them in order, but almost impossible to prevent their being interfered with by drivers. They were in practice a nuisance, because when on icy or greasy rails the wheels lost grip and spun, the rapid rotation gave the governor a false sensation of speeding and brought the engine to a stand. In some designs this difficulty was surmounted by installing a fifth wheel for the sole purpose of the governor. This wheel would roll along one or other rail (or even over the road surface) quite freely, playing no part in the traction or braking systems. It was not therefore subject to spinning or sliding and could thus give a true reference for speed purposes. This wheel would nevertheless be capable of driving the light load imposed by the governor. Governors remained a requirement until 1922, when the Ministry of Transport dropped the requirement for the Wolverton and Stony Stratford tramway.[21]

Operator: **Highgate Hill Tramways Company**
Location: **Highgate Hill, Highgate, London**
Date: **31 July 1884**

For further examples of runaways, we now move south, and the next two cases were runaways on the busy cable tramway on Highgate Hill in North London. The former of these two happened only a few weeks after the opening of the line in May 1884, when dummy[22] no. 6 towing car no. 3, ran away and at the bottom of the hill came into

Dummy car 6 with trailer 3 on the Highgate Hill cable tramway.   **These vehicles were involved in the accident which occurred on 31 July 1884.**

Courtesy: Transport for London

collision with dummy no. 5 and car no. 1, which were standing at the terminus, forcing them some 21 yards down the road. Fortunately injuries to staff were slight. The latter accident occurred only 16 weeks later. This time it was a pile-up at the same place when bogie car no. 8 collided with a cartload of ashes belonging to the local authority – the Islington Vestry Board. Nobody was hurt; neither was the horse. There were no men with the tram – they had jumped off as soon as they realised they could not stop it.

The line was worked by eight cars, which were housed in a depot containing also the engine house, at a point described by Major-General Hutchinson, who inquired into both accidents, as "nearly a quarter of a mile from the top on the left-hand side going down". The cars were either towed by horses or manhandled into and out of the depot on to the main line. Nos. 1, 2 and 3 were four-wheel open-top double-deck cars similar to the normal horse trams of the period, and were towed by dummies nos. 4, 5 and 6, which were shorter four-wheel vehicles fitted with apparatus for gripping the cable in the conduit through a slot in the roadway. When gripped, the moving cable propelled them and enabled them to tow and control a trailer car. As will be seen in the illustration, a dummy had accommodation for a few passengers on cross-benches with back-rests adjustable for the direction of travel. In fact no. 6 had six people aboard when in collision. The dummies had to run round their trailers at the termini. Two further cars were bogie vehicles equipped with a cable gripper at each end, one for each direction of travel, and controlled from the leading platform. These were nos. 7 and 8.

All the cars had brakes applied to their wheels from the platform, but on the dummies and bogies, *i.e.* the cars with grippers, these brakes were worked by treadles to enable the driver to have his hands free to deal with the gripper, but (just like the footbrake on a modern motor car) there was no means of holding the brake "on" if the man released his foot pressure. The bogie cars (7 and 8) and the trailers (1, 2 and 3) had "sledge" brakes – blocks of poplar wood 24in long, 2½in wide and 3½in deep (when new) – which bore on the rails. This brake, more usually known as the slipper, figured largely in hill working on tramways. The dummies had no slipper brakes, but the driver worked the slipper on his trailer through a connection which had to be uncoupled and recoupled at each terminus during running-round.

The line on 3ft 6in gauge was approximately three-quarters-of-a-mile (1,380 yards) long on the hill varying in gradient from 1 in 11 to 1 in 28 connecting Highgate Village, at the top, with the road junction at the bottom known from the name of the tavern there as Archway – the scene of another tram accident a few years later. The lower half mile or so (900 yards) was double track, but above there was a single line with two passing loops, at one of which the depot containing the engine house was situated.

The cable was driven by a stationary engine by which it was governed to a maximum speed of 6mph. Provided that a car was properly gripped to the cable, it could quite obviously not go faster than the speed of the cable. It was of course necessary for the

---

[21] It was only in 1890 that it became a requirement to fit a "child or life protector" on the front of every engine. This normally took the form of a bar extending the full width of the engine, pivoted to the lower edge of the skirt which, at a moment's notice, could be dropped to rail level by the driver from his foot-plate.

[22] A dummy was a tractor car designed to house the gripper gear and to haul a passenger trailer car. It might also itself be equipped to carry passengers. The term originated with early steam tramway operation, in which the engine was disguised to look like an ordinary tramcar so that it would not frighten horses.

(Copy) R. 6159

Railway Department
Board of Trade
1 Whitehall, London, S. W.
20th Sept. 1884

Sir,

I have the honour to report, for the information of the Board of Trade, in compliance with the instructions contained in the Order of the 26th ultimo, the result of my enquiry into the causes of the collision which occurred on the 31st July at the foot of Highgate Hill on the Highgate Hill (Cable) Tramways.

In this case the 10·5 p.m. Dummy (No 6) and Car (No 3) which dummy the driver had failed to connect with the Cable when passing the Engine house on their downward journey, were allowed to attain too high a speed for the driver to be able to control them with the break power at his command, and ran with continually increasing velocity till they dashed into another Dummy (No 5) and Car (No 1) at the foot of the hill where the Tramway ends.

Out of 6 passengers in the runaway dummy and car one inside and one outside the car were injured - the former (a woman) severely.

The passengers in the stationary dummy and car jumped out before the collision, and escaped injury.

The driver of the runaway dummy and car who remained on the dummy till the collision occurred, was injured in the ribs and legs.

The conductor was thrown down in jumping off the dummy to try to get to the car slipper break soon after the dummy and car began to run away. He was not hurt.

Another Company's servant (a splicer) who was riding on the dummy, also attempted to get to the car slipper break after the conductor failed. He likewise fell down in getting off the dummy, and injured his head and arms.

Comparatively little damage was sustained either by the dummies or cars which ran back together about 20 yards after the collision. Dummy (No 5) the stationary one, was most damaged.

Description

Railway Inspectorate report of the accident dated 31 July 1884 at Highgate Hill, London.

Description

The Highgate Hill Cable Tramway, which was inspected on the 19th May last, and opened for traffic shortly afterwards, is nearly 3/4 mile long, of which about 1/2 mile (from the bottom of the hill) is a double line, and the remainder to the top of the hill is (on account of the narrowness of the road) a single line with passing loops. The gauge is 3 feet 6 inches. The Cable is carried in an underground tube between the rails, and the engine house from which the Cable is worked is situated nearly a quarter of a mile from the top of the Hill on the left-hand side going down the Hill. Opposite the Engine House, where the Cable has necessarily to leave the track for a few yards to pass round the wheels by which motion is imparted to it, the gripper has to be released from its hold, and the car has to descend by gravity for these few yards until the Cable can be again seized by the gripper. The greatest care is consequently necessary both in first releasing and in then again seizing the Cable at the proper points, and special attention is directed to this in the working rules.

The rolling stock in use is of two descriptions (1) a dummy car, (which contains the gripping arrangement) drawing another ordinary car; and (2) a bogie car with a gripping arrangement at each end of it. In both descriptions besides the ordinary wheel breaks the car is provided with a slipper or sledge break, applicable either by the driver or Conductor to the rail itself, but in the case of the dummy and car the slipper break chain requires uncoupling and re-coupling at the end of each journey when the dummy has to run round its car, and there is consequently more risk of the slipper break being out of order in the case of the dummy and car than in that of the bogie car.

The gradients on the hill are very severe, varying between 1 in 11 and 1 in 28, and the speed of the Cable is restricted to a maximum of six miles an hour (the stationary engines being provided with an automatic arrangement to prevent this speed being exceeded) and there is a strict rule against the cars being allowed to descend by gravity except in cases of emergency, and then only at a very slow speed.

Conclusion.

This collision, which was happily attended with much less serious results

results than might have been anticipated, was primarily due to the negligence both of the driver and conductor of Dummy N° 6 attached to Car N° 3, before commencing the downward journey from the top of the hill, in failing to have the slipper break on the car properly coupled to the dummy before starting. It was the Conductor's duty to have coupled up this break before commencing the downward journey, and his excuse for not having done so was that the coupling chain had got twisted on the previous down journey, and that he was, in consequence, unable to release it from the hook. He states that he informed the driver of this, who, in reply said, "Never mind the —— thing". The conductor further excuses himself for not having reported to the fitter when they stopped at the dépot the fact of the break being out of order, as it was his duty to have done, on account of the driver having previously said "Never mind". Whether there really was this difficulty in coupling up the break it was impossible to tell after the collision, as the break gearing was more or less damaged.

The driver denies having been told by the Conductor that he could not couple up the break, and in this he is to some extent corroborated by a Company's servant who rode in the car from the top of the hill to the Dépot, and thence on the Dummy beside the driver, and who says that he did not hear the Conductor make any remark about the break not being connected, nor did the driver make any allusion to the fact. However this may be, it was the driver's duty to have ascertained for himself that the break was connected, and for not having done so he is much to blame.

The dummy and car then proceeded to the dépot with the driver under the impression (as he declares) that the slipper break was connected. On reaching the dépot the gripper was properly released and the dummy and car stopped for a moment, then allowed to descend by gravity, and then stopped again at the place for re-attaching the Cable. The driver then proceeded to do this, and, under the impression that he had done so, proceeded on his journey. He states that he had not gone more than 5 or 6 yards before he discovered that he had not gripped the Cable, whereupon he used the means for applying both Wheel and slipper break, and rang the bell three times — the signal for telling the Conductor to apply the car breaks. The Conductor states that he did not

hear

hear the bell, but on coming on to the dummy to collect the fares, he felt the dummy and car shoot forward, and the driver at the same time asked him to go and apply his break; that he jumped off the Dummy for the purpose of getting off the car to do so, but, in consequence of the speed and the roughness of the road he tumbled down, and before he could recover himself the car had got too far away for him to overtake it. On finding what had happened to the Conductor the splicer then attempted to reach the car by unwisely jumping off the dummy (instead of trying to get to the car by getting from the dummy on to the front platform.) This man also tumbled down and failed to get on to the car. The dummy and car then ran on to the bottom of the hill with the driver sticking manfully to the dummy break (which of itself could not control the speed when it had once exceeded a certain amount) until the collision occurred with the Dummy and Car waiting to ascend the hill.

The second cause of the collision was therefore the failure of the driver to seize the cable before starting from the dépôt; and, on discovering this, his allowing the speed to become too great before ringing for the Conductor's assistance.

To guard against the recurrence of a similar collision it is desirable (1) that the dummies themselves should be supplied with slipper breaks; (2) that a responsible officer of the Company should be charged with the duty of seeing that, before leaving the dépôt on every downward journey, the cable is properly gripped, and the slipper break connections are in proper order; (3) that the Conductor of a dummy and car should not leave the car on the downward journey, so as to be always ready to supply his break if required to do so.

It appears to me also that the printed rule should be made more explicit than it now is as to its being the duty of both driver and conductor to see that the breaks are properly coupled before starting from either terminus.

The Secretary
Railway Department
Board of Trade

I am &c
(signed) C. S. Hutchinson
Major General.

cable to leave the line somewhere to go round the winding wheels of the driving engine, which meant a gap in its continuity in the conduit. This gap was on the down-hill line, and cars were permitted to cross this short gap by gravity, and there was a strict regulation that this must be the only place where it was to be done.

The first accident originated when the driver, after having let his dummy roll over this gap by gravity, did not succeed in regripping the cable. Not being aware that this operation had failed, and thinking all was well, he released the footbrake, but the car, lacking the restraint of the cable, gathered speed which he was unable to check because he got no reaction from his attempt to apply the slipper on the trailer. The brake on the trailer had not been connected to the dummy when coupling up at the top of the hill! This was the real cause of the accident, but both driver and conductor denied any blame. The latter alleged he told the driver he was having difficulty in coupling, and the driver replied "Never mind the ****** thing". This the driver denied, but it is to his credit that he remained at his post, and with two of his passengers, was injured in the collision. The conductors on these cars had to collect the fares on both vehicles, and on this occasion the conductor was on the dummy and fell into the road while trying to get back to the trailer to apply its brake.

Operator: **Highgate Hill Tramways Company**
Location: **Highgate Hill, Highgate, London**
Date: **8 January 1885**

The other accident on the Highgate Hill cable line occurred during the first winter of operation, and was caused by a flagrant breach of the regulations by no less a person than the manager of the company. In order to save an unremunerative journey to the bottom of the hill and all the way back to the top to get the car in position for its first revenue-earning trip, he had told his men to gravitate it down to the stretch of single line 45 yards away, and there to attach the ascending cable. It will be remembered that it was only across the gap in the cable that gravitation was sanctioned. By the time the car reached the single line, it was travelling too fast for the men to be able to attach the cable, and it continued to gain momentum and sped right down the hill. The morning was cold and the rails were coated with rime so the brakes had failed to hold when the men had tried to stop the car on the single line.

At the bottom of the hill, the speed of the car was checked somewhat as first one gripper and then the other struck the end of the slot and snapped off. The car was bogie no. 8, and it is obvious from the report submitted by the Inspector (again Major-General Hutchinson) that it had cushion seats – "the fitter did not display much fertility of resource when, after failing to arrest its progress by throwing a cushion in front of the car, he might at least have tried to put another in front of the hind wheels where it would have had more of a chance of being of use"[23].

So much for these two accidents, but it is worth mentioning that following another serious one in December 1892[24], the tramway was closed for five years. Although it was so short, the line ran in three boroughs. Two of them, St Pancras and Islington, were agreeable to its re-opening after repairs, but the third, Hornsey, insisted on the whole tramway being relaid. In consequence, the line, which had cost £59,277 to build, was offered for sale, whereupon the LCC, by that date empowered to acquire tramways, offered £2,000, but they were outbid by £500. The Council's offer was raised, but it was too late and the line went to a businessman who had it reconstructed, and it restarted in 1897. Before the service resumed, the cars had been fitted with brakes which came into operation automatically were the cable, gripper, or other mechanism, to fail. I have not been able to find details of this apparatus, but gear, with very similar functions, was fitted to the cars of the Great Orme cable tramway[25], which is described later on.

Before we quit this cable line to look at another mishap on a steam tramway, a few other facts are worth inclusion. During the 12 months ending 30 June 1886, the line operated 104,331 car miles (which means about 139,108 journeys) on which 642,083 passengers were carried. The tramway was not a money spinner however and, when it was losing money and facing the Bankruptcy Court, its chairman said the line "had fared badly between the Vestry and the BoT, and was a prime example of public prejudice. The fare downhill had been reduced to 1d", he said, "and the fare uphill was 2d, but even at 1d the people were afraid to ride down; they thought it more dangerous than going up"!

The designer and chief engineer during construction of the Highgate Hill line was William E Eppelsheimer, who claimed to have built the world's first successful cable line – the Clay Street Hill Railroad in San Francisco in 1873[26]. He regarded the cable system as suitable on roads too steep for steam traction, but admitted that it was not easy to apply in narrow winding roads. We shall meet regenerative braking later on with electric cars[27], but in passing let us note that Eppelsheimer must have been the first man to visualise the economy which is, in theory, possible from this form of brake. He realised that half of the power station output was absorbed in moving the cable itself, and could see that a car descending dragging on the cable was helping to pull the cable along, and in so doing eased the task of the power house in moving other cars up the hill.

No further serious accident on the Highgate Hill line was recorded, but it will not be out of place to finish off the story of this unusual tramway. It eventually became part of the LCC tramway system and was promptly regauged and electrified on the underground conduit principle. The four-wheel class M cars, which maintained the hill service for many years, were equipped with a specially-designed brake utilising shoes which bore on special reinforced rails laid beneath the slot rails. It was a gripper with a difference, and was lowered from the car into the conduit through hatch plates at the bottom of the hill. The car stopped over the hatch, the plates of which were opened by the operation of a lever on the footpath. The driver, after having applied the hand brake, dismounted, taking with him the power handle from his controller, which he placed on a horizontal spindle and wound the brake down from its housing

---

[23] It is not clear what use this strategem could have achieved, wherever the cushions were deployed.

[24] The Inspectorate report for this accident has not come to light.

[25] It is possible that the brake took a similar form to that adopted by the Great Orme Tramway in 1902, as described in connection with the accident of 23 August 1932 (*qv*), but the brake would presumably have had to have been activated by a governor, assisted by springs, fitted to each car.

[26] Credit generally goes to London-born Andrew Smith Hallidie (1836-1900) for the installation of the Clay Street line, but its mechanical ingenuity was apparently the work of Epplesheimer: see *A Treatise upon Cable and Rope Traction*, by J Bucknall Smith, 2nd ed, published by Owlswick Press, Philadelphia, 1977.

[27] In the case of cable traction, the concept is one of "energy recovery" rather than "regeneration", since no generation occurs as is the case with electric traction.

A rare view of a steam tram accident brought about by a runaway.   Trailer car 21 of the Bradford Tramways & Omnibus Co on 4 December 1889, at Four Lane Ends.

Courtesy: National Tramway Museum

within the car. The hatch plates were then closed, the driver regained his platform, and the car proceeded up the hill. Once in the conduit, the brake was actuated by the driver in the manner usual for slipper brakes, *i.e.* by turning a basin-shaped wheel placed below the hand-brake handle and rotating a concentric tube (see fig 5 on page 58). On the return trip, the brake was taken out through the hatch at the foot of the hill by a reversal of the insertion procedure.

From this hill, on which Dick Whittington heard Bow bells – some four miles distant – to return to become thrice Lord Mayor of London, and on which nowadays one can hardly hear one's own voice thanks to the din of tramless traffic, we go north to Birmingham, for our first non-runaway accident.

Operator: **City of Birmingham Tramways Company**
Location: **Camp Hill/Bradford Street, Birmingham**
Date: **2 February 1898**

A steam-tram mishap occurred in Birmingham in February 1898 on a line which had not been laid at the time of the accidents at Huddersfield and Wigan: the line dated from the early part of 1885, having been laid by Birmingham Corporation and leased with other lines to the City of Birmingham Tramways Co later in that year.   The report of the Inspectorate, which was now installed at 8 Richmond Terrace, Whitehall, records that Kyotts Lake Road depot turned out 19 cars each morning, and reminds one that since the early days of steam traction, when authority to use mechanical means of propulsion was valid for a period not exceeding one year, there had been a change of policy based on experience, and a new licence was then required only at seven-year intervals.   On this tramway, the licence dated from October 1891.

The double-deck top-covered passenger tramcar in the case, no. 23, was designed to carry 54 passengers: 26 inside and 28 outside. The body was 19ft ½in long, with an overall length of 27ft 6½in. Its width was 5ft 6½in and height 13ft 6in. The car was carried on two 4-wheel bogies, the distance between centres being 18ft 3½in. The wheels were 20¹³/₁₆in in diameter (when new) and were 3ft 6in from centre to centre. It was being hauled by a steam engine in a northward (downhill) direction. The engine and the leading bogie of the car correctly took the line into Bradford Street, but the rear bogie of the car continued along Camp Hill, thereby "splitting the train". The vehicle consequently "spreadeagled" the lines with its bogies more or less at right angles to its body and on a downward slope. In this extremely unstable state, it rolled over on to its right side, injuring 26 out of the 31 people who were on board. It was very fortunate that nobody was killed, and this was due most probably to so few being on the upper deck. Credit must also be given to the driver, whose quick action stopped the car in the few seconds between derailment and overturning. It was this man's habit to watch his trailer at such places, so he was at once aware of trouble.

Without possibility of doubt, the derailment had been the result of a piece of the flange having broken off the right (off)side leading wheel of the rear bogie. There was a gap of 8in in the flange, and the missing portion was never found. There was a dummy point (*i.e.* one without a moving blade) on the nearside rail, so for a few inches there was no guiding power against the wheel on that side, and reliance was placed on the other wheel which, by that element of coincidence necessary to produce disaster, had no flange just where and at that instant it was most needed. In effect the Inspector, Lt-Colonel Yorke[28], blamed the management for letting the wheel get into such a deplorable state, and thought it unreasonable to expect one fitter to make a thorough examination of the 152 wheels each morning with the light of only a hand lamp in the short time available. The Inspector also questioned the stability of cars as tall as 13ft 6in[29] on the narrow 3ft 6in gauge, and proffered the opinion that check chains on the bogies would have prevented them from getting athwart the car and so might have obviated the overturning.

Industrial archaeology is a fashionable (and, in my view, a very necessary) study, and in the interest of this science, I add the following information from the report. According to it, the wheels were solid steel whereas iron was the usual material for tramcar wheels at that time: castings with "chilled" rims, ribs or spokes on their inner sides[30]. Their average life in use was about ten months, covering some 20,000 miles. Unlike the wheels of later days, they had no renewable tyres, and were considered unserviceable when the tread had been worn down to the depth of the chilling.

---

[28] Sir (Henry) Arthur Yorke (1848-1930), Inspecting Officer 1891-1900, Chief Inspecting Officer of Railways 1900-13.

[29] It was a feature of such cars that their bogies were placed at the extreme ends and the leading bogie was coupled directly to the engine so as to augment stability.

[30] At that date, tramcar wheels were generally made of cast iron, with the circumference of the tread chilled so as to crystallise the iron to a depth of ½in to ¾in to form an extremely hard surface on the tread where wear takes place. Steel tyres and centres came into general use later, having been pioneered by the South Staffordshire tramways in 1894. Steel is an alloy of iron and carbon with small amounts of other materials, making it extremely hard and of high tensile strength.

Operator: **Bradford Corporation**
Location: **Great Horton Road/All Saints Road, Bradford**
Date: **19 September 1898**

We now embark on consideration of a further series of runaways, the first occurring in Bradford on 19 September 1898 and the first in this review to involve electric traction. At about 10.30am on that day, car no. 16, a four-wheel, 6ft wheelbase, open topper on 4ft gauge, with hand and electric braking, was proceeding from Horton Bank Top into the city when, at a short distance above the curve from Great Horton Road into All Saints Road, the driver lost control of the car, which accelerated to a speed estimated to be about 20mph. It left the rails at the curve and landed against the wall of the Grange Congregational Church, causing injuries to several passengers, of whom two died later.

The inquiry Inspector, Major Cardew[31], had declared the line fit for traffic less than a month before. In his report on that inspection, he had drawn special attention to the steep gradients (steepest 1 in 14.24) and sharp curves (sharpest 46ft radius) on the line, and had advised against trailer operation. He had also recommended that the maximum speed on the steepest gradients should be 6mph and, around curves, 4mph, with a number of compulsory stops.

On the day of the accident, the rails were greasy and there was extra traffic in connection with a circus. The car had been put into service after having been held in reserve, with a driver with only a fortnight's driving experience and a conductor who was a shedman and fitter. The Inspector calculated that the timetable for operating the service on the route was such that it was virtually inevitable that the 6mph speed limit was exceeded.

At the earlier coroner's inquest, the jury had questioned the sufficiency of the brake power on the car. Major Cardew therefore arranged for a number of tests to be conducted, including the testing of slipper brakes on a car which had already been equipped with them. Intrepidly allowing the car to run free on a grade of 1 in 14.24 for a distance of 72 yards and then making a brake application, the respective stopping distances were:

by the slipper brake alone	- 179½ yards
by the hand brake alone	- 64½ yards
by the electric brake alone	- 37 yards.

The Inspector had this to say about the slipper brake:

> *From these tests it appears that the slipper brake alone, as now fitted, is the least effective of all as an emergency brake . . . considering the small fraction of the whole weight of the car that can be possibly brought to bear upon this brake, I doubt greatly whether it can be made as effective an emergency brake as the other brakes which act upon all the wheels, and which, therefore, bring into play as a retarding force a friction due to the whole weight of the car.*

> *It has, however, an advantage in that it applies a surface of wood to the steel rail, the coefficient of friction between wood and iron or steel being generally greater than that between iron and iron. The fact is that if a car be allowed to acquire such a speed as 20 mph on a steep gradient, no brake acting by friction on the running rails will stop it in a distance that could be considered safe.*

34

There appears to be an impression that a slipper-brake is quite without influence upon the wheel brakes. This is not the case, whatever proportion of the weight of the car is utilised for the slipper brake must be lost for the wheel brake, and it will be found that the wheels skid more easily on the application of the hand brake if the slipper brake be pressed down. Moreover, to the extent to which the slipper brake relieves the weight on the wheels, it tends to increase the risk of the wheels leaving the rails at curves and facing points.

The real advantages of the slipper brake appear to me, as before remarked, to be found in the use of the block of wood pressing on the rails whereby a greater coefficient of friction is secured, and the destructive action inseparable from the dissipation of energy by means of friction is to a great extent concentrated upon a cheap and easily replaceable fitting.

After all this, the Inspector's conclusions were that the accident had been caused by a combination of factors: the speed limit had been greatly exceeded; the presence of greasy rails; the pressure of extra traffic; the unfortunate combination of a driver with little experience and a conductor with none, but with a little knowledge "which is proverbially a dangerous thing". The driver had used his brake power in an injudicious manner. The conductor put on the hand brake, depriving the driver of full control of the brake power, and had removed the trolley from the wire, depriving the driver of the power of reversing, which might have prevented the accident. He considered the existing brake power to be ample, provided that the speed limit was not exceeded.

However, he approved of the addition of slipper brakes to the cars, as recommended by the jury: not as an emergency brake but as a brake continuously in use, since this would assist in the regulation of speed and diminish the strain on the motors and excessive wear on the wheels. A further jury recommendation, that each platform should be fitted with two sand boxes so that both rails could be sanded, was cautiously welcomed by the Inspector, but he felt it better on some occasions to sand only one rail to prevent the possible loss of electrical contact in the case of upward journeys. Finally, he recommended that the timetable for the down journey should be extended to 35 minutes (in place of the existing 30 minutes) to make it easier to observe the speed limit. Nothing was attributed to the employment of the narrower, 4ft gauge.

Operator: **Huddersfield Corporation**
Location: **Somerset Road/Wakefield Road, Huddersfield**
Date: **28 June 1902**

We now we go back to Huddersfield where, in June 1902, only a few weeks after electric working commenced on the Almondbury route, there occurred another accident involving a runaway. It will be recalled that Huddersfield had previously had an accident causing fatalities on a steam line only then recently opened (see the accident on 3 July 1883). On this occasion, it was electric car no. 40, a four-wheeler, that ran away out of control down the hill in Somerset Road, after leaving a passing loop. It managed to pass another car waiting at the next loop and then derailed at the bottom of the hill and crashed into a shop, killing two pedestrians. A passenger later died of injuries sustained

---

[31] Philip Cardew (1851-1910), Inspecting Officer of Railways 1894-1910.

in the accident and 15 other people suffered injury. The driver claimed that the brakes of the car had failed, but the hand, rheostatic and slipper brakes were all found to be in order. The Inspector, Major Druitt[32], came to the conclusion that the slipper brake had not been used and, if it had, the accident could not have occurred. He recommended that more training be given drivers and that they be formally allocated a period of time to test the equipment on their cars before taking them out on the road.

Only a month later (on 29 July) a second car of the same type – no. 32 – went astray at the foot of East Parade, Huddersfield, but luckily caused no serious injuries. Information on this accident is sparse, but in due course we shall come to an accident of a very different sort in this town – an accident of which there is a full report[33].

Operator: Glasgow Corporation
Location: Renfield Street, Glasgow
Date: 6 September 1902

For a very spectacular runaway in the same year, we cross the Border to Glasgow, where, on 6th September, three cars of the then most numerous fleet in the Kingdom became locked together. Car no. 690 originated the trouble and then got involved with, successively, nos. 755 and 585[34]. No. 690 had successfully climbed the 1 in 22 gradient in Renfield Street and the driver had shut off power preparatory to stopping the car at the compulsory stop before turning the corner to join the line in Cowcaddens Street and was about to apply the hand brake *when the handle came away in his hand*! He was so taken aback that he overlooked the simplest thing to do, which was to re-apply power and continue to move ahead. Instead the driver applied the electric brake (or thought he did), but the car started to roll back and gathered speed rapidly. After crossing Sauchiehall Street and continuing down a gradient of 1 in 94, it came into head-on collision with no. 755, which was standing there with its hand brake on. The pair of cars then went together down the road and ran into a third one – 585 – standing on a 1 in 24.6 slope with its hand brake applied. The trio, locked together, ran back for a further 165 yards to the junction of St Vincent Street where they all derailed, mounted the pavement and damaged a shop. No. 690 had run back 572 yards – 27 people had been injured, but not on the cars – they had hurt themselves in jumping off.

After the accident, a series of brake trials were made under the supervision of the Inspector, Major Druitt, with no. 691, which was identical to no. 690, having British Thomson-Houston equipment, and no. 956, with Westinghouse equipment and magnetic brakes. Like many of the interesting dissertations in these reports, there is no space to say much about these trials. In this case, we must be content to mention that they showed that both the electric brake and the magnetic brake were effective in checking a runaway if the driver did not lose his head and forget to put the controller into reverse.

As to the initial cause of the pile-up, it was analogous to the parable of the missing nail

---

[32] Edward Druitt (1859-1922), Inspecting Officer of Railways 1900-18.

[33] This concerns an overturning trolleybus at Outlane on 4 October 1938.

[34] Glasgow no. 585 was later to be preserved, as a representative of the British tramcar, in the national collection at the Science Museum, South Kensington, London. Regrettably the car is now in storage at Wroughton, Wiltshire.

36

Tramcar hand brakes

This type of brake is operated by manually rotating a "swan-neck" crank handle (or, more rarely, a wheel) on a column located on the platform.

This brake applies cast-iron brake blocks to the wheel treads of the car.

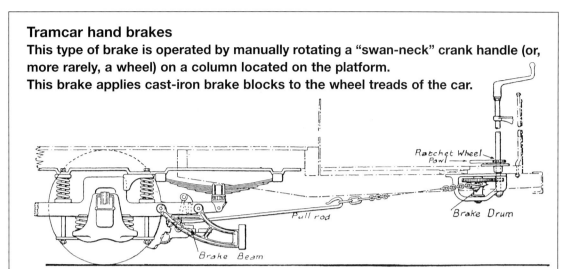

Figure 1

Brake gear on a single-truck car. The brake blocks are fixed to transverse bars, called brake beams, to which pull rods are connected to the platform operating gear by a short length of chain. The brake is applied by winding the chain around a brake drum, unwinding being prevented by a ratchet wheel and pawl on the operating column.

Figure 2

The handbrake column, with its above-floor ratchet and foot-operated pawl (or "dog"), is geared to a secondary shaft below the platform. This carries a "snail" cam to which the brake pull chain is connected. The two "cog wheel" illustrations show the underside view of the mechanism in the released and applied positions. The gearing gives mechanical advantage to the driver's effort and the snail-cam shape provides for the quick take-up of slack and maximum force transfer when the brake blocks are in contact with the wheel treads.

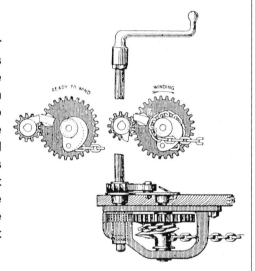

Figure 3

Brake gear on a bogie car. In the case of maximum-traction trucks, a mechanism of the type shown for a reversed 39E-type truck has to be employed. With this arrangement, the forces applied to the brake blocks are in a similar ratio to the car weight distribution on to the two axles.

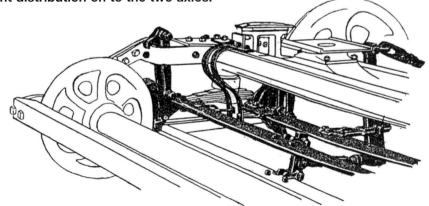

from the horse's shoe – a small pin or grub-screw only 1½in long and ⁵⁄₁₆in diameter, which should have prevented the brass Brill ratchet handle from parting from the spindle, was not in position. The mystery of why it was not there was not solved, or why its end was not seen protruding from the handle as it worked loose during the 16 hours the car had been at work in the hands of three drivers. It was never found.

Guard wires (the purpose of which are described in the Wakefield accident of 29 January 1920 (*qv*)), cropped up here in Glasgow. One of the three dewired trolleys pulled some guard wires down, but they "shorted" against the live overhead wires and "threw" the substation circuit breaker.

Operator:	**Chatham and District Light Railways Company**
Location:	**Westcourt Street/Dock Road, Old Brompton**
Date:	**30 October 1902**

Let us now go south to Kent, where four people lost their lives and "about 50 others suffered more or less seriously" in another runaway on a steep hill. At Glasgow there had been human failure to take the correct action following a small mechanical failure, but at Chatham there was nothing but human lapse. The line was the Chatham and District Light Railway. Its name was really only a legal nicety as it was, to all intents and purposes, a normal electric tramway of 3ft 6in gauge.

We can draw a fairly complete picture of what the BoT report describes as "this lamentable accident" to car no. 19, when it suddenly attained a dangerously high speed and turned over at the foot of a hill. The route carried a heavy traffic, and the company found it necessary to run four times as many cars for dockyard workers as they were obliged to do under their Light Railway Order; so the rails were well used. But the car which came to grief was the first to go down the hill on the morning in question, when it was damp and the rails slippery.

Through many years' acquaintance with railway and tramway accident reports, I have noticed an inquiry often elicited facts about dubious practices and goings-on which, although not the prime cause, may have contributed to what happened. In this case several circumstances and facts came to light.

The official plans showed a gradient no steeper than 1 in 11 and a minimum radius of 60ft in the curve at the bottom of the Westcourt Street hill, yet a survey of the gradients after the accident revealed that there were no less than 34 yards at 1 in 9.5 (a drop of as much as 3ft from end to end of the car). Several yards of the curve were sharper, and what was worse – instead of any superelevation, cant or banking, call it what you will – making the outer rail higher than the inside rail, as it should have been, the outside rail of the curve was more than ½in *lower*. It is truly remarkable that no car had turned over previously.

The driver, a man of only five months' standing, got the blame for "locking the wheels by unskilful application of the brake power" so that the car skidded down the hill on the slippery rails. Well aware of the danger of this steep hill, the company had appointed two very experienced "pilots", and decreed that the driver of every car down the hill should be accompanied by one of these men. The company, however, had failed to bring the pilotman on duty early enough to sand the rails as he was required to do before the first car was due. The tram driver waited for four or five minutes for the pilot to arrive to ride down with him, but rather than delay his passengers on their way to work in the docks, he took a chance and went on. This was his first mistake, and from then on everything he did with the brakes was wrong.

It is well known in railway and tramway circles that the retarding effect of a wheel sliding or skidding on rail is very much less than when the wheel is braked with such force as will just allow it to continue to revolve[35]. With an electric tram, it also deprives the car of electric braking, because, without rotation of the wheels, the motors will not be revolving, and consequently can generate no current. It was therefore in the company's operating rules that the hand brake must be released before putting on the electric brake. There was, in addition, a rule which stated that "in going down a gradient with hand brake…hold the brake by the hand, but do not lock it by ratchet and pawl in case of skid". In the particular circumstances of Westcourt Street, there was a rule "that the slipper and electric brakes alone are to be used". Yet after the accident the hand brake was found to be locked in the "on" position – so the driver had broken four rules. His bungling had cost the lives of four people and injuries to 50 others.

The Inspector was Major Pringle[36], who made a similar comment to that of Colonel Yorke on the earlier Birmingham accident about the instability of double-deck cars on the 3ft 6in gauge. On this occasion, car no. 19 was carrying about 65 men. Its seating capacity was only 50, and men were standing on both decks – about six of them upstairs. Says the report – "the worst position for standing passengers……not only do they here run greater risk of injury to themselves in the event of an accident, but the additional weight at that elevation increases any tendency to overturn which a car may have acquired owing to centrifugal force".

It is worthy of note that as result of this disaster, the lines were re-routed along a somewhat more suitable street. Also, although not required to do so, the company immediately equipped all its cars with Westinghouse magnetic track brakes. Car no. 19 later re-emerged with a home-made body fitted out as a van for permanent way services.

Operator: **Isle of Thanet Electric Tramways & Lighting Company**
Location: **Belle Vue Road, Ramsgate**
Date: **12 August 1903**

Proceeding in date order, the next accident about which I have worthwhile facts also happened in Kent where, on the 3ft 6in lines of the Isle of Thanet Light Railway, we meet our first case of an electric bogie car in trouble. It happened on 12 August 1903 and concerned an American-built (St Louis Car Co) double-deck car with maximum-traction bogies. There had been several mishaps during the first few months of operation and opponents of the tramway had demanded a BoT inquiry. On 12 October 1902, Major

---

[35] This proposition was established by Captain Sir Douglas Galton (1822-1899), Inspector of Railways and Secretary of the Railway Department of the BoT 1850-57, as a result of experiments made by him in 1878 and described in papers read by him before the Institution of Mechanical Engineers on 24 October 1878 and 24 April 1879.
[36] Sir John Wallace Pringle (1863-1938), Inspecting Officer 1900-16, Chief Inspecting Officer of Railways 1916-29.

Pringle had recommended that track brakes be fitted to all cars. This proved to be relatively easy to implement in the case of single-truck cars, but it could not be done in the case of the bogie cars because of the unusual design of their trucks. So the Company devised, as a substitute, what can only be described as a "Heath Robinson"-type[37] of brake. A steel-shod scotch was hung under one wheel at each end. The scotch was intended to be used in emergency and could be dropped by a lever on the relevant platform. When ascending a hill, the conductor lowered this gadget at his end so that it dragged on the track behind one of the trailing driving wheels. Should the car stall and begin to run back, the scotch came into action under the wheel. Likewise, in the forward direction, the driver could lower it as an emergency brake.

There were some theoretical advantages in having the pony (smaller) wheels in the outward positions and the driving (larger) wheels in the centre – generally referred to as "reversed maximum-traction" – and these cars had this arrangement: the scotch being between the wheels of the bogie.

The accident took place on a relatively unusual example of track alignment. Normally, where there was not enough room for the two lines of a double track with adequate clearance, they were brought together through points into a single line, or were interlaced, but in Ramsgate, where the carriageway was narrow near the bottom of Belle Vue Road, the two lines were merely brought close together, without any overlap[38]. Of course this meant that cars could not pass one another, so there was a rule that if cars approached from opposite directions at the same time, the car going uphill had preference.

On this occasion, the car going down could not stop, and although the driver of an ascending car tried to set back, the cars met in violent, almost head-on, collision. No fewer than 30 people were injured, some of them being catapulted into the road from the upper deck of the runaway by the impact.

As so often was the cause of runaways, the driver had let the car run too fast and, in trying to check its speed, had applied the hand brake too vigorously and locked the wheels, depriving himself of the electric brake. What might perhaps be called a "nostrum" – the locally-designed scotch – had no effect as the car was already skidding! This had been assisted by the rails being wet – the result of road watering, which was at one time a very common practice, but which generally disappeared with the universal adoption of stone and wood blocks and tarmacadam road paving. Previous to the employment of these materials, most roads had surfaces of waterbound macadam or gravel kept more or less compacted by the wide steel tyres of cart wheels. The surface was naturally gritty when dry and fresh dust was always being formed by the interaction of steel and stone plus horse dung finely powdered by passage of wheels and horse hooves. A strong wind on a dry day would raise clouds of swirling grit and dirt. To allay this, the roads were watered, and some tram concerns had their own road watering cars (*e.g.* Cardiff, Chesterfield, Dublin, Gloucester, Reading and Rochdale).

The statutory tramway area was often bordered by such road surfaces which were watered every few hours. This was done by horse-drawn tank carts which sprayed a fan of jets of water to their rear. When the water level in the tank was high, the jets spread water far beyond the limits of the roadway – on both pavements and tram lines.

Here, at Ramsgate, the rail was wet from a fresh watering, and the same thing happened with the Highgate collision described later. The Inspector, Lt-Colonel von Donop[39], found that the condition of the rails compounded the driver's lack of skill so as to cause the accident. The report ended by pointing out that had track brakes been fitted, as recommended earlier, the accident would not have occurred and the company was directed to discontinue the use of the bogie cars until track brakes had been fitted. Given the choice between equipping the cars with new bogies capable of taking track brakes and shortening them to take four-wheel trucks, the company decided on the latter course and the whole batch of bogie cars underwent this conversion.

Car 6 of Yorkshire (Woollen District) Tramways Co in Dewsbury Market Place on 20 May 1904 after a series of collisions. *Courtesy: National Tramway Museum*

Operator: **Yorkshire (Woollen District) Electric Tramways Company**
Location: **Halifax Road, Dewsbury**
Date: **20 May 1904**

Back to Yorkshire for the next case: there, on the Spen Valley Light Railway, tramcar no. 7 belonging to the Yorkshire (Woollen District) Electric Tramways, ran into trouble in the shape of a dray loaded with mineral waters, then a cart and subsequently another tramcar. Eight people, including the tram crew, were injured.

Major Druitt's report records that the car was a four-wheel covered-top double-decker with the usual hand brake and the Westinghouse magnetic track brake, its controllers being of the Brush HD-2 pattern. Also fitted were "Spencer scotch" brakes and Tidswell life-guards; the latter information being quite gratuitous as it had no bearing on the

---

[37] William Heath Robinson (1872-1944) was an English cartoonist of World War I days and later, famous for his drawings of complex mechanisms improvised from the strangest mixtures of "Do-it-Yourself" materials - bedsteads, bicycle chains, biscuit tins, mangles and so on - designed for absurd purposes.

[38] Other examples existed at Ashton-under-Lyne, Ilford, Liverpool and Oldbury.

[39] Pelham George von Donop (1851-1921), Inspecting Officer 1899-1913, Chief Inspecting Officer of Railways 1913-16.

occurrence. (This scotch brake was an unusual item and of a different type to that referred above in connection with Chatham.)

Until two days before this accident, the car had been in its depot having new wheels fitted. It was taken on a trial run in the hands of the shed foreman who pronounced it fit, and it went to work giving no trouble on the day before the accident. On the next day it ran satisfactorily from Dewsbury to Cleckheaton and back but, on the return leg of a second trip, the driver lost control descending Halifax Road, the steep parts having successive 1 in 8, 1 in 11 and 1 in 9 gradients. There is little doubt that the driver had somewhat mismanaged the magnetic brake and had let the car get going too fast (though not out of control) to stop short of the dray – or so the driver thought – so he applied the scotch which acted so smartly that it skidded the wheels, depriving the driver temporarily of his electric brakes.

A driver with presence of mind could still have slowed the car, even if he could not have stopped it, but this man panicked and jumped off. His conductor stuck to his job and was commended for his action in preventing scared passengers from jumping off and injuring themselves. The onrushing car left the rails, went on to the opposite line, and collided in Dewsbury market place with a tramcar from Birkenshaw. The front of no. 7 was wrecked and "the controller thrown into the street".

The Inspector judged the braking equipment of the car to have been in good order and he concluded that the accident was caused by the driver's anxiety to prevent the first collision, after which he lost his head. He added that a much higher standard of driver-training was required.

Operator: **Stalybridge, Hyde, Mossley & Dukinfield Tramways & Electricity Board**
Location: **Ditchcroft Hill, Millbrook**
Date: **11 October 1904**

Next, to the west side of the Pennines, to the SHMD Many tramway students rattle off these initials, but not so many can tell you what they signify. The accident on this system was one of the few occasions when a single-deck car was in serious trouble. There were relatively small numbers of such cars in this country, so they were not likely to be in the news very often. They were thought to be safer on hilly routes than double deckers, especially on the narrow gauge, and it was this quality which caused them to be used for example on the Walkley route in Sheffield and most probably on the Alexandra Palace line (Metropolitan Electric Tramways) in London, although neither was narrow gauge. There were of course places where they were used because of height limitations, such as the lower deck of the High Level bridge connecting Newcastle and Gateshead[40], and the Kingsway Subway, as originally constructed, in London. Manchester had a large batch of cars to cope with low railway bridges on its route 53. Seaside towns also favoured single-deck cars and Blackpool had (and has) the largest number on any British system. Smaller systems, where the traffic was thought not to warrant double-deckers, adopted them. Perhaps another factor was that single deckers were marginally cheaper to build and maintain. In the case of demi-cars (as to which see the following accident), there were savings to be derived from their being driver-only[41].

Now to the accident, as a result of which a little boy of four was killed by falling debris and the tram driver seriously injured. He was a very capable driver, specially selected to drive on the hill on which his car ran amok. He had been with SHMD for only one month, but had gained varied experience driving on the systems at Brighton, Chatham, Bath, Weston-super-Mare and the Isle of Thanet. This was in the days when men moved about to keep in employment – the Englishman's will to work not having been sapped by "doles" and State mollycoddling.

Car no. 33, a four-wheeler equipped with hand brake and magnetic track brakes, had already descended Ditchcroft Hill (a place which was to gain a bad reputation in tramway annals), in Millbrook, safely and without trouble three times on the morning of 11 October 1904 in the hands of Driver Knell. It was it seems a case of three times lucky, for on the fourth descent the car got out of control and, attaining a great speed, derailed on the 100ft radius curve at the bottom of the hill, demolishing the stone cottage into which it crashed. Leaving the top of the hill to go down 83 yards at 1 in 15.3, followed by 146 yards at 1 in 11.4, the driver had put the controller on to the magnetic brake notches and let the car roll, but it failed to respond as he expected, and it quickly gained speed. We can picture Driver Knell leaning over the front of the accelerating car, with great presence of mind pouring sand on to the rails from a bag. This and other measures he took, vouched for by witnesses, were of no avail.

The handling of the brake was called into question at the BoT inquiry, which was conducted by Lt-Colonel von Donop. Brake operation is a sort of *leit motif* running through many accidents, and I will not dilate on it now but explain it when we come to a more widely-known incident in Archway Road in London.

Operator:　　**Halifax Corporation**
Location:　　**Horton Street, Halifax**
Date:　　　　**14 October 1904**

It is well-known in tramway circles that the Halifax tramway system had more hills and undulations per route mile than any other in the Kingdom. It was also one of the first to see the possible benefit the use of demi-cars (small purpose-built one-man trams) could have on services with lower traffic potential. Such cars were being promoted by Raworth Traction Patents, the first car of this type having been introduced at Southport early in 1903.

Halifax Corporation purchased two such cars, becoming nos. 95 and 96 of their fleet but, unlike the Southport car, which had a single traction motor, Halifax's gradients made a two-motor version a necessity. Whilst there is nothing unusual about using two motors, Raworth's demi-cars broke new ground in the tramway world by being regenerative. There is much kinetic energy in a train or tram running with power off and, if running downhill, gravity adds to it. Braking or slowing down means absorbing this energy and the usual ways of accomplishing this generally means producing heat which goes to

---

[40] Strictly speaking, the High Level bridge could (and did) accommodate double-deck cars: it was a railway bridge over Wellington Street at the Gateshead approaches that limited the headroom to single-deckers.

[41] Single deckers have been universally adopted in modern systems at home and abroad, although double deckers are still to be found on "traditional" systems, such as Blackpool and Hong Kong.

waste. It has long been an ideal of electrical engineers to put this energy to use and so save power bills. Electric motors, of the types used on trams, trains and trolleybuses, can usually be turned into dynamos by simple changes in their connections. By the use of traction motors with shunt- or compound-wound field systems, instead of the otherwise universal series-wound fields, it made it easier for electrical energy produced during electric braking to be returned to the overhead line, whence it could be distributed to other cars on the system which were drawing current via the power station busbars. For electricity to be returned to the power station, it was fundamental that the connection between the regenerating tram and the station busbars remained intact.

No. 95, in the charge of motorman John Rhodes, was (according to his account) descending the 1 in 14 gradient of Horton Street at a slow speed, being held in check by the regenerative brake. Unfortunately for him, the automatic circuit breaker on the power station switchboard for the Horton Street section tripped out, for a reason not established, disconnecting the supply. As there was no longer anywhere for the regenerated power to go, the retardation caused by the generation immediately ceased and the car began to accelerate down the incline. Motorman Rhodes repeated the routine for establishing regenerative braking, unfortunately to no avail, and the car continued to accelerate. He then applied his hand brake, but was unable to avoid colliding with the other demi-car, no. 96, which was approaching on the single track on to which Rhodes' car had run. Rhodes was injured in the collision and, as a result of further colliding with a dray, the driver of the latter vehicle was also hurt.

The inquiry established that Rhodes was unaware that the controllers on the car had an "emergency" position for the reverse handle to cater for loss of power connection which, had it have been operated, would have provided a powerful short-circuit brake on the car. In addition, the car had a hand-operated slipper brake which Rhodes did not use or attempt to use. The Inspecting Officer, Lt-Colonel Druitt, drew attention to the failure on the part of the management to ensure their motormen were properly instructed, and reminded them that there was a BoT regulation in force in respect of Halifax, to the effect that their trams were required to be fitted with a run-back brake, whereas the two demi-cars were not so fitted. It seems likely that Halifax also realised that this was true for others in the fleet, and the undertaking subsequently implemented a programme of modifications to other tramcars to achieve this. We shall come across this modification again in respect of an accident three years and a day later, also on the Halifax system (at Pye Nest Road, Sowerby Bridge).

The report into the Horton Street runaway contains several details of the controllers fitted to the car at the time. They appear to be of the rare HG-2 type made by Brush, though unfortunately this point is not specifically mentioned. Detailed technical information on Brush tramcar traction equipment is scant compared with that of other manufacturers and, unlike other suppliers, no Brush tramway traction hardware seems to have survived the 1930s. But using a known description and circuit of the Brush H-2 controller, upon which the HG-2 was based, and the details given by Colonel Druitt in the report, it is possible to work out the likely form of working and operation of the HG-2.

The H-2 was a simple two-motor series-parallel controller without graduated rheostatic braking, but with an "emergency brake" facility obtained by putting the main handle to "off" and pulling the reverse handle from "forward" through "off" and "reverse" into an emergency position. In this respect it was similar to British Thomson-Houston 'K' and

English Electric Manufacturing Co 'DE1' types. However the H-2 did not, unlike the others, have an equivalent fifth position for the reverse handle giving reverse emergency braking beyond the "forward" setting. In motoring and emergency braking, the motors would be pure series machines, but the change to regeneration would require them to become shunt-wound machines, with their armatures connected permanently in series. With the HG-2 controller, the fifth position for the reverse handle was introduced to achieve this change to the motor field windings, so in clockwise sequence the handle positions became: forward regeneration; forward motoring; off (where the handle could be removed); reverse motoring; emergency brake (forward motion only). The usual interlocking would have been provided, requiring the power handle to be in the "off" position before the reverse handle could be changed in its position but, in addition, there would have been an additional restraint on the power handle preventing progression beyond the full-series notch when in the forward regeneration position.

In understanding the procedure which the motorman would have had to follow to use the regenerative brake, as described above, it is convenient to assume the car to have stopped on a downward slope. Before starting the car, the motorman would have had to move the reverse handle anti-clockwise one position from "forward" to "regen"; this would prepare the motor fields for being energised from the line as shunt-wound machines. Leaving the power handle in "off", he would allow the car to start rolling under gravity and then feed up through the usual series resistance notches until by full series he had the car running downhill at about 6mph (this was the BoT speed limit on the Horton Street gradient) and regenerating into the line. Notching back would introduce resistance into the motor circuit and allow the car to run faster, so, in order to stop the car, he would have had to apply one of the friction brakes to take over as he notched back or threw off.

This conjectural outline as to how the HG-2 controller was designed and used prompts the thought that confusion at times of stress might have occurred and in part explains why, when motorman Rhodes lost retardation from the regenerative braking, it took significant time for him (using both his hands) to repeat his attempt to apply it, consuming much of the 26 seconds available to him (as calculated by Colonel Druitt) before the first collision.

But it is possible to consider a different scenario which also takes in another feature of the incident about which Colonel Druitt makes observation but no comment, although he may well have explored it. If motorman Rhodes had forgotten to change the reverse handle from "forward" to "regen" when he started down the hill, his notching up to engage the regenerative brake would instead have acted in motoring mode and so accelerate the car. On realising this, his likely reaction would have been to throw to "off", then move the reverse handle into the "regen" position and apply the regenerative brake as quickly as possible to recover the situation. In a state of anxiety, he probably would have done so by swinging the power handle to the "full regen" position ("full series" on the controller), without pausing on the intermediate resistance notches. The chances are that the car's speed would have been well in excess of the usual 6mph. At 10mph, the generated voltage of the two motors in series would have been of the order of 840 volts and, on striking the full series notch, this would become paralleled to the power station busbars which were of course operating at only 500 volts. In these circumstances, it is no surprise that the feeder circuit-breaker for the Horton Street section tripped out on the resulting momentary current overload. Whilst this is speculation, no one else seems to have offered any explanation for the tripping of the feeder circuit breaker at exactly this crucial time.

The question might well arise in the minds of readers "Why didn't the circuit breakers on the tram trip as well?". The probable answer is that there weren't any. Demi-cars were intended to be cheap to build and operate. Provision of two non-automatic canopy switches and a traction fuse was a cheaper option than circuit breakers. In the circumstances of the Horton Street incident, it would have been quite reasonable for the power station circuit breaker to have responded more quickly than a tramcar fuse to a sudden, but short, overcurrent[42].

Operator: **Isle of Thanet Electric Tramways & Lighting Company**
Location: **Madeira Hill, Ramsgate**
Date: **3 August 1905**

Going on into 1905 brings us back to Thanet, where a tramcar unexpectedly landed on the beach of the popular resort of Ramsgate. This spectacular stranding occurred on 3 August, when four-wheel double-deck car no. 41 on this 3ft 6in gauge line leapt from the rails when running down Madeira Hill, mounted the kerb, crossed the pavement to break through the railings and fall over the cliff on to the beach 32 feet below. One passenger – fortunately there were only six – and the driver, were seriously injured, the car body being wrecked and wrenched from its truck.

Just like the earlier case on the SHMD, the car had previously made three safe and normal descents of the hill in question before coming to a grievous end on the fourth. From a compulsory stop at the top, Madeira Hill dropped away continuously for 230 yards on

Isle of Thanet Electric Tramways Co car 41 deposited on the beach at Ramsgate, after careering down Madeira Hill on 3 August 1905.

Courtesy: National Tramway Museum

46

slopes varying from 1 in 13 to 1 in 16. Not so very steep for a tramway hill, but it was complicated by bends and, on a reverse or "S" bend, the car parted from the rails at the point where the curve changed from 66ft radius left to 73ft radius right with no straight piece in between and, with the rail superelevated in the wrong direction! This would not have mattered if the car had not been going faster than the 3mph stipulated, but having failed to stop at the top of the hill, and gathering speed far in excess of this, it had no chance. The end throw of the car, 28ft long on only 6ft wheelbase, will also have lent instability on the reverse bend.

The car had slipper, rheostatic and hand brakes, but there is not much doubt that the driver had locked the wheels with the hand brake and so had deprived himself of electric braking. The company was "hauled over the coals" for permitting such a callow driver to work cars on the tricky Madeira Hill – the man had only worked as a regular driver on four days previously.

It is worthwhile noting that on cars of this type, the slipper brake was applied by a lever on the platform instead of the usual hand wheel and, because there could be no graduation of the brake pressure, the levers had "on" and "off" positions only, which made no allowance for the wear of the blocks. There was, so said the report by Lt-Colonel van Donop, "certainly a screw…..adjustment, but it was…..crude….and could not be made use of in an emergency". The sanding gear had also failed to operate and its design was criticised because sand did not fall on the rails when the car was going round a curve.

Operator: **Liverpool Corporation**
Location: **Leece Street/Renshaw Street, Liverpool**
Date: **22 January 1906**

Most tramway systems, even those well-administered, having a steep hill, sooner or later had an accident on that hill[43]. However well-organised or how good the standard of maintenance of track and cars may have been, somebody or something ultimately lets them down. Liverpool Corporation had an electric tramway system operated to a high standard relatively free from trouble, but one of those typical runaways occurred on their Leece Street line on 22 January 1906.

On that day, car no. 447 – 28ft long on a 6ft wheelbase – carrying 73 people down the slope of from 1 in 22 to 1 in 17.5 in Hardman and Leece Streets, failed to stay on the rails on the curve at the bottom of the hill leading into Renshaw Street. With a full complement of passengers (64 sitting and nine standing), and on perfect track which consisted of 96lb rails laid only the previous year, the car got out of control. The resulting overturn, on to the left-hand side of the car, wrecked the upper deck but scarcely

---

[42] The information contained in this account has been supplemented by material supplied by J D Markham, who is co-author with Dr Struan Jno T Robertson of a book entitled *The British Regenerative Braking Story* to be published by the Scottish Tramway & Transport Society.

[43] It is noteworthy that Sheffield, which was a particularly hilly system, does not feature in any of the Inspectorate's accident reports. According to *Trams in Trouble* by Brian Hinchliffe, published by Pennine Publications, Sheffield, 1990, not a single passenger of the several billion carried received a fatal injury whilst on a Sheffield tram (*op cit* at p 3).

The accident in Leece Street, Liverpool, which took place on 22 January 1906, with overturned car 447. *Courtesy: National Tramway Museum*

scratched the lower regions, and the car was towed away on its own wheels. Between 40 and 50 people were hurt, but by good fortune only one was seriously injured.

The Inspector, Lt-Colonel von Donop, came to the view that the driver started off from the top of the hill at a somewhat high speed and that, in order to check this speed, he reversed his current, thus blowing the canopy switch. He then restored the switch and reversed the current again, with the same result. The driver then appeared to have lost his head for, by his own account, without cancelling the switch, he applied the reverse current. But with the switch out there would have been no line current flowing through the motors, and no response could therefore be expected until the parallel notches were reached. Meanwhile, neither the hand brake nor the electric brake were being applied, so it was not surprising that a high rate of speed had been attained. When close to the curve, the driver had applied the hand brake but by then the speed was too high and the derailment and overturning ensued.

The Inspector also urged the Corporation to consider rearranging the roadway at the junction, so as to provide suitable superelevation of the outer rail at that point.

Operator:	**South Staffordshire Tramways (Lessee) Company**
Location:	**Birmingham Road, West Bromwich**
Date:	**5 May 1906**

Before considering further the catalogue of runaways, let us have a look at a very different tragedy. It was not so much that a child was run over by a tram – this was no rarity especially among cyclists whose wheels got caught in the lines – but the apparatus which should have saved her failed in its purpose. This accident happened in West Bromwich on a line over which cars of the South Staffordshire Tramways Company operated. No. 20, of that Company, a reversed maximum-traction bogie car (*i.e.* the pony wheels were outward), *en route* from Dudley to Birmingham, was approaching the West Bromwich/Handsworth boundary on a wide straight road down a slope of 1 in 120.

Running at 6 to 8mph and nearing the Woodman Inn, the driver saw three children in the middle of the other track but, as they were quite clear of his car, he did no more than sound the gong. He was getting close to the children "who appeared to have been engaged in picking up horse manure from the road", when the little girl of the trio suddenly ran to join her brother who was standing on the opposite footpath. Fate intervened, she stumbled and fell in front of the tram. The driver at once applied the electric brake but had not the slightest chance of stopping short of and avoiding running over the child.

The "trigger" type of lifeguard dropped, but the tray failed to scoop the girl whose mutilated body was found underneath the leading bogie. It is not our purpose to dilate on the gruesome details, but to note the point the report makes about tramway equipment. The Inspector took the view that the lifeguard was not effective because the girl fell flat on the road surface with her arms outstretched. Her hands were apparently the first part of her to reach the tray and were small enough to pass under it rather than being scooped up. According to this hypothesis, the tray then rose above the remainder of her body, leaving her to the mercy of the wheels.

Lifeguards took several forms; on steam trams only the engines had the equipment (as already noted). This could be a deep fender, not unlike the "cowcatchers" so familiar and conspicuous on pictures of trans-prairie railway engines, which were intended to prevent people from passing underneath the wheels of the trams. There was no equivalent on horse cars as the horses were leading and anybody unlucky enough to be down on the road would be trampled on before the car reached him[44]. On electric cars there were many designs of lifeguard. Some were nothing more than a V-shaped plough, as favoured by Liverpool in its early days. Others were metal-framed with mesh surfaces and some had side valances. The most common took the following form. There was, under the foremost part of the platform, a vertical gate comprised of horizontal wooden slats athwart the car and free to swing on hinges at its top. Behind the gate was a horizontal tray, also of wooden slats, parallel with the gate. The action was such that as soon as the gate hit an obstruction, it swung inwards and in so doing released a catch which allowed the leading end of the tray to drop. Assuming the obstruction to be a person, the tray would have shovelled him or her up, the tray having a vertical fence at its rear to prevent the victim from going any further. The side valances, where fitted, were hinged so as to retract when the gate swung inwards[45].

It is very obvious that being at the extreme ends of the car, severe end-to-end pitching would bring the gates into contact with the road, and thus trigger the tray. The usual inward and visible sign on the driver's platform was the head of a plunger normally lying

---

[44] According to *Horse Trams of the British Isles* by R W Rush, published by The Oakwood Press, Usk, 2004, lifeguard protection was applied to horse cars from the 1890s. This generally took the form of either a blunt-pointed wooden "cowcatcher" or metal plates set at an angle in front of each wheel so as to deflect objects clear of the wheels. At the end of the 19th century, wooden slats were often adopted, rigidly-mounted and suspended across the width of the cars forward of the wheels (*op cit* at p 43). The horse-operated Edinburgh Street Tramways Company provided lifeguards of wire mesh, fitted in front of, and between, the wheels of the cars.

[45] The report does not state the make of the lifeguard in question, but most likely it was of the Hudson and Bowring type, which was trigger-activated (see fig 4). With another type, the tray was not activated by the gate but was cam-operated. The Phillipson lifeguard, with which Bolton no. 66 (preserved at, and operating on, the Blackpool tramway) is equipped, is reset by a lever, not a pedal. Others employed a toggle or latch. Blackpool tramways have some lifeguards which are pneumatically reset.

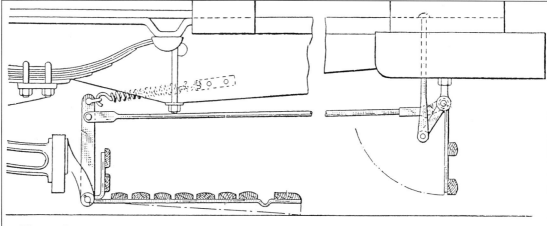

Figure 4

A falling-tray lifeguard by Hudson and Bowring of Manchester, which was widely used on tramcars in the UK and USA. The latch holding the tray clear of the road surface takes the form of a resettable toggle, which is pushed over centre to release it by the action of the gate at the front being swung back.

flush with the floor. Whenever the gate and tray triggered, the plunger rose and projected several inches above the floor. To reset the apparatus, the driver had to depress the plunger by stepping on it heavily, and on a car on a rough track or one with a sensitive trigger, it was not at all a novelty to see the driver performing this antic. It is worth noting in passing that motor buses were not compelled to wear these encumbrances, although they did have a sort of angled fence of horizontal slats intended to steer obstructions, which the front wheels missed, clear of the rear wheels. Nowadays rubber-tyred juggernauts, the wheels of which are right in front and which travel at speeds unheard of on public roads in earlier tram days, have no protective device whatever.

After this digression, let us return to the accident report which recognised that, although the BoT stipulated self-acting lifeguards, no standard height had been specified for the simple reason that it varied with the different types of car, "some of which pitch more than others". To those who remember riding on numerous four-wheel cars on various systems, this seems a rather too obvious statement. Allowing for this pitching, the Inspector, Lt-Colonel Yorke, thought that four-wheel cars should have a clearance of four inches. Apart from the pitching motion, he had to take into account the uneven levels of granite setts, if the lifeguards were not to be everlastingly tripped by the setts. On a smooth-riding bogie car, he opined that the height could be as little as 2½in[46].

A long delay in getting the child's body from beneath the car pin-pointed the question of lifting jacks. The driver quickly went to the nearby Handsworth tram depot and fetched one, and later another, only to find that they were intended for depot use and were too high to apply under a bogie truck on the road. The problem was solved by a jack borrowed from a motor wagon which happened to be passing. Strangely enough, all cars in neighbouring Smethwick did carry jacks in compliance with City of Birmingham police regulations [47], and it was mentioned in the report that all cars on the LCC Tramways carried jacks.

The reference to horse manure quoted in the report brings to mind a once very familiar sight, and although it has nothing to do with tramway history, I hope a digression into social history will prove interesting. The practice of collecting dung from the streets in

Two views of the Swindon accident (above and overleaf) that occurred on 1 June 1906, which resulted from a brake failure of car 11.   Five persons were killed and over 30 injured.

Courtesy: National Tramway Museum

our towns was still prevalent in my schooldays, and many boys from the poorer areas spent Saturday mornings scraping this substance from the roadways and hawking it for pocket money.   There was a ready sale in the adjacent better-off roads, where it was valuable in the small gardens, and a two-gallon galvanised bucketful would fetch a penny – a lot of money to children then.

Operator:	**Swindon Corporation**
Location:	**Victoria Road, Swindon**
Date:	**1 June 1906**

We now turn to another, but more compact, 3ft 6in gauge system, that of the Swindon Corporation Tramways.   We have met cases of drivers with only a few days' experience on the road being faced with a sudden cataclysm and being unable to meet it; in other words, a "brand new" novice driver, but this time we meet a "brand new" car coming to grief.   This happened in Swindon in the town which owes its existence to rail transport: the choice of a sleepy agricultural location in which to place the workshops of the up-and-coming Great Western Railway (GWR).   Swindon's trams have long since gone (in 1929), and the final faint beat of its atrophied railway heart has now been stilled too.

The hill on which we are interested in its tramway days was a long one in Victoria Road, on the route from the Corn Exchange to the GWR station.   Descending, its slope was no steeper than 1 in 24 for the first 400 yards, but after that it became 1 in 14 and 1 in 15.8. It was down here that the driver of car no. 11 lost control.   For Swindon the day was an exceptional one, being the occasion of the Bath and West of England Agricultural Show. Consequently the traffic on the tram route to the railway station was unusually heavy,

---

[46] Glasgow used a device on its four-wheel cars which was designed to raise and lower the leading gate so as to maintain the minimum clearance.   Glasgow no. 812, at the National Tramway Museum, Crich, Derbyshire, is so equipped.

[47] If this statement was true, it seems odd that the police should have required the presence of jacks on cars operating on the Birmingham-Dudley route via Smethwick, but not on the Birmingham-Dudley route via West Bromwich.

Another view of the Swindon accident.   *Tomkins and Barrett*

which was doubtless the reason a car built to seat 26 inside, 32 upstairs, and seven standees downstairs – total 65 – was carrying not many short of 80 people, some of whom filled the rear platform.   Nearly all of them were injured to some extent, and from the scene of the crash, at which two were killed, 35 were taken to hospital where three more succumbed.   The conductor was concussed for 48 hours and could not afterwards remember the occurrence.

No. 11 first went to work on the Corn Exchange route on 30 May.   On its next day out, disaster overcame this glistening vehicle, purchased only a few months before and resplendent as it must have been with its pristine varnish, paintwork and brass fittings, so characteristic of cars from Falcon Works at Loughborough.   What nowadays are referred to as teething troubles on new items are shown to be nothing new because, owing to a defective lighting circuit, no. 11 did not go to work until 11.40am, when it replaced its sister, no. 10, which was suffering from a controller defect.

Lt-Colonel von Donop's report covers no fewer than seven printed foolscap pages in explaining what went wrong with no. 11.   The gist of it follows.   On his very first run down the hill, driver Lyons found the magnetic brake was not "acting well", and he told the traffic manager.   Lyons then drove the car down the hill six or seven times more before being relieved for tea by driver Stallard, and before which he had reported the brake for a second time at about one o'clock.   Stallard made three journeys, on the first and third of which the car stopped with a jerk every ten yards or so when the magnets were applied.   On his second trip all was well.   This driver also reported the trouble to the traffic manager, who, after inspecting the brakes, offered to substitute another car. Stallard replied "That would be best, sir, as she is not safe as she is", to which the traffic manager responded "Very well, do another journey and I will have one ready for you when you are next down".   So driver Stallard made another journey and, neither traffic manager nor relief car being in evidence on his return, made yet another.   After this journey he found the traffic manager and a fitter waiting, but the latter was without tools! While the fitter went to get spanners, the car departed on still another journey by which time driver Lyons had taken over again.   The fitter, now with tools, got on the car on the way up, and on arrival at the Corn Exchange found that the brakes did need adjustment, but failed to do anything to them on the weak excuse that he could not do so while the hand brake was "on" as it had to be to hold the car on the incline at the terminus[48].

Then the heavily-overloaded fatal journey began. The first stop was at Prospect, where the magnets brought the car up with a bad jerk, and at Brow, a loop 170 yards further on, the car was stopped without difficulty by the hand brake alone. From this point the driver started away by releasing the hand brake and applying the magnets, but not until 35 yards had passed did they act with one big jerk, followed by a jolt a few yards further on. After a momentary application of power to set the wheels turning in case they were skidding, the driver put the controller to the fourth braking notch, but without the slightest effect. The car rapidly gained speed and on reaching the curve in the track, derailed and then turned over on to its right side.

The fitter, who had been riding on the footstep because there was no space on the platform, observed the track magnet jumping up and down and to and fro. That the magnets were pulling on the track was proved by the fact that their springs were found to be stretched to double their length when the magnets still clung to the rails as the car pulled away from them as it rolled over. The inquiry paid great attention to the evidence of a GWR engineer who examined the car as it lay on its side, and several witnesses gave prominence to the fact that the driver had removed his overcoat during the descent and, while so doing, "let go of his levers altogether".

However the crucial cause of the accident was the brake linkage, which was out of adjustment. It got worse and worse with each successive jerk so that in the end the magnets had no effect on the wheel blocks. The report lashed out right, left and centre: on the drivers' not insisting on withdrawal of the car; on the traffic manager for not withdrawing it; on the fitter for not being prepared and then for not making an effort to remedy the defects he knew to exist; and on the management in general for error of judgement, as it was considered injudicious to employ a novel type of car and an unproven one at that, in charge of drivers who had never previously handled it on the most exacting route on the Corporation's tramways, and on a day when it was known that traffic would be exceptional and that the cars would be likely to be heavily-loaded.

Operator: **Metropolitan Electric Tramways**
Location: **Archway Tavern, Highgate, London**
Date: **23 June 1906**

We next turn our attention to London where, only 22 days after the tragedy in Swindon, a car ran away providing more injuries, some fatal. Highgate once more was the site of a serious tramway collision following a runaway, and possibly for the reason that it occurred in the metropolis, this accident attracted wide attention and was much discussed in tramway circles.

The Archway Tavern is at the bottom of what were two tramway hills converging on an

---

[48] Since the magnetic brakes were of the Westinghouse-Newell type, with the wheel shoes operating on the inner side faces of the wheel treads, while the hand brake worked wheel shoes on the outside faces of the treads, the fitter's excuse had no merit since the linkage concerned would not have been involved in holding the tram stationary.

The accident at Archway, London, on 23 June 1906, with Metropolitan Electric Tramways 115 in collision with another car of the company.

F Wilson

important crossroads. One hill leads down from Highgate Village (the route of the cable tramway, the troubles of which appear earlier in these annals), the other, known as Archway Road, comes down from the direction of Barnet and passes under the Archway – the high bridge carrying Hornsey Lane. On the day in question, type A car no. 115 of the Metropolitan Electric Tramways' (MET) fleet careered down this hill, colliding with a hearse, a furniture pantechnicon, a motor bus and a cab, as well as another tramcar. Three persons were killed and 20 injured – some seriously – among people moving about in the street. Nobody was hurt on any of the vehicles involved, though a few people who jumped off the runaway received slight injuries.

The tramway on which the accident happened was the three furlongs of track belonging to the LCC, and was not only their first piece of electric tramway on their Northern Section, but it was their very first stretch of "overhead" anywhere[49]. It was isolated from most of the LCC system and remained so until November in the year following this disaster. Even then, LCC cars coming along Holloway Road terminated at the Tavern, and it was to be another seven years before through working was established and LCC cars worked over it as a result of pressure from 'bus competition. At the time that no. 115 ran away, the LCC line was leased to the Middlesex County Council and the MET company operated the trams by agreement with that authority.

We go back to Lt-Colonel Yorke's report to obtain the following facts: the line, of 4ft 8½in gauge, was straight and dropped down sharply to the Tavern at an inclination of 1 in 22 for the first furlong and then at 1 in 23. The next paragraph, culled verbatim from the report, epitomises the BoT attitude to such slopes:

> *Gradients such as these are by no means severe or exceptional, and tramcars can be, and usually are, controlled upon them by means of hand brakes only. In many parts of the country, tramways have been authorised by Parliament upon inclines of 1 in 10 and 1 in 9, and in such cases it is necessary to use some description of track brakes (either mechanical, magnetic or pneumatic). The practice of the officers of the Board of Trade is to insist upon track brakes being fitted to all cars which run over gradients of 1 in 15 or steeper, unless they are very short, and to*

cause the speed of the cars while descending ordinary hills to be limited to six miles an hour as a maximum, or in the case of steep hills to be limited to four miles an hour. It is also usual for all cars to be stopped at the top of all hills with gradients of 1 in 20 or worse.

The car had seats for 30 people inside and 38 outside. Empty, it weighed 12 tons divided equally between two maximum-traction bogies, the pony axles of which were outward, each carrying about two tons. Some details in these accounts may be of little or no relevance to the accidents, but are included as they give information of general interest to the tramway student and are not readily available elsewhere.

Let us see what happened. In keeping with the BoT dicta about hills, there was a compulsory stop at the Archway with a twofold object: "to ensure that cars shall enter upon the gradient….at a low rate of speed" and "to give the motorman ample time to apply his magnetic brake before starting down the hill". The latter seems a strange explanation as it would be a matter of only a split second to move the controller handle on to the prescribed notch[50]. All MET cars were equipped with electric magnetic brakes, and it was laid down that before starting away from the compulsory stop at the Archway, the controller should be set at the second notch as this would result in the speed of the car not rising above the 6mph maximum referred to two paragraphs earlier[51]. With this type of brake, the retarding power was proportional to the speed so as soon as speed increased, so would the current generated by the motors rise and increase the drag of the magnets which would slow the car down. (In later years I rode down this hill on MET and LCC cars many times and never once saw this instruction obeyed; in fact, without exception, the drivers gave the cars a couple of notches of power to speed them on their way!)

Going back to the report and the driver's own evidence at the inquiry – near the Archway the rails became very slippery owing to the road having been recently watered and, on trying to make the compulsory stop with the hand brake, the wheels skidded. He released the hand brake, applied the magnets, and put down sand, but the wheels failed to start rolling, so the car continued to slide past the Archway on the 1 in 22 gradient down which it gathered speed. Realising that the car was getting out of control, the driver signalled to his conductor to apply the hand brake at the rear end. This was done but, having no effect, it was released whereupon the driver put the controller into "reverse" and turned it to the first power notch. This, of course, "blew" the circuit breaker, and the driver then correctly put the controller on to the eighth (highest) power notch which, by connecting the motors in parallel, forced them to generate current against one another which should have produced a strong braking effect. Again nothing resulted because the wheels were not revolving and consequently the motors were not generating.

---

[49] It is a minor mystery as to how the LCC managed to get powers to build the overhead line there: the London boroughs had the power of veto over the installation of overhead wires and, without exception, rigidly used it until 1908.

[50] It is for conjecture whether the Inspector really intended to say: "to give the motorman ample time to determine that his magnetic brake has become established".

[51] From the report, it would appear that the journey between Whetstone (where the car began) and Archway was over five miles and that this was covered in 27 minutes: an average speed of 11.4mph. To achieve such a high speed suggests the MET might well have been using the magnetic brake for service stops, particularly given that a significant section of the route had a 6mph speed limit. This point was not taken by the Inspector.

The car, gaining further speed, soon hit a funeral hearse, which it badly damaged and swept out of the way (we are not told whether it contained a corpse), and was rapidly approaching a large furniture van. The driver, as a last resort, turned the controller to the sixth (maximum) magnetic brake notch, and then jumped off. The car had attained what he called a terrific speed, but seeing that he escaped without a scratch, he must have exaggerated. After wrecking the pantechnicon, the tram continued to increase speed and ran into a "Vanguard" motor bus, forcing it into the premises of a jobmaster and a restaurant. The next vehicle in its path was another tram of the same type, standing at the terminus at the bottom of the hill. The runaway car became locked into the stationary one, which it propelled some 40 yards along Holloway Road where, after knocking down an electric lamp standard and the bollard of a refuge, the pair eventually stopped against the kerb of the nearside pavement.

The word "jobmaster" may not be known to younger readers of this book, so, as it is of transport interest, an explanation will not be out of place. Jobmasters were not unusual in my childhood: they were tradesmen who hired out carriages and other conveyances with horses and, more often than not, liveried coachmen. Their nearest present-day equivalent is the man who provides hired chauffeur-driven cars for weddings and other outings. Generally part of the same business was a "livery and bait" stable. At such place, one could get accommodation for trap or carriage and food for one's horse, if one's own horse, or that of one's host, had no stabling. Their counterparts today are the garages and filling stations, and, from what I have read, comparable roguery to be found at some of these places is basically unchanged. In place of not giving animals the food for which they charged, or perfunctory grooming or carriage washing, we now hear of falsifying mileometers, skimped servicing, botched repairs, and charging for changing sump oil when it hasn't been done.

After this digression, let us return to the MET car and see what went wrong with it. The report is unusually long but wastes no words: it is interesting from beginning to end and, containing so much, it is difficult to *précis*.

The car had been out of service for about three weeks during which time it had been overhauled and repainted. It should therefore have been in "apple-pie" order, and it had accomplished a test run satisfactorily on the day before the accident. In going into the reasons why an apparently perfect car came to grief, Colonel Yorke is scathingly critical of tramcar brakes in general, of sanding gear and of the paucity of attention given to brakes and their manipulation during the training of drivers, and of the difficulty of avoiding putting inexperienced men on the road where their mistakes can affect not only their passengers but other road users as well. He compares the training of a tramway driver with the thorough grounding of the railway driver of those days, who served on the footplate for years before being put in charge of an engine; even then gaining experience as a shunting driver, progressing to goods trains prior to being put on passenger trains.

On tram brakes, the report said that the car in question had had brakes which were in better condition than most, but they possessed "all the unmechanical features (*sic*) which are characteristic of most tramcar hand brakes". Their adjustment was "rough and ready", made of parts knocked up in a forge when needed. In all respects they were what was used on light, slow horse cars, and no part was designed or made with the precision required for mechanical apparatus. Everything was wrong, he said, with the sanders which dropped sand too far away from the wheels, even if the sand arrived on the line at all. The accident was blamed on the driver's inexperience, but the report did ask why, with electricity to hand, he should be expected to do so much in an emergency. It is a fact that the driver, whilst keeping his eyes on the road, had to use his feet to apply sand, sound the gong, control the dog or pawl on the hand brake pillar, and perhaps deal with the life-guard pedal. His left hand would be on the controller and his right on the hand brake, and he might have to ring the bell to alert the conductor to assist with the brake. *All this* possibly having to be done *simultaneously* – a physical impossibility even for an agile quick-thinking man.

What the Inspector believed happened was that the driver applied the hand brake with too much pressure, and that the newness of the blocks and the greasy condition of the rails caused the wheels to skid; that though the driver released the hand brake he did not succeed in doing so completely, with the result that the rear driving wheels continued to skid[52]; that he then got confused and turned the handles various ways without knowing exactly what he was doing; and that his nerves completely failing him, he jumped off the car, and left it so far as he knew without any brakes on at all. So far as the equipment was concerned, apart from the general comments given above, the Inspector concluded that the origin of the trouble was that the brake blocks were new and were adjusted with insufficient, and probably unequal, clearances from the wheels.

It was the Inspector's view that if the driver, immediately on finding that the wheels were skidding, had been careful to release the hand brake completely, and to give a plentiful supply of sand to the rails so as to cause the wheels to revolve, and had then applied his magnetic brake with gradually increasing force, the car would have been under proper control and would have descended the incline with perfect safety. Even at the time that he jumped off the car, if he had placed his reversing key in the forward position before applying the magnetic brake, it was probable that speed would have been very much reduced by the time the car reached the foot of the hill.

In this case, and in others, the Inspector recommended that consideration should be directed to giving the magnets current from the power supply, and before this account comes to an end, we shall see how a car was treated in this way, causing it to run away and turn over 28 years later (see the Eltham accident on 25 March 1934).

It will perhaps be thought that too much is being written about this one case, but it attracted a lot of publicity at the time, and was regarded as important in tramway circles. Similar disasters, which were in the public mind at about the same time, had focused a great deal of attention in Parliament and the press on tramway brakes[53]. Much adverse criticism had been let loose, it being averred that tramway authorities had failed in their duty, and they should immediately "be compelled to use the most instantaneous and efficient method of arresting the progress of a tramcar". The Inspecting Officer wryly commented: "It is perhaps fortunate that no means are available whereby the progress of

---

[52] With both motors in use, the electric circuit arrangements required to ensure load balance in braking between the motors did not at that time enable one motor to generate whilst the other was skidding. On car no. 115, a skidding motor would have deprived the other motor of the ability to "self-excite", which is a vital process in the establishment of electric braking.

[53] In connection with the Swindon accident, which had occurred earlier that month (*qv*), news of it had reached the national press. A leading article in the *Daily Mail* entitled "The Scandal of Preventable Accidents", alleged that more passengers had been killed in 1902 by runaway tramcar accidents than on the entire railway system.

a tramcar can be instantaneously arrested, as the result would be as bad as a collision".

The Inspector was also astringent about "emergency" brakes, saying that "in tramcar driving, the emergency is ever present and a driver should be permitted at all times to use the most powerful braking at his disposal". We know, of course, that this advice was not universally adopted, and that those systems on which rheostatic was the only power brake could not adopt it for all stops without overworking the car motors.

Before leaving this case to pass on to a disaster at Halifax, I would like to mention the evidence of the chief officer for the LCC Tramways, A L C Fell. (When I was a lad, this gentleman's name was painted in full on both sides of about 1,900 trams, as well as on a fleet of internal service cars and ancillary road vehicles.   Sometimes, as schoolboys walking home along the tram route, we would declaim or chant "Aubrey

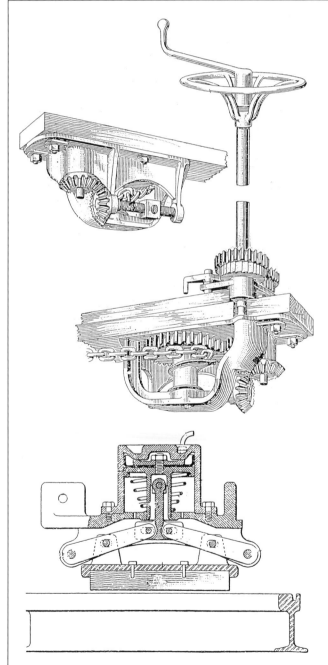

Tramcar track brakes:

Mechanical

This type of brake takes the form of a mechanical application of wooden or cast iron brake blocks, or slippers, bearing directly on to the rails.   The pressure on the brake blocks may be applied manually or by compressed air.

Figure 5 (left)
A combined hand wheel and track brake column.   The track brake is operated manually by rotating the wheel, which is mounted on a sleeve concentric with the hand brake column. The rotation applies the brake through the bevel gear and worm nut illustrated to which the pull rod of the track brake is attached.   This type of brake utilises a portion of the weight of the car as the retarding force.

Figure 6 (left)
A cross-section of an air track brake.   When compressed air is admitted to the cylinder at the top, the piston is driven down to press the brake block on to the rail.   Compressed air may also be employed to apply brake blocks to car wheels.

Tramcar track brakes: <u>Magnetic</u>

This type of brake consists of two or more electromagnets which, when energised, are attracted to the rails by magnetic force. It may also be arranged to operate wheel brakes or be combined with mechanical operating gear so that the latter is also capable of pressing the magnet blocks on to the rails.

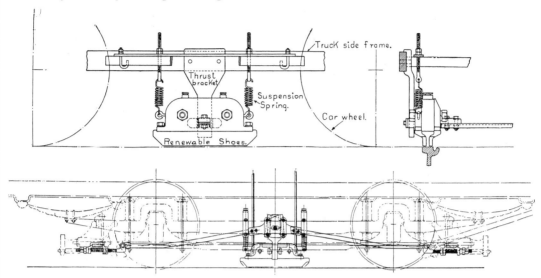

Figure 7 (above)
The upper illustration shows the simple brake magnet suspension where the brake thrust is taken directly by the truck frame. It should be noted that the "thrust bracket" must be made of non-magnetic material to ensure the magnet does not adhere to it but is attracted to the rail when it is energised.

The lower illustration shows one of the various mechanisms whereby the drag of the magnet is used by way of a moving thrust bracket, cams and pull rods also to apply ordinary wheel brake blocks.

Figure 8 (right)
The mechanical operation of track magnets and slipper brake blocks work in a similar way and a typical system is shown here. A system of levers giving mechanical advantage is employed and arranged, by means of a floating central sway-bar in this case, to equalise the downward pressure on both rails irrespective of the end of the car from which it is applied.

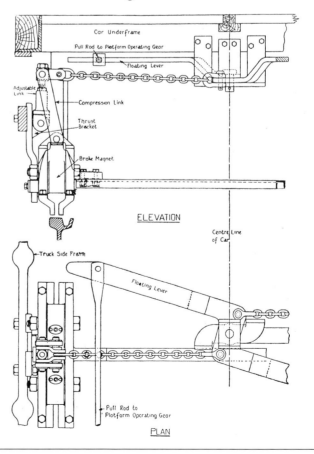

Llewellyn Coventry Fell, Runs the Trams from Here to Hell.")   He was indeed a power in the tramway land, and Colonel Yorke had attended a series of "careful experiments" which Fell had made on LCC cars on which magnetic brakes were used for all service stops, and he agreed with Fell on the desirability of a brake which "does not depend on the rotation of the wheels".   Fell said: "I shall not be satisfied until a supplementary attachment is provided so that the magnet shoes can be operated by hand, if necessary".   In the event it was not long before his ideal was attained for, only five months later, a slipper-cum-magnet shoe was in use on the steep Dog Kennel Hill in London, on which hill we shall in due course come across another accident to dissect (see 31 July 1925).

Operator: **Halifax Corporation**
Location: **New Bank/North Bridge, Halifax**
Dated: **1 July 1906**

The eight killed and 57 injured in June tramway accidents were quickly added to by two more dead and 12 injured on 1 July, when Halifax Corporation car no. 94 (the newest in the fleet), a vehicle 27½ feet long on the short wheelbase of 5ft 6in, ran away and turned over on North Bridge.

The car, which was 6ft 3in wide, with its top deck 9ft 6in above rail level, had been, since 1.15pm, in the hands of driver Chadwick, who had brought it down the hill without trouble on his five previous journeys from Shelf.   Lt-Colonel Druitt's report sheds light on running time for, by stating that the car left Shelf each time at 45 minutes past the hour, we can deduce that the journey time was about 26 minutes from Shelf into Halifax, assuming turn-round time at termini to have been four minutes.   There was a shower of rain which had wetted the rails, but did not clean them before Chadwick made his sixth descent.   After stopping correctly on the 1 in 16 slope at the top of the hill, he could not thereafter control the car which gained speed and derailed on the 90ft-radius curve at the bottom.   The rear wheels came off first before the car rolled over on to its right side, due it was thought to the slipper brake being applied so hard that it took a large proportion of the weight from the rear wheels.   Summing it up, the driver failed to make allowance for the changed condition of the rails.

Great trust seems to have been placed in slipper brakes for their efficiency on hills, but in point of fact their value was very limited, as Major Cardew pointed out in his braking trials in Bradford after the accident there on 19 September 1898 (*qv*).   When one thinks about them, it is obvious that they were, by pressing down, acting to some extent as lifting jacks and, by so doing, robbed the wheels of adhesive weight so very necessary for the hand brake to be effective.   Magnetic track brakes had the opposite effect as their action was to clamp the car down[54].

This accident spoilt a good record in Halifax, where, in eight years of operation, the trams had carried more than 100 million passengers without a fatality, although there had been some runaways (see particularly the accident in Horton Street on 14 October 1904).   The Corporation had also taken the additional precaution of installing sprinklers on their steepest tram hills, and two of these appliances existed on the hill in question.   It would be interesting to know whether they were fixed or portable, and if the former, how they cleaned the track by "running water down the grooves and over the rails"[55].

Two photographs taken at North Bridge, Halifax, after the accident of 1 July 1906, when car 94 overturned after a runaway.

(top) Courtesy: Alan Brotchie

(bottom) Courtesy: National Tramway Museum

After some moderately caustic comments on the relative instability of cars on the 3ft 6in gauge, the report mentions three side-effects of the Tramways Act 1870 that encouraged the adoption of this narrow gauge. It occupied less road width, which enabled it to be

---

54 The magnetic track brake clamps the shoes down rather than the car. The additional downward force on the tram is only that needed to extend the magnet support springs until the shoes make contact with the rail. This may be only of the order of 100-150lb per magnet, whereas the vertical force between magnet and rail may be over a ton.

55 Presumably if the groove was kept full of water, the passage of a wheel flange would displace water from the groove (fed presumably from a track fountain) and spread it over the head of the rail.

laid in streets where the statutory clearance between rail and kerb could be attained without the expense of widening, which would have been desirable. Secondly, the punitive requirement of paving a roadway was minimised – on a double line the adoption of narrow gauges meant a difference of at least 2ft in width of road surface for the tramway undertaking to lay and repair. Thirdly, although the cars were a few inches slimmer, they were almost as commodious as those on standard gauge.

In regard to the present case, after carrying out thorough checks to the equipment, the Inspector thought that the accident was entirely due to driver Chadwick. He had applied the hand brake too hard, thus locking the wheels, and had applied the slipper brake too late and too vigorously, thereby virtually jacking the tram off the track. In the light of the Inspector's report, Chadwick was dismissed. This action gave rise to a strike, but the management's action prevailed.

Following this accident in New Bank, the Halifax cars had another four runaways within the next nine months or so, all fortunately without causing deaths – 13 October in Burnley Road; 15 October at Pye Nest Road (a place we shall hear of again), car no. 61; 14 December in Wharf Street, car no. 67; and on 5 February 1907 (another case of a car from Shelf causing alarm at New Bank – this was no. 52).

Operator: **South Metropolitan Electric Tramways & Lighting Company**
Location: **Park Lane/Ruskin Road, Carshalton**
Date: **1 April 1907**

The tram route from Croydon to Sutton, following for part of its length the valley of the sluggish polluted river Wandle, would hardly seem to be the locale for a runaway and overturn. Yet this is what happened on a veritable artificial pimple – no long decline from a massif but the slope from the top of a bridge spanning the then London Brighton & South Coast Railway crossing this flat part of Surrey.

It was at 3.30pm on "All Fools" day that no.19, a four-wheel open-top car belonging to the undertaking generally known as the "Southmet", heavily-laden with bank-holidaymakers, turned turtle, injuring 36 people, of whom two died, on the curve between Park Lane and Ruskin Road.

Major Pringle submitted a very detailed account. Large flatted places on the wheels and discolouration of the metal proved that the wheels had been locked. Once again it proved that skidding wheels make for very poor braking. Once again the driver was deprived of electric brakes. Once again it was a case of a "greenhorn" driver who, to quote the report, "cannot with his record of service have acquired such judgement of speed, intimate knowledge of brake effects as a tried motorman will possess".

This accident was a good example of the proverb about too many cooks – the conductor realising the car was going too fast down the hill, left his fare collecting on the top deck and, rushing downstairs, screwed the hand brake on as hard as he could from the rear platform. By so doing he took control of the car out of the hands of the driver who, left to himself, might have mastered the situation – might have!

It might be thought surprising that a car should overturn on so modest a gradient. The

Southmet 19, which overturned at the corner of Park Lane and Ruskin Road, Carshalton, on 1 April 1907.
(top) Courtesy: Alan Brotchie
(bottom) Courtesy: National Tramway Museum

Inspector's conclusion was that it was caused by a combination of excessive speed, an unbalanced distribution of passengers (22 inside and no fewer than 47 persons on top, 14 of whom were standing), and the application of the hand brake by the conductor. According to the Inspector, this last action caused the wheels to jam in the rail grooves, imparting an overrunning motion to the body. This, coupled with centrifugal force, including the displacement of the live load on the top deck, combined to overturn the car.

Operator: **Sunderland District Electric Tramways**
Location: **Mill Hill Bank, New Silksworth**
Date: **29 July 1907**

Now to the north-east, to a brace of runaways on the same hill in the evening of the same day in July 1907. These were cars on the 4ft 8½in gauge Sunderland & District Electric Tramways from Grangetown to Houghton, descending Mill Hill Bank (also known as Botcherby Bank), on gradients varying from 1 in 30 to 1 in 10.9, but mostly at 1 in 12. At the bottom was a curve of 100ft radius and, as was so often the case on hillsides, the superelevation of the curve was the wrong way about, *i.e.* the outer rail was lower than the inner. This was not necessarily bad engineering. Apart from the influence of the levels of side roads running into the main road accommodating the tram route, it would often have been impossible on the side of a slope to bring the two rails level, let alone give them some superelevation.

The location had been the site of an earlier tramway accident. Only three days after the line had opened in 1905, car no. 8 had got out of control on the same hill, derailed at the bottom curve, hit a stone wall and overturned. Upper deck passengers were thrown out and a 14-year old boy was killed[56]. On the later occasion, the first car in trouble was no. 27 – a four-wheel double-decker, with a short top cover without end canopies[57], built to carry 48 passengers, of whom 26 were accommodated upstairs. The second car, no. 19, was an identical vehicle, and rather unusually for a British concern, the cars were made in France, by Établissements Arbel of Paris. Neither overturned: the first one was brought to rest by a stone wall, the second one jostled against the first one some little time later, injuring six people out of the day's total of 13. Whilst attempts had been made to reverse it, both drivers muddled their use of the magnetic brake, and the questionable instruction as to which notch to set it on at the start of a descent was again raked over at the inquiry, in this case conducted by Lt-Colonel von Donop.

The migration of drivers from one tramway to another was again evident. The driver of one of the runaways had served one year at Cheltenham, and two at Bath, before coming to Sunderland, while the other man had worked for six months at Glasgow, three-and-three-quarter years at Stockton, and two years at Gateshead[58].

Operator: **Bradford Corporation**
Location: **Church Bank, Bradford**
Date: **31 July 1907**

Only two days later, there was an overturn in the neighbouring county on the system of Bradford Corporation, where there were steep hills on all the tram routes. This was not another instance of a driver getting in a muddle with the brakes, but the result of the front axle breaking as the car rounded the curve from Otley Road into Barkerend Road.

As soon as he sensed that the car was going too fast, the conductor applied the slipper but, in the words of Lt-Colonel Druitt, in his report, "unless the slipper brake is applied before a certain rate of speed is reached [it] will not stop a car on a steep gradient". The driver's efforts with hand and rheostatic brakes were of no avail.

The report gives copious details of the dimensions and chemical composition of the axle;

64

The runaway which occurred on 31 July 1907 at Church Bank, Bradford, caused by an axle failure to car 210. *(top) Courtesy: National Tramway Museum (bottom) Sachs*

all of great value and interest to the industrial archaeologist, but too lengthy and technical for inclusion here. It is surprising to read (I should think it would have been alarming at the time) that in a year 21 axles similar to this one under car no. 210 had broken. It must have been pure luck that no other incidents like this had resulted. Lucky also that

---

[56] See *The Tramways of Sunderland* by S A Staddon, published by The Advertiser Press, Huddersfield, 1964, at p 145. No Inspectorate report of this accident has come to light .

[57] Further reference to cars of this type of upper-deck design is to be found in footnote nos. 98 and 121, *infra*.

[58] A problem facing peripatetic drivers is that each system tends to have its own layout of platform equipment. Whereas controllers and hand brakes occupy the same relative positions, the location of foot controls do not: ratchet dogs work to the left or right; gong, sand and life-guard reset pedals have no standard positions (some life-guard reset pedals are under the stairs) and sometimes there is also a back-sander pedal to be accommodated.

only ten passengers were slightly hurt, but unlucky that a fortuitous participant, a bystander, should have been severely injured, as were the driver and conductor.

How science advances! When Colonel Druitt said in his report "it is of course quite impossible to detect hidden flaws in axles", neither the electro-magnetic flaw detectors of the 1920s, nor the electronic and ultrasonic detectors of today, were as yet dreamt of.

As a tit-bit of information on Bradford's trams, it is of interest that the cars accomplished an average of 550 miles a week in the days of this accident. It is of course well known that this system ran on the unusual gauge of 4ft and some of the cars were equipped (for a time) with an arrangement of adjustable axles to enable them to run on to the Leeds tramways, which were of standard gauge. The variable-gauge axle problem, which seems to have been more or less satisfactorily resolved in this case, has continued to tax the ingenuity of railway designers, notably on railway lines between France and Spain and between Russia and Poland. In these two cases, the change of gauge is effected by employing carriages capable of taking bogies of both gauges, a set of bogies of one gauge being exchanged for a set of the other gauge at the point where the gauge-change occurs.

Operator: **Birmingham Corporation**
Location: **Warstone Lane/Icknield Street, Birmingham**
Date: **1 October 1907**

The year 1906 was, as we have seen, a bad one in which ten people were killed and 78 injured in runaways. The next year was destined to be another bad one, during which nine died and 109 were injured. After the two fatalitics at Carshalton in April, there followed seven in October, two in Birmingham, and five in Halifax.

Lt-Colonel Yorke conducted the inquiry into the Birmingham accident, in which car no. 22 of the Corporation's fleet was descending Warstone Lane on the Lodge Road route when it ran loose and turned over at the corner with Icknield Street. It was a double-decker, 27ft long on four wheels, with a wheelbase of 6ft, and, as is noted elsewhere, the track gauge was 3ft 6in. The hill was virtually straight, but not so steep as some we have met, and at its worst was only 1 in 17. At the bottom, the curve, from which the car departed, was of only 40ft radius, but its superelevation reached 1¾in. There were compulsory stops at the top and at the foot of the hill prior to rounding the curve.

The car left Rosebery Street depot at 4.15am on 1 October. Motorman Mountford checked the equipment before starting out, finding nothing wrong and the sand boxes full as they should be. On the way to Edmund Street, the city terminus, to commence his first journey to Foundry Road, the outer terminus, using no. 2 controller, the driver tried the magnet brakes only to find that there was no response whatever on the first and second notches, uncertain behaviour on the third, but on the fourth the car was brought up with a jerk. He went on to Foundry Road on this controller and descended Warstone Lane easily and safely on the hand brake alone, eschewing the use of the dubious magnetic brake. Changing ends, he drove back using no. 1 end controller, from which the magnets worked well, and, as the car went round a loop terminus at Edmund Street, he continued on again to Foundry Road on the same (good) controller. Before leaving, he reported the difficulties he had had at no. 2 end to inspector Hall, who arranged to

66

meet the car when it next came back from Foundry Road as it would then, by reason of reversal at Foundry Road, have no. 2 (defective) end leading.

Thus it came about that the car left on its third trip to Foundry Road in the hands of the inspector, whose driving was to end a few minutes later in tragedy. (From the times given in the report, one can calculate the running time on this route as being about 18 minutes.) Going down the incline in Summer Row, the inspector had exactly the same experience as had motorman Mountford on his initial run from the depot: the same nasty jerk when the brake ultimately applied at notch four. Undeterred by this, Hall very foolishly went on to take the car down Warstone Lane on the magnets. This time they failed to act at all, and the inspector's attempts to bring the car under control by the various ploys available all failed. The car rushed forward, derailed, and turned over. In doing so, it threw the upper deck passengers on to the pavement where one

Two views of the accident in Warstone Lane, Birmingham, on 1 October 1907, resulting in the derailment and overturning of car 22.   *(top) Midland Photo Press*
(bottom) Courtesy: National Tramway Museum

of them was crushed and killed between the car and an overhead standard against which it fell.

As we have seen proved by the driver's having done so on his earlier trip, the car could have been taken down the hill in perfect safety on the hand brake, provided it had not been allowed previously to become out of control. The tram inspector's stupid action was therefore the immediate cause of the accident, but the probable reason the magnets did not work may have been a broken resistance grid. It was one of those cases of egg v chicken: did the grid break beforehand and, by depriving the brakes of current, result in the accident, or did the derailment break the grid? One was as likely as the other[59].

Operator: **Halifax Corporation**
Location: **Pye Nest Road/Bolton Brow, Sowerby Bridge**
Date: **15 October 1907**

For the last of the disasters in 1907, we return to Halifax where, it will be remembered, the Corporation had received a pat on the back in 1906 for its freedom from fatal tramway accidents up to that time. Now it had a far worse one, resulting in five deaths and 37 injured. It happened on 15 October to car no. 64, a four-wheel open topper on the 3ft 6in gauge, and this time it was the case of a runback for a distance of more than three-eighths of a mile culminating in derailment, striking a stone wall and rolling over, leaving car body above window-sill level and truck 20 yards apart. Let us go back to the start of the sequence of events.

After satisfying himself that his car was in proper order, for which 15 minutes were allowed after he booked on duty, driver Simpson departed from the depot at 4.45am to go to Halifax and thence to the terminus at Triangle. To get there, he had to go down the long Pye Nest Road, much of which was straight and on gradients varying between 1 in 10 and 1 in 18. This decline was safely negotiated, as was the 200ft radius curve at the bottom. On the return journey, all seemed to be going well except for slight slipping after the car left the bottom of the hill with a full load. There were only some 20 people outside, but inside there were the 22 for whom there were seats as well as several standing because it was a damp morning when people sought to be inside.

In these conditions the car climbed the hill much as usual, but when it was 690 yards up, the power supply ceased owing to the circuit breaker at the central generating station having blown. Simpson's instant reaction was to turn the controller to "off" and apply the hand brake but, as this did not hold the car, he put the key to "reverse" and put the controller to full brake. Before he had time to see whether this had any effect, power was restored, so he quickly replaced the controller to forward power, but the trolley then parted from the wire and he was bereft of power again. (Incidentally, in case the reader is wondering how the driver knew of the restoration of power, it can be noted that there were no street lights at this hour of the late autumn morning. The utter darkness into which he had been plunged by the loss of power would be relieved by the coming on again of the car lights when the power station switch had been reset.) Resorting to the electric brake once more, there was no effect. The driver had lost control and the car continued on a headlong acceleration course backwards towards destruction.

As a precaution against the risks of this hill, a man was employed to clean the rails each

TRAM SMASH AT SOWERBY BRIDGE.
OCTOBER 15TH 1907.

THE CAR BASE.

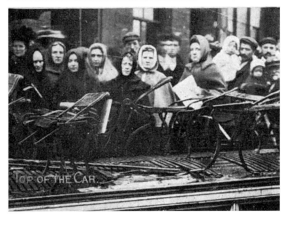

TOP OF THE CAR.

Views at the scene of the accident at Pye Nest Road, Sowerby Bridge, on 15 October 1907, involving the run back of Halifax Corporation car 64.

(top) Courtesy: National Tramway Museum

[59] Since the car had only one set of resistors, the fracture of a grid would have resulted in the same defect manifesting itself at both ends of the car. In such a case, it is highly probable that the first two series notches in motoring would not have worked. The symptoms suggest that it is far more likely that there was a defect in the no. 2 end controller.

morning before the passage of the first car in each direction. Having done this, the man was waiting at a point near the summit to board no. 64, the first car to climb the hill. He jumped on just as the car was about to run back. With a quick realisation of what was happening, he started to apply the slipper brake and intended to drop sand, but before he had managed to apply the brakes, the conductor rushed on to the platform and pushed him out of the way. Almost at the same time, a passenger dashing down from the top deck, no doubt with the idea of jumping off, also collided with the would-be brake-applier and hurled him into the road.

Many of these accidents have explanations compounded of several factors. In this case both the conductor and the driver were at fault. The former, in breach of the regulation which stated that he should be on the rear platform on steep hills and arrange fare collection accordingly – he was however inside or outside (the evidence varied) at the critical time and so was unable to comply with another rule which laid down that in the event of runback, his first duty was to drop sand and continue to do so until the car stopped, and to apply the slipper as quickly and as hard as possible. Unfortunately he spoiled the efforts of somebody else who had taken over his neglected duties: he was to pay a heavy price for his neglect, being one of the five persons killed.

The driver could not have been more wrong in what he did with the controller both times the power was cut off. The car in question was one of a batch set aside for the especially difficult Pye Nest route as they had higher powered (35hp) motors. (As built, the Halifax cars were under-powered for such terrain – only 20hp motors.) In view of the generally hilly nature of the tramways in Halifax, all the trams were being modified to incorporate a run-back circuit in the controllers. Using a modified controller, all that was necessary to obtain braking, if the car ran back, was to put the main handle to "full brake" without altering the reversing lever. The letter B was painted in two places as an indication to the driver that the controller had been wired in this way. But it was taking a considerable time to make the alterations to all cars. Preference for dealing with both ends was being given to cars which had to mount hills in both directions. Since the same cars were always allocated to the Pye Nest route (because of their more powerful motors) and because the cars on that route always operated the same way round, as a temporary expedient the cars had only one controller equipped with the device: the controller at the end leading when the car was ascending the gradient. This "half-and-half" affair may have confused the driver, or being in the dark he did not see the letter B. However that may be, he reversed as would have been correct with an untreated controller (to put it in phase with the direction of motion) and turned the main handle to the brake notches. There was no braking effect![60]

The report of the inquiry submitted by Lt-Colonel Druitt speaks of the desirability of instantaneous application of slippers and suggests compressed air or strong springs as possibilities. A few accidents further on we shall meet a contrivance of this sort. The Pye Nest accident was another question of precedence of chicken or egg? A broken connection behind the controller could have been the primary germ of the disaster, or it could have resulted from damage done in the overturning[61].

Going on to 1908, we find another bad year which includes the worst accident, judging by the yardstick of the number of people killed, of the electric traction period so far: two in Glasgow, two in Birmingham, and seven in Bournemouth. The accidents were of different kinds – one a runaway and collision, one a turnover without running away, but the third was similar to so many described in these pages.

Operator: **Glasgow Corporation**
Location: **High Street, Glasgow**
Date: **3 January 1908**

In Glasgow the year started badly. The excitement of hogmanay had scarcely subsided when on 3 January 1908, Corporation tram no. 986 got out of control when descending Bell of Brae: it ran on for about 100 yards and came to rest in Saltmarket where the track was almost flat.

No. 986 was a four-wheel open-top double-decker fitted with the usual hand brake, magnetic track brakes, Westinghouse Type 90 controllers and one sander at each end. Some of this equipment became the subject of criticism in the report on the accident. Compared with many tramway hills, this one was not unduly steep, the only section at all severe (between Rotten Row and George Street) having short lengths of 1 in 16, 1 in 18 and 1 in 26 and, unlike so many of these runaways, the car in this case did not overturn; it did not even leave the rails, and none of

Damaged car 986 at Coplawhill works, after its runaway and collisions in High Street, Glasgow, on 3 January 1908.

Courtesy: National Tramway Museum

its passengers was killed. One of the dead however was the driver, the man who would have been the key witness to what occurred.

The car left Langside depot at 5.17am and worked all day between Mount Florida and Springburn until it ran into disaster at 5.0pm, when it was dark and foggy, but not so

---

[60] It is stated in the report that this absence of braking followed from the special nature of the controller circuitry, but it is submitted that while the driver's action would have defeated the run-back circuit, it would have provided him with rheostatic braking if the controller had not suffered from the internal connection failure postulated in the following footnote.

[61] It is highly probable that the broken connection *was* the "primary germ" of the accident. This failure was a result of overheating sufficient to melt the solder that had secured the cable termination lug to its terminal within the controller, the overheating being such as would have been derived from a sustained electrical load (as could occur with a heavily-laden tramcar ascending a long and steep gradient). The soldering might well have taken place during the run-back modification to the controller carried out by Halifax's own technical staff. Support for this contention is provided by the tripping of the power station switch, which might well have been brought about by the resultant short circuit on the car.

foggy as to obscure street lamps and other landmarks. So it was presumed that driver Dolan knew where he was and that the reason he failed to observe three obligatory stops was that he was unable to stop the car. The three drivers who had had the car before Dolan had found no fault with it, and Dolan drove it without difficulty from Mount Florida to Springburn and back, then went again to Springburn. On arrival there he wanted to leave the car for a few minutes (we can guess why) and asked a driver McKenzie, who chanced to be there, to take the car through the crossover ready for the journey back to Mount Florida.

On his return, he found the car exactly where he had left it and standing in the way of cars waiting to go on to Bishopbriggs. McKenzie had not moved the car because he could not get the reverser key off the controller at no.1 end. The two drivers and the conductor joined forces and were trying to remove the handle when two supervisors – a time-keeper and an inspector – turned up. They too had no success, even after removing the cover of the controller to seek the cause of the difficulty.

Why, why, why, did they not send the car to the nearby Possilpark depot for attention? In the realms of transport there is, or should I say was, a pride in punctuality and a sense that "the show must go on", apart from the slating one could expect from higher authority (who not only had the same pride but had to fend off public moans and complaints) for delays and cancellations. Short cuts and an element of taking a chance are great temptations in the circumstances, and at this stage inspector Muirhead adopted an expedient which involved Dolan in a breach of the rules which proved fatal to the driver and an innocent victim.

Muirhead, knowing that the main handle could be removed without placing the reversing key to "neutral", did so and mounted the handle on no. 2 end controller and, with a pair of pliers instead of the proper key, turned the reversing handle at that end. The reversing handle was left in the forward position at the no. 1 end. Driver Dolan, being assured that the position of the key at no.1 end was immaterial, set out on what was to be his last journey alive.

Dolan was a careful reliable man who had never failed to qualify for the safe driving bonuses, so, although the attempt to remedy the controller had made him several minutes late leaving Springburn, it was very unlikely that he was taking any dubious chances in order to catch up on his timetable. All went well until he omitted stopping to operate the Bundy time recorder at Cathedral Street and then ran past first one and then another stopping place on the hill. By the time he passed the second one, the speed of the car according to witnesses, including a policeman, was going at 25 to 30 mph, with the driver blowing his whistle, ringing the bell and working the two handles. Very shortly afterwards the car hit four lorries in rapid succession. Between the second and third collisions, driver Dolan fell from the platform head downwards on to the road and died later in hospital. It had to be assumed he fell as a result of injuries received in one of the collisions.

After this, the car careered on, without striking anything, though it went through a busy cross-roads, Glasgow Cross, until it eventually struck four more lorries and was finally brought under control by the conductor using the hand brake. At that point, a well-meaning passenger removed the trolley from the wire, no doubt thinking to deprive the motors of power, but the only result was to put out the lights.

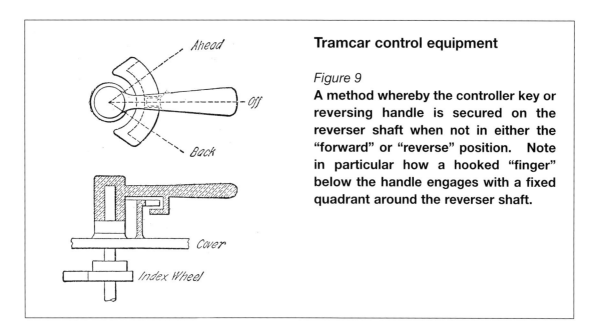

Tramcar control equipment

Figure 9

A method whereby the controller key or reversing handle is secured on the reverser shaft when not in either the "forward" or "reverse" position. Note in particular how a hooked "finger" below the handle engages with a fixed quadrant around the reverser shaft.

Ahead

Off

Back

Cover

Index Wheel

The other person killed was a van-boy knocked from a lorry. (The term "lorry", used in the report, is not referring to a motor vehicle but to one that was horse-drawn.)

Now, what was a Bundy recorder? It may still exist in the world of buses[62]. It was a machine installed at convenient or strategic points along a route in order to keep a check on time-keeping. The driver, or conductor, had a key bearing either his number or the car number. Arriving at the machine, he would dismount, insert and turn the key in the machine, which would cause a bell to ring as the mechanism stamped the time and the key number on a tape. In Glasgow, it was the duty of the driver to operate the machine, but it was a rule that he should not leave his car without first removing the reversing key from the controller.

It was significant that Dolan had not operated the Bundy on the outward trip, which strongly suggested that he had not even then been able to get the key off the controller. On the way back, there was no point in stopping there, because, as will be remembered, he had no reversing key to remove as the spindle had been set with inspector Muirhead's pliers. Thereafter his failure to hold the car in check was the total failure of the magnetic brake. Placing his faith in this usually reliable brake, he discovered too late that it was ineffective. Why then was he unable to rein the car in on this not particularly steep incline? As the reader will have read, perhaps *ad nauseam* as it crops up in so many of these runaways, there were two other electrical methods of braking a tramcar *in extremis*. Both of these needed the change in position of the reverser, but Dolan had no key on his controller. This unfortunate man had virtually signed his own death warrant when he acquiesced in the inspector's makeshift strategem.

But why did the magnetic brake let him down? Muirhead had been quite right when he said that the position of the reverser made no difference. On the Westinghouse Type 90 controller in use on this car, the reversing contacts did not meet until the main handle was on either "power" or "brake". Colonel Yorke, the Inspecting Officer in this case, puzzled by the fact this theory was confirmed by the makers, whereas Dolan's controller had been found to be at "full brake", made some tests on Salford Corporation and LCC cars on which

---

[62] A Bundy time recorder is on exhibition at the National Tramway Museum, Crich, Derbyshire.

the same type of controller was used, and came to the conclusion that it was possible to take the main handle away when it was not truly in the "off" position. If only a fraction of an inch towards the brake notches, it moved the reversing barrel and prevented any magnetic braking from the other end, and as a result of this finding, it was decided to alter the design to incorporate (on the controller top) the familiar raised ring beneath which a claw on the handle travelled, and from where it could be removed, only in the true "off" position, where there was a gap in the ring (see fig 9 for an example of such a device).

Colonel Yorke also had this to add:

> *It is the custom on the Glasgow Corporation Tramways to use the hand brake for ordinary stops, and to reserve the magnetic track brake for emergency stops and when coasting down hills. As I have said on a previous occasion, I do not regard this as a proper manner in which to employ the magnetic or any other form of 'power' brake. I am disposed to think that it is a mistake in tramway practice to regard any brake as an 'emergency' brake, and as one which is only to be used on rare occasions. When this custom is followed, there is a risk that the brake will either be wrongly applied or, for some reason or other, will fail, when the occasion for its use arises. In tramcar driving, the 'emergency' is ever present, and the motormen should be instructed to use at all times the most powerful device at their disposal.*

Readers old enough to have travelled on LCC trams will recollect seeing the word "interlock" on the cover of every controller, and there is reason to believe that it had its origin in the Glasgow tragedy. No LCC car was allowed to leave the overhaul works until its controllers had been tested to ensure that they did not quarrel with one another and there could be no accidental attempt to drive from both ends at the same time. As soon as the car had line current, men would go aboard and apply a reversing key to each controller. If both keys were away from neutral at the same time the circuit breaker should blow. When, and not until, the breaker had been blown by all four combinations of reversing key positions, the word "interlock" was stencilled in white on the black cover of each controller. Then the car could be taken on to the road.

Operator: **Birmingham and Midland Tramways**
Location: **Brades Lock, Dudley Road, Rowley Regis**
Date: **20 February 1908**

Interrupting the long saga of steep hills, we come to an overturn brought about by something very different. Car no. 6 of the Birmingham and Midland Tramways, on its journey from Dudley to Birmingham, was entering a passing loop situated at the canal bridge at Brades Lock between Tividale and Oldbury at 3.20pm when the unexpected happened. The car was a typical four-wheel covered-top double-decker on a 6ft 6in wheelbase and had appeared to be in good order when it left Spon Lane at 2.50pm. It had given no trouble during the ten hours it had been running that day.

This tram was nearing the bottom of the incline down to Brades Lock bridge at about 7mph when the driver of a trap, with a restive horse, signalled the tram driver to stop. This he did some 100 yards short of a loop and, after the horse and trap had passed, restarted and went on through the points at a shade over 4mph. The tram immediately came off the rails and turned over without any previous warning. Of its 26 passengers, nine were injured amongst whom one died from the effects.

But where was the conductor? A bystander suggested he might be underneath the car, and sure enough, there he was found after several who had gathered at the scene raised the car by hand to look for him. In falling over on to its left side, the car had squashed and killed its conductor, who, it was presumed, had got down while the car was travelling slowly with the intention of walking ahead to speak to the driver as soon as they had come to a stand in the loop.

It did not need a searching inquiry, although one was carried out by Lt-Colonel Yorke, to find the reason for this sudden tragedy. The nearside trailing wheel had collapsed when its spokes broke. The spokes were of peculiar construction – another design feature which would interest industrial archaeologists – and the wheel, suffering from what nowadays would be called "fatigue", could not withstand the change in its loading when for a few inches it rose on its flange instead of on its tread during its passage through the blind point of the turn-out.

Operator: Bournemouth Corporation
Location: Poole Hill/Avenue Road, Bournemouth
Dated: 1 May 1908

To the south coast for the next of these unfortunate incidents. We have peeped at accidents to cable, steam and overhead electric trams, and we now pass for the first time to an electric conduit line. The system of current collection had little to do with this deplorable disaster, which we shall see was man-made inasmuch as it resulted from neglected maintenance and dubious management methods. This accident, which ranks among the worst on British tramways, caused the deaths of seven people and injury to 26 others – some very serious.

The Bournemouth Corporation Tramways were laid to the 3ft 6in gauge and embodied a few miles of conduit track and, except at junctions or at change pits, where the slot was in the centre between the rails, the conduit was situated under one of the running rails. The components were almost identical with those of the first sections of the great LCC network, being conceived on the drawing board of the same engineer. To rephrase an account from a book of 1911 – Bournemouth adopted conduit as a token of civic pride. Thrice the Corporation had declared it did not want tramways of any kind within its gates, but when public opinion eventually forced its consent, it was arranged that no unsightly overhead wires should appear in the Square and other lines in the central area. After not many years, the conduit was abandoned, because of its high working costs, and wires were erected – "the public had got used to the wires on other routes but had not got used to trams which produced a heavy loss".

The Bournemouth trams ranged the nine miles or so from Christchurch to Poole as well as some branches, and on the two routes into Poole crossed the Hampshire/Dorset boundary. Poole had no cars of their own[63]. It is easy to think of trams of one authority

---

[63] Poole & District Electric Tramways had operated cars between 1901 and 1905. In the latter year, the undertaking was acquired by Poole Corporation, which leased it to Bournemouth Corporation.

which journeyed on to neighbouring systems, but there were fewer municipal systems which provided the *only* cars in the area of another authority[64].   Incidentally, these two Bournemouth-worked lines in Poole comprised the only street tramways in Dorset, unless one includes the lines used by railway trains from Weymouth Town station along public roads to the harbour.

I made the journey from Parkstone to Christchurch in 1912, four years after this accident: it had made a vivid local impression and was still a topic of conversation, and I well remember my aunt telling my mother all about it as we travelled down the hill itself;

Three dramatic views of the runaway down Poole Hill, Bournemouth, on 1 May 1908, when car 72 derailed and plunged down a bank into a garden, causing the death of seven persons.

Courtesy: National Tramway Museum

women don't usually talk on transport topics! I have vivid memories of many tram trips made as a little boy, but this one stands out not because of the unusual (for a Londoner) thrill and excitement of watching a trolley pole, or wondering which way we were going when we approached a junction, but because I sat in indescribable discomfort from Boscombe to Christchurch. A sudden uncontrollable urge came upon me, but as my mother had paid the fares for the four of us, we were certainly not going to get off the car! No more interest in the wires or the lines – I was filled with apprehension as to what fate I had in store when the full truth of my plight was revealed at the terminus!

In Bournemouth, the Square (which is not square!) is situated in the valley of the rivulet or bourne which gives its name to the town. Into this valley, the tram lines converged from east, north and south down fairly steep hills, and it was on one of these that car no. 72 ran away out of control on 1 May 1908,

became derailed, crossed the footpath and plunged down a bank into a garden where it came to rest lying on its right side on a steep wooded slope.

As is customary with the BoT reports, this one by Major Pringle is full and lucid, and has been reproduced here.

A very unusual feature of the system was that its cars were not allocated to a "home" among the four depots on the system. Their timetables could land them in any depot and, on the day before the disaster, the car in question had set out from Central depot and finished at Parkstone depot. On the fateful day, it started from Parkstone depot at 4.56am and until 6.50pm, when it turned over, it had travelled 99.4 miles in the hands of six different drivers. It is from reports such as this that we can glean tramway facts not found elsewhere. For instance, the figures just quoted show a service speed in Bournemouth (if we allow only five minutes in each hour as terminal standage) of 8mph.

---

64 Several other examples existed, notably in the Birmingham, South-east Lancashire and Glasgow areas.

The report also throws light on the rostering of drivers' duties – the first man had the car from 4.56am until 1.14pm (a turn of duty of more than eight and a quarter hours without a meal break, unless the car stood idle while the men fed). The second man had the car from 1.14pm until 4.30pm and, in the 50 minutes following this, there were three drivers in quick succession who were filling in "split turns". After this, the man who was to meet with catastrophe took over.

In those days of split turns (a day's work divided into quite separate periods: for instance three hours for the morning rush and five hours for the evening) were more of an accepted part of transport duties than nowadays, when jobs are arranged to suit the whims of staff rather than to run an efficient economical service. The unfortunate driver Wilton, who stuck to his post and sustained broken ribs when the car turned over, was on a split turn having come on duty at 10.40am until 12.40pm and again from 4.40pm with a view to finishing at 11.32pm – a total of eight hours 56 minutes. Quite incidentally, we learn that it was a run of 48 minutes from Landsdown, where he took over and drove to Poole. (The report does not tell us, but Landsdown, which was then a conduit tramway junction, is at the summit of the hill on which the car came to grief half a mile to the west of the Square.)

Here was another analogue of the parable of the kingdom, which was eventually lost because of an initial defect in one horseshoe nail (see the accident at Glasgow on 6 September 1902 for the previous example). On this tram, the seeds of the runaway were sown nearly two years earlier in August 1906, when the car was only three months old. At that time it got out of control on Poole Hill and was saved only by the use of the "reverse power" brake, the principle of which was explained in the Archway case of 23 June 1906 (*qv*). A controller defect was found to be the cause of that narrow shave, and the controller barrel was replaced by a second-hand one which fitted loosely[65]. Three times during the month before the accident, the controllers had given similar trouble involving a failure of the magnetic brake when descending Boscombe Hill.

Early in the afternoon of the fatal day, the controller at the Poole end had jammed and the car had to be taken into Parkstone depot for attention. Driver Wilton was not told of this and drove without bother or suspicion to Poole, where he reversed in the usual manner and left again in about two minutes. His journey as far as the conduit change pit was uneventful: there were no sharp inclines and no emergency stops so he had no need to use anything but the hand brake. He had not tried the magnetic brake on this journey, but he had used it satisfactorily to descend Constitution Hill on the westward trip.

On arriving at the conduit pit, "the plough was attached to the underground conductor". This uncharacteristically vague wording in the report refers to the operation of changing from overhead to conduit current collection. This procedure had no bearing on the accident but it is, I think, not amiss to explain it here. The car was brought to a stand with its centre over the hatch plates in the slot (which at this point was in the middle of the track). The plates were then raised on their hinges by means of a lever in the roadway. The "plough", the current collector, was then lowered into the conduit from the truck by winding a handle working a chain and gear device, after which the hatch plates were restored to the position flush with the road surface, and the car went on its way, its trolley stowed, with the plough sliding between the slot rails of the conduit and in contact with conductor rails within it.

Leaving the change point, the driver restarted his car with a notch or two of power, and then let it roll to Par's Corner, where he turned the controller to the brake notches. There was no response and the car began to speed, but the driver was not perturbed as it had happened with him on other occasions that the magnets did not always work on the first application, so he put down some sand and turned the handle to the brake notches again. Once more nothing happened and he next tried using his reversing power by throwing the controller into reverse, applying power as explained earlier. The automatic circuit breaker (that switch on the ceiling of the canopy which produced such a startling sneeze and flash when it operated) blew, as was to be expected, but the car's career remained unchecked. It was now running round the curve at Robson's Corner at about 25mph and about to start on the steepest part of the hill on a gradient of 1 in 12.5 or 1 in 14. Eyewitnesses averred that the car tilted so much on the curve that they expected it to fall over there. The driver could now do no more than put on the hand brake, but this was hopeless on such a slope at this speed. He said afterwards that if he had known or suspected that the magnets would let him down, he could have got the car quite safely down the hill on the hand brake alone.

Something serious went wrong – what?

The rails could have been in better condition, but they were good enough for normal speeds, and in fact tests made by the Inspector showed that cars went safely round at 12mph, which was double the permitted figure. Nor was it Highgate Archway all over again because the wheels never ceased turning. It was simply a freak connection in the rear controller which cost seven lives.

Most tramcar controllers were designed with interlocked handles: power and reverse. The power handle could not be moved from the "off" position until the reverser was set either "forwards" or "backwards", and it could not be removed from the controller unless it was in the "off" position. The reversing key could not be moved unless the power handle was in the "off" position and could not itself be removed unless it was showing "neutral". On some tramways, the power handles were fixtures and only the reversing key was carried from end to end of the car, but in Bournemouth the driver took both with him when he changed ends. The controller he was using when the car became out of control, no. 2, proved to have very little wrong with it, but in no. 1, at the rear, several components were extremely worn so that it had been possible to take off both handles while the reversing barrel was not properly in its "neutral" position. The circuits this made instead of being in unison with no.2 were such as to make driver Wilton's actions useless. This was somewhat similar to the January Glasgow collision, but for a different reason.

Who had been responsible for this state of affairs?

Major Pringle's report, as I read it, was a "rocket", and to continue the present-day metaphor it had multi-warheads. Its target was the whole of the town's tramway set-up. It advised the Corporation to appoint a qualified tramway manager. Up to that time, the trams were the job of nobody in particular; several officials, including the Borough Engineer, had fingers in the pie.

---

[65] It was not the main barrel of the controller which was replaced, but one of the two barrels which were assembled on the reverser shaft. Each of these two barrels served one motor for reversing, power-brake changeover and motor cut-out functions.

The report reminded the Corporation that the BoT licensed the lines only on the understanding that full equipment would be available and that "public safety depends on the highest possible efficiency and not the second best". This cutting remark was prompted by the fact that the capsized car had only three of its magnet brakes connected; the fourth had been isolated for weeks; no material on hand, or being obtained, to put it right.

Things were so slack that nobody could be tied down for letting the car go to work with controllers in such a state, and nobody knew that controllers like this were death traps. The cars went into and out of all depots willy-nilly, so nobody knew what work had been done, and it is more than likely that nobody wanted to know. Digressing for a while, this reminds me of the same sort of thing, but with a wider scope, I came up against on the railway during World War II. As hostilities wore on, traffic increased, engines became scarce, the blitz made things worse, and necessity encouraged the system of using the first engine to hand, never minding where it belonged, to "keep the wheels turning" to move food, troops, bombs, petrol and all else to destination. In doing this, engines were as often as not sent on trips which took them still further from home. Shortage of artisans, materials and time meant that depots dodged doing more than makeshift repairs, so the engines drifted round the country without the "stitch in time". If one could patch things up enough to get the engine out of the shed and land it safely on somebody else it went!

I can clearly visualise the Bournemouth Tramways at the time of this accident, being a miniscule version of this sort of cycle. Nor did the track, the sanding arrangements on the cars, or the training of drivers escape the Inspector's lash.

"Training is not given the attention it deserves" may seem to be an overstatement to the lots of people who thought, and many probably still so think, that tram driving is only a matter of turning two handles. So it may have been, but in the big town, in particular, it was a specialised skilful turning of handles on which public safety depended and which demanded alertness, good eyesight, good judgement, good physique and stamina. It will be remembered that the report on the Archway accident remarked on the likelihood of a driver having to apply all his limbs simultaneously to separate jobs. It was no mean physical feat for eight hours, with little or no protection from the weather, constantly pulling on a brake pillar and rotating a stiff controller, the handle of which on many older cars was uncomfortably-placed below waist level. The so-called science of ergonomics had not then become fashionable.

As a boy, I was told that it was the heavy strain on the body, particularly in operating the hand brake, which precluded women being employed to any great extent on tram driving during World War I. As another tramway sidelight on that war, I was told that quite early on, tramways experienced a shortage of drivers because so many patriotically answered the call, volunteering as military drivers. They were disillusioned when they found their skills were of little use for driving motor vehicles and they were drafted as ordinary infantrymen. A tram driver's specialised knowledge and experience were of little use elsewhere except in Glasgow on the Subway, where men were used for whom the daily turmoil of Sauchiehall Street had become too exacting.

On the general subject of driving, it is often overlooked that the tramwayman could not cause his vehicle to swerve to avoid a collision. He was also in the forefront in case of danger, although it must be conceded that his vehicle had a pretty good battering ram at the front in the shape of a substantial fender and sheet-steel rampart around some two-

BOURNEMOUTH CORPORATION TRAMWAYS.

Board of Trade (Railway Department), *1/5/08*
8, Richmond Terrace,
Whitehall, S.W.,
29th June, 1908.

Sir,

I have the honour to report, for the information of the Board of Trade, in accordance with your Order of the 2nd May, the result of my enquiry into the cause of the accident which occurred on the Bournemouth Corporation Tramways about 6.50 p.m. on the 1st May.

In this case, car No. 72 was descending the incline from St. Michael's Church, Poole Road, into Bournemouth Square, viâ Poole Hill, The Triangle, and Avenue Road, when the driver (Wilton) lost control. The car attained a dangerously high speed and eventually left the rails at the right-hand curve in Avenue Road near the School of Cookery. It then crossed the left-hand footpath and plunged down a bank into the private garden of Fairlight Glen House, where it came to rest on the steep wooded slope, lying on its right side.

I regret to say that the casualty list was long and serious.

There were at the time from 35 to 40 passengers on the car—ten inside and the remainder on the upper deck. Of these, seven were killed, or died very shortly afterwards, and 26 were injured, some of them very seriously. The driver, who remained at his post, sustained a fractured rib and other injuries.

Car No. 72 was a double deck (without top cover) bogie car, with eight wheels, and maximum traction trucks (large wheels leading). It weighed about 12 tons unloaded, and I, understand, about 75 per cent. of the load was carried on the large wheels. There was seating accommodation for 30 inside and 34 outside passengers. The principal dimensions were as follows :—

	Ft.	Ins.		Ft.	Ins.
Length over all	35	6	Wheel base of bogies ...	4	0
Length over body ...	23	6	Diameter of driving wheels	2	7¾
Width over all	6	6	Diameter of pony wheels	1	8

The braking equipment included :—

1. Hand wheel brake working cast-iron blocks on all eight (steel) wheels. The gear is of the usual type, an upright staff carrying a cranked handle with a ratchet head. A chain connected with the rigging is wound up on the lower end of the staff, under the platform, when the handle is revolved, and the blocks thereby pressed against the wheels.

2. Electro-magnetic track brake, with four shoes, two on each rail. Each shoe has two steel blocks placed in line over the rail, and acts as a powerful electro-magnet when excited by current supplied by the motors acting as generators. The drag of the shoes on the rails, caused by their magnetic adhesion, brings pressure to bear upon the wheel brake blocks by a system of levers. The brake acts, therefore, both upon the track and upon the wheels. It is also similar to the ordinary rheostatic electric brake in the retardation of the motors themselves due to their acting as generators.

3. In addition there was available the braking effect obtained by reversing the motors and using power either in series or on the highest (parallel) notch.

The car was fitted with four sand boxes, one at each corner, of the non-automatic type. The sand valves, operated by pedal or foot tramp from the driver's platform, were intermittent in action. The sand was discharged through india-rubber pipes at a distance of 24 inches from the wheel contacts.

The tramways in Bournemouth have the 3 feet 6 inches gauge. Through the centre of the town, the lines are worked by electric traction on the underground conduit (side slot) system ; outside the centre, overhead conductors with trolley arm connection are used. On the west the change from trolley to conduit is made in Poole Road, about 100 yards east of St. Michael's Church. All cars travelling from Poole to Bournemouth have, therefore, to come to rest at this spot, in order that the conduit plough, for making contact with the underground conductor, may be fixed

The track is double in Poole Road and Poole Hill. At Par's Corner the tracks diverge. The descending track, with which we are concerned, traverses The Triangle and Avenue Road, and was authorized as Tramway No. 1 of the Bournemouth Corporation

Railway Inspectorate report of accident dated 1 May 1908 at Poole Hill, Bournemouth.

Act, 1901. The lines from St. Michael's Church to the square were constructed in 1902, and I inspected them on behalf of the Board of Trade in January, 1903.

From the conduit pit in Poole Road to the scene of the accident is a distance of about 460 yards. The route winds considerably, and has continuous falling gradients. The principal curves and gradients are as follows :—

Yards from Conduit Pit.	Gradients.	Name of Thoroughfare.	Yards.	Direction of Curve.	Radius in Feet.	Remarks.
0–17	1 in 108	} Poole Road				
17–33	1 in 45		0–176	Left	Very easy	
(a) 33–67	1 in 24					
67–83	1 in 19	} Poole Hill				
83–133	1 in 14·5					
133–183	1 in 19		176–206	Left	100 and 150	Par's Corner.
183–233	1 in 14·6	} The Triangle	206–261	Left	350	
233–300	1 in 17		261–293	Left	150	
300–333	1 in 13		293–345	Right	100	Robson's Corner.
333–366	1 in 18		345–426	Left	400	
		} Avenue Road	426–448	Right	300	
(b)366–466	1 in 22		448–458	Right	150	
			458–464	Right	120	Derailment at 460 yards.

The average gradient on the incline between (a) and (b) is about 1 in 18. The steepest actual gradient (as measured) is between yards 300 and 317, where the inclination is 1 in 12·25. The route as a whole is not one which, from the point of view of either curvature or gradient, can be described as exceptional for tramway working.

The superelevation on the sharper curves was as follows :—

Curve at Par's Corner—100 feet radius ... ... From 1 to $2\frac{1}{4}$ inches.
Curve at Robson's Corner—100 feet radius ... From $\frac{1}{4}$ to $\frac{1}{2}$ inch.
Curve at derailment—150 feet radius ... ... From $\frac{1}{4}$ to $\frac{3}{4}$ inch.
Curve at derailment—120 feet radius ... ... From $\frac{1}{2}$ to $\frac{5}{8}$ inch.

The Board of Trade Regulations governing the traffic on the down hill route are as follows :—

1. Speed limited to six miles an hour in Poole Hill, The Triangle, and Avenue Road as far as Fairlight Glen House, just above which the derailment took place.
2. All cars have to be brought to a standstill at the top of Poole Hill.
3. The track brake must be applied on all falling gradients of 1 in 15 or steeper.

In addition to the above, the Corporation had imposed the following compulsory stops :—

On Poole Hill at Par's Corner.
In Avenue Road at Robson's Corner.

My enquiry was held in public in the Council Chamber, and lasted several days. In addition, I acted as assessor to the coroner at his inquest.

Judged by the number of fatalities, this accident is the most serious which has occurred on tramways in the United Kingdom. The general circumstances, however, are not peculiar. A long steep incline, a car out of control attaining a dangerous velocity, and consequent derailment on a curve at the foot of the hill—these are features common to most tramway accidents. The deplorably long list of killed and injured in this case was due, firstly, to the large number of passengers who happened, by reason of the warm weather, to be travelling on the upper deck of the car, and, secondly, to the unfortunate contingency that, just at the point of derailment, there was nothing more substantial than the kerb of the footpath and a light iron railing to prevent the car from plunging down the embankment and overturning.

The car in question (No. 72), together with the maximum traction (Brill) trucks, was built by the Brush Electrical Company, Loughborough, and was delivered in May, 1905. It was first taken into service in May, 1906. The controllers (series-parallel, No. 90 M type) were made by the British Westinghouse Electric Company, and the same Company supplied the electro-magnetic track brakes. These, together with all the electrical equipment, were fitted to the car in Bournemouth. Between May 21st, 1906, and November 2nd, 1907, the car ran 34,348 miles. In August, 1906, it got out of control on Poole Hill, but the driver eventually regained control by using the reversing power. On this occasion there was a dirty contact found in the leading controller. The car was in the shops for general overhaul and repair in November and December, 1907. Between December 14th, 1907, and May 1st, 1908, the mileage worked by the car was 10,302. On three days in April, 1908, complaints were registered regarding the working of the controllers. No. 2 controller fired on the 2nd April owing to fingers requiring cleaning. On the 6th there was trouble owing to the catch of the reversing barrel (No. 1) being stiff and out of position. On the 28th the magnetic brake (No. 2) failed to work on the journey down Boscombe Hill owing to dirty contact at the bottom of the controller. On the night of 29th April the controllers were examined and tested by assistant fitter Grimwood in the Central Depôt; and brakesman Fry examined the brake equipment, as regards clearances and mechanical details, in Parkstone Depôt on the night of 30th April.

On the day of the accident (1st May) No. 72 car was driven by six different men, and travelled 99·4 miles. From 4.56 a.m. until 1.14 p.m. it was in charge of driver Bartlett, who made three descents of Poole Hill, and found all the brakes efficient. Driver Copelin took charge at 1.14 p.m., and at 3 p.m., in trying to reverse from No. 1 end, he locked the controller, and was unable to drive any further from that end. Eventually, by cutting out one of the motors, he was able to drive the car from the rear (No. 2) end into Parkstone Depôt. He reported that No. 1 controller was out of gear, and he could not use power from that end. Inspector Rushton examined the controller, and found the motor barrel out of position. He threw it out of gear, re-adjusted the barrel, and replaced the pinion gear which had over-ridden. He then tested the controller by means of the handles, and found it worked properly.

At 3.30 p.m. Copelin again took out No. 72 car, and, accompanied by a conductor who was learning to drive, drove it to Christchurch Station. Copelin took the car twice down Poole Hill, once before 3 p.m. and once after. On both occasions he found the magnetic brake working properly. Drivers Sackley and Dewar, who were in charge from 4.30 p.m. until 5 p.m., had no occasion to use the magnetic brake, and cannot speak as to its efficiency. Driver Allen drove the car from 5 until 5.20 p.m., and used the magnetic brake in descending Boscombe Hill, and on several other occasions. He found it worked perfectly, and had the usual retarding effect.

At 5.20 p.m. driver Wilton took charge of the car at Lansdown. He was not informed by Allen that anything was amiss. Copelin, who alone of the drivers was aware of No. 1 controller having got out of order at 3 p.m., did not hand on the information to Sackley, who succeeded him in charge of the car. Indeed, as the car was sent out again at 3.30 p.m. by Inspector Rushton as being in working order, there seems no reason why Copelin should have reported the occurrence to his successor.

Wilton drove the car from No. 1 end westward to the terminus at Poole, where he arrived about 6.8 p.m. He used the magnetic brake on this journey in descending Constitution Hill, and found it worked perfectly. About 50 yards from the terminus he shut off power, by moving the large controller handle into the " off " or neutral position. After coming to a standstill he brought his small handle or reversing key at No. 1 end from the forward into the " off " position. He then removed both handles, and took them to No. 2 end. He had no difficulty in doing this, and noticed nothing unusual in the movement of the handles. It is not possible, owing to the interlocking, to remove either of the handles until the pointers of both have been brought round into the " off " position as indicated on their respective dials. Wilton left the terminus at Poole, on his eastward journey to Bournemouth about 6.10 p.m., driving from No. 2 end. As far as the conduit pit in Poole Road, about 4½ miles from the terminus, the journey was uneventful. No emergency stops were made, and there is no steep decline, so that Wilton is perfectly certain that he did not use the magnetic brake on this return journey. The hand brake was sufficient for all purposes, and acted well. The car was brought to rest at the conduit pit, and the plough attached to the underground conductor. Wilton restarted the car, by using one or two notches of power, until a speed of three or four miles an hour was attained. Power was then shut off, and the car allowed to run a little distance without power. He applied three notches of magnetic brake opposite the Pembroke Hotel, in the vicinity of an arc lamp post on the left of the roadway, which is situated about 65 yards from the conduit pit. There was no effect, and Wilton's first impression was that he had missed making contact on the notches. He worked further notches on the brake side, and used sand, but there was still no effect. By this time the car was close to the usual stopping place at Par's Corner, and had attained a speed of ten or twelve miles an hour. He realized that the brake had failed; but was so confident that it was only a temporary failure, that he brought his controller handle from the brake into the " off " position and allowed the car to run freely round Par's Corner. He then reapplied the magnetic brake in the same manner notch by notch, but again without effect. A little more than half way between Par's and Robson's corners, *i.e.*, about 280 yards from the top of the hill, Wilton applied his reversing power, by bringing his controller handle into the " off " position, moving the reversing key into the backward position, and then using power, notch by notch, as far as the 5th. This had no retarding effect, although the automatic canopy switch was blown, and the car had attained a speed of twenty to twenty-five miles an hour at Robson's Corner. Wilton then used his hand-brake, which he had held in position ready, to apply it all down the hill, but the speed was so great that there was little or no retardation, and the car left the rails on the curve above Fairlight Glen House, as has been described, about 460 yards from the starting point at the top of the hill. Wilton's explanation for relying so long upon his magnetic brake was that on another occasion, about a year previous, the magnetic brake failed the first time he tried it, but worked beautifully on the second attempt. If he had known that the magnetic brake was not to be relied on, he could have taken the car down the hill in safety with the hand brake only.

Wilton's tour of duty on 1st May was from 10.40 a.m. until 12.4 p.m., and from 4.40 p.m. until 11.32 p.m.—a total of 8 hours 36 minutes. He had been employed by the Corporation from December, 1902, and had been a permanent driver for over four years, after serving as cleaner, conductor, and spare driver. Although more frequently employed driving on other routes, he was fully conversant with the route *via* Poole Hill and Avenue Road, and stated he had driven cars down the incline in question many hundreds of times. The evidence given by Dr. Spinks, who saw him after the accident, by Chief Inspector Palmer, and other witnesses, proves that Wilton was absolutely sober on the 1st May ; and he bears an excellent character for general sobriety and carefulness. This is vouched for by his record, which shows no entries during the last $2\frac{1}{4}$ years.

Two other tramway employés were on the car during the descent of the hill, inspector Sellars and conductor Finch. Sellars was engaged in checking the tickets on the first portion of the journey. Both these men agree that the car started from the conduit pit as slowly as usual, and that they did not observe the speed was unusually high until close to the stopping place at Par's Corner. Sellars was on the back platform, and Finch on the upper deck, and as Wilton did not signal on the bell for assistance, they neither of them, in accordance with the rules, interfered with the hand brake at the rear end of the car. Sellars was of opinion that the wheels were not skidding down the incline, and Finch estimates that the speed at the moment of derailment was 25 miles an hour. There is evidence to show that the car tilted outwards considerably in rounding Robson's Corner, and that several people expected the car to leave the rails or overturn at that point. Mr. White, who was one of the passengers on the car, jumped off it just before reaching Robson's Corner. He estimated that the speed of the car was then 18 miles an hour. Dr. Spinks' estimate of the speed at the moment of derailment was 12 to 15 miles an hour ; in Mr. Salomon's judgment it was 30 miles an hour.

I examined the permanent way on the route on several occasions during the course of the inquiry. The rails are the same as were originally laid in 1902. The width of groove was then 1 inch, and considerable wear has since taken place. At Par's Corner, from measurements taken in my presence, the width of the groove varied from $1\frac{1}{4}$ inches to $1\frac{3}{8}$ inches, at Robson's Corner from $1\frac{1}{4}$ inches to $1\frac{7}{16}$ inches. Guard or check rails have been added at various places to reduce the wear of the outer rail. On the curve where derailment took place, the original rails were taken up and relaid two or three years ago after the derailment of another car at the same place. The outer rail was then raised so as to provide some superelevation, and to prevent the continuance of the heavy wear on the head and running edge of the outside (left) rail a check rail was fitted to the inner rail in such a position that the groove was reduced to $\frac{7}{8}$ inch. The top of this check rail was about $\frac{1}{4}$ inch above the level of the running rail. When I measured the grooves at this curve, that of the left-hand rail varied in width from $1\frac{1}{4}$ inches to $1\frac{5}{8}$ inches, whilst the right-hand rail showed the groove had widened to $1\frac{1}{4}$ inches, the increase in width from $\frac{7}{8}$ inch being due to wear of the check rail by the backs of the flanges. There was a clearly marked score on the wood block paving between the rails, showing where the flange of one of the right-hand wheels had left the groove. I had sections prepared of the rails at the point of derailment. These show that the wear on the running edge of the left-hand rail amounted to about one-half of the original vertical distance between the head of the rail and the bottom of the groove. There were clear indications also that the flanges of the left hand wheels, owing to the check on the inner rails and the wearing down of the head of the outer rail, were riding on the bottom of the groove, two very clear scores being apparent.

On the 14th May certain trials were made on this particular curve, and speeds up to 12 to 13 miles an hour attained by different cars without derailment. These trials prove at all events that, notwithstanding the large amount of wear on the rails in proximity to the site of the accident, as regards speed, there was a considerable margin of safety beyond the authorised limit of six miles an hour, provided the wheel flanges were in fair condition. At the same time it is not possible, I think, to avoid the conclusion that the worn condition of the rails at the point of derailment and of the flanges was to some extent a contributory factor in the case.

I examined car No. 72 on the afternoon of 2nd May, before it had been moved from the position it occupied after the accident. It was then lying on its right side on the embankment. The hand brake was applied—two and three-quarter turns of the chain being wound round the spindle—and the blocks were bearing on all wheels. It required special effort to turn the spindle further. The hand brake rigging, springs, &c., were intact, and apparently in good order. The cast iron wheel blocks, especially those of the pony wheels, showed very considerable wear, but appeared to be in proper adjustment. There was plenty of sand, which had been upset all over the car when it overturned. The sand valves and sand pipes were in order. At No. 2 (leading) end both handles were in position on the controller, the reversing key being in the "backward" position, and the large handle at the last (seventh) brake notch. The automatic canopy switch was "out." No. 2 controller as regards contacts, fingers, mechanism, &c., was in good condition, and the movements of the large handle, and reversing key, actuated the barrels and made contacts with the fingers in the proper manner. I found one of the leads attached to the coil of the off rear magnetic brake shoe broken, the break being of old standing ; the insulation of the other lead to the same coil was damaged. Inside the car the leads to this shoe were disconnected. Only three out of the four magnetic shoes were therefore available for use. So far as I could judge, the adjustment of the shoes was correct, and the release springs were in working order. Some of the steel blocks, which form the magnet poles of the shoes, were worn away to within half an inch of the holders.

There was some indications of "flats" on the treads of some of the wheels, but the marks were all so slight that it was evident that the wheels could not have skidded for any appreciable distance on the journey down the hill. Moreover, from the Report Sheet, there were slight flats in the wheels at No. 2 end before the car was taken out on service on the 1st May. The tyres of the driving wheels showed signs of much wear. At the centre of the treads of these wheels the diameter had decreased from $31\frac{3}{4}''$ to a minimum, in the case of the right leading wheel, of $28\frac{5}{16}''$. The thickness of the tyre in this case was worn down from about $2\frac{1}{2}''$ to $\frac{3}{4}''$. The tyres of the pony wheels at the centre of the tread were only worn down to the extent of $\frac{1}{4}''$. The flanges of all the right hand wheels were much worn at the backs, most signs of wear being visible in the leading (No. 2 end) right hand wheel. But there was no actual "sharpness." The leading left hand flange was not worn at all at the back, but the thickness of the flange had been reduced from about $\frac{5}{8}''$ to $\frac{3}{8}''$ by wear at the throat.

At my request all the electrical and magnetic circuits and earth connections were tested for continuity by Mr. Bulfin, Borough Electrical Engineer. All were found correct with the following exceptions :—

1. Rear (No. 1 end) off magnetic shoe coil, the lead to which (as described above) was found broken.
2. The earth cable to the case of No. 1 motor was found torn away from its socket, the severance in this case being clearly the result of the overturning of the car.

To make these tests the cover of No. 1 controller was removed by Mr. Lait, Depôt Superintendent, and foreman Robinson, on the evening of 2nd May. They found the reversing or motor barrel of this controller was not in its proper "off" position, but midway between "off" and "reverse," and that there was contact made with several of the reversing fingers. It was not realized at the time what effect this position of the reversing barrel in No. 1 controller would have when the magnetic brake was applied from No. 2 controller. Nothing was therefore said at the time by these witnesses to anyone else regarding the wrong position of the barrel. They easily turned or jarred the barrel back into its proper "off" position.

But the fact, which the evidence establishes, that, when Wilton lost control of the car, the reversing barrel at No. 1 end was making contact with the reversing fingers, explains the failure of both the magnetic brake and the reversing power. The effect of this contact (with this type of controller), whilst the car was being driven from No. 2 end, would be to short circuit the armatures of the motors, and prevent the generation of current by the motors. Consequently there would be no magnetization of the steel blocks forming the shoes, and no attraction would be set up between the shoes and the rails. Similarly there would be no retardation when the reversing key was placed in the backward position, and the controller handle used in the highest power notches.

On the 5th May I was present at trials that were made in Bournemouth on a car fitted with controllers similar to those on No. 72. When the reversing barrel in the controller at one end was placed in the midway position above described, so that there was contact with the fingers on the reverse side, no appreciable braking effect could be obtained, either from the magnetic brake or reversing power, when the car was driven from the opposite end. At the time No. 72 car got out of control, it did not therefore matter whether there were three or four magnetic shoes available, for all would have been rendered useless by the position of the reversing barrel at No. 1 end.

There are two possible causes to account for the incorrect position of the reversing barrel of No. 1 controller :—

    (*a*) Ill-use or mismanagement of the handles by driver Wilton.

    (*b*) Wear and tear of the moving parts of the mechanism, resulting in excessive slackness and freedom of movement in the barrel itself.

Ill-use of the handles, *i.e.*, rotating them together, instead of separately, would cause overriding of the teeth in the gearing and result in locking the controller. This, no doubt, was what occurred to the same controller at 3 p.m. on the day of the accident, when driver Copelin was in charge. It was then necessary, in order to unlock the controller, to throw the barrels out of gear, and replace the pinion wheel in its proper position. On the 5th May nothing was said in the evidence given by Mr. Lait and foreman Robinson to indicate that the controller was locked with the reversing barrel in the incorrect position in which they found it after the accident. It was not necessary to throw the barrel out of gear, in order to put it into working order, and it was easily jarred or shaken back into its proper " off " position. I concluded that they had not found any overriding of the teeth. On the same morning (5th May) I examined No. 1 controller, and found there was so much slack play in the reversing barrel, that it was possible to move it by hand from the "off" into the midway position described, without using the handles. It was also possible to effect the same result by manipulating the large handle sharply. The effect in both cases could be obtained without causing the teeth to override. On the 10th June, when re-examined, the same witnesses stated that, after the accident, they had found the teeth in the pinion gear out of place. If the rack and pinion were in at all a reliable condition, it is difficult to understand how the gearing could have been put "into time" so easily as they described. Again, the displacement of the teeth must have taken place at the Poole terminus, and must have been caused by mismanagement or forcing of the handles, by driver Wilton. But his evidence is very clear on the point that he shut off power 50 yards from the terminus, and after coming to rest brought his reversing key into the " off " position. These separate actions do not indicate mismanagement or forcing of the handles, and are unlikely to have caused overriding of teeth in the pinion gear.

Mr. Turner, electrical engineer to the British Westinghouse Electric Company, gave evidence to the effect that, when he examined, at the request of the Corporation, the controllers of car No. 72, there was a marked difference in their condition. The gearing and motor barrels of No. 2 were in good order, and no slack movement was observable beyond that which is always to be found in similar gearing. The mechanism of No. 1 controller was in a very slack condition, one of the motor barrels was so loose on its spindle that contact could be made with two or three fingers on either side by moving it with the hand. Granted contact with two fingers on the reverse side at No. 1 controller, the brake effect and reversing power when applied at No. 2 controller would be neutralized. It was possible, by sharply swinging round the controller handle at No. 1 end into the off position, to make contact on the reverse side, without any over-riding of the teeth in the gearing, and this would occur without the knowledge of the driver. He thought it inconceivable for overriding to have occurred at the Poole terminus, if Wilton used the handles in the manner he described. Nor did he think it was possible if overriding had occurred for the teeth to be reset in their right position without removing the pawl spring, unless the controller was in a deplorably bad condition.

The looseness in the working of No. 1 controller noticed by several of the witnesses may be accounted for by the fact that the original reversing barrel, supplied with the controller in 1906, had been replaced by another and older barrel, which had seen previous service. This barrel, besides having been subject to more wear and tear, may possibly have fitted the new controller with less accuracy.

My general conclusions on the whole case are as follows :—

1. The initial cause of the car getting out of control on this occasion was the incorrect position of the reversing barrel of No. 1 controller at the rear end, which rendered useless all the electrical braking equipment whilst the car was being driven from No. 2 controller.

2. Consequently the only available means of checking the speed of the car down the hill was the hand brake with its wheel blocks. These were in good order, and if Wilton had recognised at an earlier moment—say, when he was rounding Par's Corner—that the magnetic brake and reversing power were useless, he could, by careful management of the hand brake, and the use of sand, have negotiated the remainder of the decline in safety.

3. The incorrect position of the reversing barrel was not, in my opinion, due to mismanagement of the handles by the driver, but to looseness in the mechanism of the controller, due to wear and tear and want of proper maintenance.

Wilton's failure to recognise more quickly that his electric brakes were useless does not, in my opinion, amount to more than an error of judgment ; and he deserves credit for remaining at his post till the last moment.

To fairly apportion the responsibility for permitting the car to go on service in such an unreliable condition is a difficult matter. The system of stabling cars indiscriminately at any of the four depôts, in order, as I understand, to suit the convenience of the traffic, is largely at fault. No particular set of men can be held wholly responsible for the maintenance of a car which goes one night to one depôt, and somewhere else the next. The system weakens responsibility by distributing it over all the depôts. More especially as regards controllers, which are only subject to a bi-weekly examination, is it a bad system. A man who is only occasionally and possibly at long intervals called upon, as in the case of Grimwood on the 29th April, to examine the controllers of a particular car, is likely to shirk the responsibility for putting a car out of service for renewals. The records of any particular car must also be more difficult to maintain.

Mr. Barber, Traffic Manager, who is responsible for this system, considers, on the other hand, that it tends to greater efficiency and public safety, as it engenders competition between the men in the discovery of faults. But the fact remains that the system is against common, if not universal, practice on tramway undertakings.

The particular controller must for some time past have been in an unreliable condition. That its condition was not discovered by any of the controllermen, foremen, or Inspector Rushton, argues either insufficient examination or want of knowledge. Possibly the latter alternative may be the correct reason, as none of the subordinate staff questioned, or the Depôt Superintendent, were aware what effect the incorrect position of a reversing barrel (with this type of controller) would have upon the electrical braking equipment. They would therefore be unaware of the necessity for guarding against undue looseness or slackness. More careful instruction in the method of examining controllers is necessary, and more practical supervision.

There are a number of other matters to which I wish to call the attention of the Corporation. These are :—

(a) No cars should be permitted to be on service without their full brake equipment. Mr. Barber has had trials made to show that the stopping effect on a large car with four magnetic brake shoes in use is but little better than with three only. This may be admitted, but public safety demands the highest possible efficiency, and not the second best. It is only on the understanding that the full equipment is available that the Board of Trade licence working. In this particular case there were no magnet coils in store, and there was no evidence to show how long the shortage existed. But if the Corporation had given the necessary authority for keeping such necessary articles in store, the responsibility rests with the Depôt Superintendent and his staff.

(b) The position of the sand pipes in the large cars can be improved. On No. 72 they were placed 24 inches from the wheel contact. Dry sand delivered at such a distance will of necessity fall clear of the rails on a curve, and even on a straight road be more liable to be blown away from the desired spot by any current of air. The distance should be reduced by one-half at least.

(c) The rails on the curve where derailment took place require to be renewed, preferably with a wider groove than that originally used. I have referred to the worn condition of these rails and recognised that there was sufficient margin of safety for the speed authorised. But all curves at the foot of long steep declines are danger points, and for this reason it is of importance that the rails on such curves should be carefully watched and replaced when they show considerable signs of wear.

(*d*) As regards the magnetic brake, it is now generally recognised that it should not be reserved only for emergency purposes, and for descending steep gradients, but should be in common use. When used for coasting gradients, the common practice, as set forth in the Instructions to Motormen issued by the British Westinghouse Company, is to set the controller handle immediately to the last braking notch and move it back as may be required. I see no reason why the practice in Bournemouth should be otherwise.

(*e*) The training of drivers is not given the attention it deserves. At most tramway centres a regular school is maintained for the training of men, which contains full scale models of all the electrical equipment and wiring on a car. Batches of selected men are put through a regular course, first of technical education, and afterwards of practical driving under a qualified instructor, and the men are examined both in theory and practice. The method at Bournemouth of giving a conductor a permit to learn driving, during his spare time, from any permanent driver is not a satisfactory substitute.

(*f*) The organization of the tramway department is open to criticism. So far there has been no regular manager at Bournemouth. The control seems to have been divided between the Borough Engineer, the Traffic Manager, and others. No one officer is responsible to the Corporation for the administration of the whole undertaking. This cannot be a satisfactory arrangement. I strongly advise the Corporation to make a change in the organization, by selecting in open competition a properly qualified General Manager, and giving him control over the whole department. The critical period for tramways is not during the first three or four years, when equipments, &c. are comparatively new. It is later on, when mechanism begins to wear out and renewals have to be made. Previous experience of some length is then of first importance.

I recommend the Board of Trade to make the following alterations (1) and additions (2) and (3) to the regulations now in force :—

(1) The compulsory stopping-place in Poole Hill on the downward journey should be at the arc lamp-post before reaching the Pembroke Hotel.

(2) So long as the magnetic or other track brake is not used for ordinary stops it shall be applied, to test its effectiveness, before reaching any steep gradient down which the brake is used for coasting.

(3) All controllers at every terminus, before the handles are removed, shall be opened and the barrels examined for their proper " off " position.

In view of the fact that the whole question of braking is now under consideration by two Committees, I do not propose at this moment to make any recommendation regarding the addition of a mechanical method for applying the shoes of magnetic brakes.

I have, &c.,

J. W. PRINGLE, Major.

The Assistant Secretary,
    Railway Department,
        Board of Trade.

thirds of the platform. The inability to steer clear of anything in his way meant a driver must be able to use his brakes with precision – to stop on a sixpence as we used to say when we had "English" money. This was most important in London where, on the conduit system, a few inches misjudged would stop a car on a dead section with unpredictable delays to all road users, including itself.

Returning to the report: here we get an insight into what the BoT considered to be proper tramway methods: "At most tramway centres a regular school is maintained . . which contains full-scale models of all electrical equipment and wiring on a car . . . Selected men are put through a course first of technical education, and afterwards of practical driving under a qualified instructor, both in theory and practice." Bournemouth's "unsatisfactory substitute" was to give a conductor a permit to learn in his spare time from a permanent driver!

To a person such as myself, who has spent many hours, and ridden thousands of miles, on trams, choosing whenever possible a seat from which the driver could be watched, it seems that there should be a way of using the magnetic brake other than as one does on a car or a bicycle – that is to say, just as hard and just as long as necessary to slow down as desired or to stop in the distance available. Yet, at Archway the driver was supposed to leave the top of the hill in notch two, whilst in Bournemouth the Inspecting Officer said he should start with the controller on the maximum brake notch and ease it off as necessary! It is very noticeable how the magnetic brake crops up in so many reports, and this essentially tramcar brake figures in the next accident case, as it also will in an incident which happened not far short of a quarter of a century later. This wonderfully powerful, yet simple, brake has yet to find favour with railways, although I think it correct to say that some continental shunting locomotives use it, and I read of its being fitted on some railcars in Egypt some years ago.

Operator: **Stalybridge, Hyde, Mossley & Dukinfield Tramways & Electricity Board**
Location: **Ditchcroft Hill, Millbrook**
Date: **5 June 1911**

From the enervating air alleged to be so beneficial to the hundreds of chairborne invalids who flocked to Bournemouth in those days, to the more exhilerating air of the Pennines, where once again the SHMD was the tramway in trouble. This time it happened at 6.30am on 5 June 1911. Again it was Ditchcroft Hill, Millbrook, and the same BoT Inspector, Lt-Colonel von Donop, conducted the inquiry as he did that held in 1904. This time he chillingly observed: "This is now the third case which has occurred on this hill of a car having been allowed to get out of control by the driver, and there is clearly no assurance that it will not occur again"[66].

---

[66] The first case was that which occurred on 11 October 1904 (*qv*). No Inspectorate report has been traced concerning the second case, which occurred on 2 April 1908 and involved car no. 25, which ploughed through a wall and fell into a stream. Fortunately casualties were minimal. Despite the Inspector's foreboding, no further runaways took place on Ditchcroft Hill, although an even more severe accident occurred at Mossley a few months later (*qv*). After these accidents, cars operating on the hilly routes were equipped with Spencer slipper brakes and no further serious accidents occurred on the SHMD system: see *My Fifty Years in Transport*, by Anthony George Grundy, republished by Adam Gordon, Chetwode, 1997, at p 32.

The accident at Millbrook on 2 April 1908, when SHMD car 25 careered down Ditchcroft Hill, through a wall and came to rest on the bank of a stream. *Courtesy: Alan Brotchie*

The cause of one person being killed and 13 being injured was not far to seek. It was simply yet another case of a driver mismanaging his brakes. In his efforts to get the facts, the Inspector called ten of the passengers as witnesses. He wanted to establish whether the car had been brought to a stand before making the descent, as it should have been. During the inquiry one lady changed her mind. Perhaps there was nothing exceptional about that, but the evidence is a good example of the differing degrees of observation and recollection in a sample of people. Taking their evidence into consideration with the statements of the driver and conductor of car no. 44 (the runaway) and of another travelling in the opposite direction, the Inspector remained uncertain.

According to the driver's evidence, he did stop at the top of the hill and, on getting the signal from his conductor, he released the hand brake and proceeded on first power notch, then moving his controller to the magnetic brake notch. This action was in direct contravention of the regulations, which required him to start on the hill on the fourth notch of the magnetic brake. It would appear that in actuality he approached the hill too fast and that when he did try to apply the brakes, this caused the wheels to lock and the car to skid on the greasy rails.

Colonel von Donop drew attention in his report to the fact that at that time the Westinghouse Electric Company was fitting its magnetic brake equipment with an additional device, which enabled the brake to be applied mechanically as well as electrically, and suggested that the Joint Board so equipped their cars. He also called urgent attention to the curve at the bottom of the hill: its want of uniform superelevation and undesirable sharpness (at a shorter radius than that authorised), which latter to be remedied required the road to be widened. He considered that double-deck cars should not be allowed to use the route until this work had been carried out. The Board accordingly operated the line with single-deck cars (somewhat straining their resources) until the remedial work had been done, which it was by December of the same year.

Operator: London County Council
Location: Shardeloes Road, Lewisham, London
Date: 2 September 1911

I now take a brief look at the first case of an LCC car turning over on its home ground and on the conduit system: the Archway Road spill happened on what was an LCC tramway only in law. This time it is no madly careering runaway but a car travelling at about 8mph which turned turtle, killing one passenger and injuring 35 more in addition to its *two* drivers and its conductor.

Two photographs illustrating the overturning of London County Council car 110 at the corner of Shardeloes Road and Lewisham High Road, London, on 2 September 1911.

(top) Courtesy: Alan Brotchie

True to the meticulous pattern of these reports, this one is replete with interesting details. We are told the exact moment at which the car fell over, give or take a few seconds – 3.38pm on Saturday 2 September 1911. It is evident from many of these reports that the Inspecting Officer tried to be on the scene to study the mechanical features of car and track before anything was repaired or tampered with, and while the facts were still in the minds of those involved. If death resulted, he most likely attended the inquest where he acted as the coroner's assessor (to advise on technical and practical tramway aspects), and listened to evidence and thus perhaps obviated calling for it again at his own inquiry.

This particular report settles part of a controversy which has enlivened discussion on the LCC tramcar fleet for years. This large fleet started with double-deck cars on Brill 22E bogies and numbered from 1 to 100 (designated class A). One of them (and this is another point of controversy because the actual car has still not yet been identified[67]) was driven by the then Prince of Wales on the inaugural journey in 1903. Almost before these trams were on the road, another 100 cars – four-wheelers on 21E trucks (designated class B) – were being built, but instead of their top number being 200, it was 201, and this overlap of one was apparent right through the fleet numbers up to 2003. What threw this long sequence out?

The LCC's very first electric car was a sample built by Milnes of Birkenhead to display their products and to demonstrate the Westinghouse Company's exhibit of conduit track at the Tramway Exhibition in the Agricultural Hall at Islington in 1900. This specimen open-top bogie car was bought by the LCC with the sample track and its generating plant. The presumption is that this oddment was given the number 101 and the batch of new cars began at 102. There is no evidence that the sample ran in public service, nor was it seen as 101. At some uncertain date towards the end of World War I, it came into traffic cut down to a bogie single-decker. It was then renumbered 110, the same number attributed in the report to the double-deck four-wheel B-class car, the overturning of which was the subject of the report.

Whatever may be the solution of that enigma[68], no. 110, which rolled over in 1911, could not be faulted mechanically, its speed was not excessive, the rails were in good order, and the car had already gone round the same curve safely four times that day.

The report contains another dissertation on the magnetic brake, which on these cars was not coupled to the blocks on the wheels, the latter being only applied by hand. We are given a table of the speeds at which the magnetic brake took effect. This smash was ascribed to a very human cause – that the regular driver was not paying enough attention to the learner who was driving, and when he realised that the controller had not been turned to the brake notch adequate for the speed, he reached over and put it on full, applying the hand brake hard at the same time. The sudden application of both brakes, so the report says, jerked the car out of the rails on this curve of 64ft radius with a 1 in 16 dip.

The Inspector, Lt-Colonel von Donop, thought that two other issues contributed to the accident. First, the stop post at the site of the accident was situated too far forward beyond the commencement of the curve; and secondly, that it was not intended on that occasion to bring the car to a stand until it was a certain distance beyond the post. He accordingly recommended resiting the post and that the requirement for cars to stop at it should be strictly observed.

Operator: Birmingham Corporation
Location: Cape Hill, Smethwick
Date: 1 October 1911

Once again the environs of Birmingham provide the scene for a tram crash. It was 1 October 1911 on Cape Hill, Smethwick, on the route of the Birmingham and Midland Tramway from Birmingham to Dudley, that what was almost a repeat performance of the triple crash in Glasgow of 6 September 1902 was enacted. This time the "filling in the sandwich" was the car of a different authority. Birmingham Corporation had running powers over this line and it was one of their cars – no. 177 – which ran backwards down the hill, crashed into Birmingham and Midland no. 34, and this duo ran together, hitting another Birmingham Corporation car, no. 180, near the foot of the hill. This time however they all stayed on their rails.

The only man to be killed, and the two who were seriously injured, were among those who jumped off the moving cars. Of all the people who remained aboard, none was badly hurt – some 20 or so received slight wounds.

On this occasion, the report by Lt-Colonel Yorke says little about the cars, but this doesn't matter as the incident could have happened to any type of car. Cars nos. 177 and 180 were double-deckers "of the usual type on the Corporation's tramways". You will remember that at Glasgow the controller handle flew off its pillar as the driver was about to apply the brake to hold the car on the hill; this time the hand brake handle flew out of the driver's hand as he was about to make a start after having stopped to set down a passenger. To restart a tramcar on an ascent was very similar to the hand-brake start so beloved of examiners for present-day motor car driving licences. The controller was turned to the second power notch almost simultaneously with releasing the hand brake gradually. The driver of no. 177 said he applied power, but as he was in the act of releasing the brake, its handle suddenly slipped out of his hand and spun round. The car did not react to the power but began to run backwards.

Instead of grabbing the handle and screwing the brake on again, the driver applied the magnetic brake, thinking it would act with greater rapidity. The car did not respond. The driver went through the gamut of expedients – or thought he did – but failed to stop and soon collided violently with no. 34, which had been climbing about 150 yards behind no. 177.

The driver of no. 34, seeing the other car coming at him, decided to stop and reverse, but could not get to the far end in time, so he jumped off leaving the hand brake hard on. Just as in Glasgow, the two cars went on together and hit no. 180. The three, jammed together, ran on until brought to a stand. The body of the one in the middle suffered very little damage, but both its platforms, canopies and staircases were destroyed.

There is little doubt this was yet another case of failure to set the controller in phase with

[67] According to volume 1 of *London County Council Tramways*, by E R Oakley, published by the London Tramways History Group, 1989, it was A-class car no. 86 (*op cit* p 188).

[68] According to Oakley (*ibid* pp 259 and 303), the B-class car no.110 was renumbered 101 post 1911. A car of this class, no. 106 (with a trolley pole added), forms part of the collection of the National Tramway Museum, at Crich, Derbyshire.

the direction of travel ("an operation which in a moment of excitement or anxiety a motorman may omit to perform" wrote Colonel Yorke). Would it be possible, queried the Inspector, for magnetic brakes to be so designed as to be available at all times irrespective of the direction in which the car was travelling? It is not mentioned in this case, but is worth recalling that the LCC, always ready to try anything once, had in point of fact found a way to achieve this, but did not adopt it because they considered the cure was as bad as the disease. From time to time, the suggestion came up of making brake magnets independent of the motion of the car by connecting them to the line current. This was obviously all very well whilst the car received current, but if the supply failed, or the pole left the wire, the car would be bereft of brakes. Tramway authorities knew better than to fall for this suggestion until, in their unwisdom, the London Passenger Transport Board did. Their action led to the overturn of a car of the once-proud LCC fleet they had inherited – but we will come to that later (at Eltham on 25 March 1934)[69].

Operator:	**Stalybridge, Hyde, Mossley & Dukinfield Tramways & Electricity Board**
Location:	**Stamford Road, Mossley**
Date:	**20 October 1911**

Back yet again we go to the unlucky SHMD after a lapse of only four months since their last fatal runaway. On this occasion a most spectacular disaster befell, when on 20 October 1911 no fewer than six people were killed and nine seriously injured. It was eight weeks before the driver recovered sufficiently to be able to explain what had happened at the inquiry held by Lt-Colonel von Donop.

Single-deck SHMD car no. 24 was seven years old when a few weeks before this accident it underwent a major overhaul "though not fitted with new controllers". Since this attention, it had worked without trouble and, on the day before the tragedy, had been in the hands of three drivers and made six safe descents of Stamford Road, Mossley, as well as ten descents of the worse Ditchcroft Hill, the scene of previous runaways. The car was taken into Mossley depot after finishing work, and from there it was taken out at 5.00am next day by driver Houchin, who little knew that within an hour he would be lying, seriously injured, in hospital. Leaving the shed, the car went empty to Haddens to begin its first passenger journey from there at 5.30am. Both these trips entailed reversing *en route*, so the driver had opportunity to try all his brakes from both ends of the car.

Houchin was an old hand, having served on the St. Helens trams for 14 years prior to his joining the SHMD three years before this accident, and both he and his conductor were described as sober, attentive, industrious and efficient – neither of them likely to take chances or be slap-dash in their duties. At the point where it had to reverse to go back along another road, *i.e.* at Brookbottom, the car was stopped on a rising gradient of 1 in 21 and held there on its hand brake. The driver walked through the lower deck with his controller handles, while the conductor changed the points and walked the trolley pole to the other end, after which he used his whistle to signal the driver to draw down on to the Stamford Road branch. The conductor remained on the ground, as he had to change the pole from one wire to the other, when the car stopped again.

When the conductor returned to his platform, he gave the bell signal to start. This the driver did by gravity – releasing the hand brake with the controller set at notch four magnets in accordance with this oft-recurring instruction. This done, the motion of the car should have very soon been checked, but it wasn't, and the driver's efforts were of no avail. Gathering speed on the 1-in-16 hill, the car entered the right-hand curve to the south and there its trolley pole parted from the wire, putting the car in darkness and depriving the driver of any chance of using reverse power as a brake. Not having derailed, the car sped wildly down the 650 yards towards the next curve, continuing to accelerate on a gradient of 1 in 18, steepening to 1 in 15.8. At one of the passing loops on this otherwise straight stretch, the car jumped the points but, as occasionally happens but at much lower speeds, got back on to the rails. At the bottom of this slope was a small radius curve to the left to take the road over the cutting of the London and North Western Railway. There was no hope of the car travelling at such a high speed negotiating the sharp corner. It left the rails, broke through a wall and nose-dived on to the railway, where it blocked both lines. What might have worsened the tram disaster, and superimposed a railway one on it, was averted by the railway signalman putting the signals to danger to stop an approaching train.

The tram landed upside down, its truck across one of the railway tracks with its wheels uppermost, its body reduced to matchwood. Four passengers were killed outright, and another, as well as the conductor, died soon afterwards. Many other passengers and the driver were severely injured.

The mechanical and electrical equipment on the car was so badly damaged that no fair or reliable deduction could be drawn from it. The conductor was dead and, understandably, after eight weeks of illness, the driver's recollection of detail was hazy. From the scanty evidence, and bearing in mind that the wheels showed none of the unmistakable signs of skidding, it was surmised that the cause was the same as it had been at Bournemouth, when the two controllers quarrelled with each other and vitiated the driver's action. The accident bore two other similarities – the high casualty list – and the upturning of the car down a bank[70].

Operator: **Rawtenstall Corporation**
Location: **Manchester Road, Accrington**
Date: **11 November 1911**

Still in 1911, we next turn our attention to part of a nest of 4ft-gauge tramways in the County Palatine of Lancaster just north of the large Manchester web, namely Rawtenstall/Accrington, where on the eleventh day of the eleventh month in the eleventh year there occurred a runaway finishing with a collision. Rawtenstall Corporation's car

---

[69] Notwithstanding these strictures, Birmingham Corporation did equip many of its fleet of trams with the means of energising the track brake magnets from the overhead line supply. An additional switch (known colloquially in Birmingham as the "lineswitch") was fitted under each canopy which, when operated by the driver, or the conductor at the rear, energised the track magnets from the overhead supply via a nine-ohm resistance. This was done in such a way as to allow the magnets still to be energised from the motors in the usual manner. The problem of trolley dewirement was appreciated in Birmingham and it is understood to be one of the reasons why cars on the Lodge Road route, with its many sharp bends and gradients, were equipped with bow collectors at an early stage.

[70] This accident has been the subject of further research by J D Markham, which suggests that there are grounds for believing that some of the evidence may have been tampered with so that Colonel von Donop was denied the opportunity of reaching a definitive conclusion: see the note at Appendix C *infra*.

no. 14, descending the fairly steep hill in Manchester Road, Accrington, on a single line, jumped the points of the passing loop and hit, corner to corner, its sister car no. 11 which was waiting there.

The car had run unchecked for 356 yards. Twenty people were injured and both vehicles badly damaged. The top deck of no. 14 was torn off completely and fell on the roadway some distance in the rear of the place where the lower deck came to rest against an electric lamp standard on the far side of the road. This happened on one of the few tramway systems using Raworth's regenerative control[71] which, as outlined earlier in relation to the Horton Street runaway in Halifax on 14 October 1904, was designed to serve as a brake. Many times we have come across the precept of coasting down hill by carefully starting by gravity with the controller preset to a prescribed brake notch, or on slipper and hand brakes, but the Raworth system involved a very different driving technique. This car began its descent of a 1 in 20 gradient with its motors in full parallel! This was quite normal with this control system, which was, it seems, the only commercial scheme of its ilk. Unlike the vast majority of trams and trains, which run with series-wound motors, the Raworth cars contained motors with shunt-wound field magnet windings. The significance of this would take several pages to explain, and the extent to which it might be understood would depend on one's basic knowledge of electro-dynamics, so an explanation will not be attempted[72].

The driver had, in starting the car, worked the controller round from off, clockwise, in the usual way to notch 13, at which notch it should have been going at a steady 10mph, but unexpectedly it "shot away at high speed". Despite all his efforts, the driver, assisted by an Accrington inspector who chanced to be on the car and who applied the slipper from the back platform, could not bring the car under control. The sudden surge forward had been brought about by the fusing (*sic*) of one of the shunt magnet field coils, giving the motors a high freak current and at the same time robbing the driver of any vestige of electric braking. This reason, too complicated to explain here, was accepted by the Inspector, Lt-Colonel Druitt, who said the driver was free of all blame. Somewhat paradoxically, the Inspector gave it as his opinion that this type of braking was unsuitable for hills, which was the precise locale in which the theoretical benefits of such a system were expected to be obtained[73].

The report gives an interesting sidelight on labour conditions at the time. The driver was guaranteed 60 hours a week, but he actually worked more. The Inspector's sole criticism was that his duties were spread from 5.30am until 11.30pm. He started at 5.30 to run an early morning workman's service and went home again at 6.30am, and then took duty from 1.15 to 11.30pm, which allowed him only six hours rest after a ten-hour spell before the workman's trip. Most men of today would faint at the thought alone, but in 1911 men had an incentive and will to earn their living.

Operator: **Newcastle upon Tyne Corporation**
Location: **Elswick Road/Westgate Road, Newcastle upon Tyne**
Date: **21 June 1913**

Tramway accidents seem to have had a tendency to happen either in the early mornings or late at night – that at Accrington occurred at 11.00pm, as did the next one to be considered. Judging by the gap in the reports, it would seem that 18 months elapsed before another tramway accident occurred bad enough to warrant a BoT inquiry, and so we pass over 1912 and come to a case in Newcastle in 1913, on the tramways of the Corporation. Here was an instance of an empty car running away on a 1 in 13.5 hill through the usual bungling with the brakes, causing injury to some half-dozen people when it collided with cars nos. 172 and 160.

The car at fault was no. 117, a four-wheel covered-top car, 28ft 8½in long, 6ft 10½in wide, 13ft 8½in high, weighing 9 tons 4cwt, accommodating 34 people inside and 36 upstairs. It departed from Elswick Road terminus at 9.36pm to go on the Chillingham Road route – a circular journey via Byker. When it reached the "big lamp" at the junction of Elswick Road and Westgate Street, the driver reported to the inspector there that his conductor had noticed something amiss with the hand brake under his platform. (In fact one of the links in the chain had snapped.) The driver was instructed by the inspector to change to another car at Byker depot, but the driver pointed out that he was on a circular route back to Elswick Road without changing ends. So off he went, and in due course returned. In the meantime, a fresh car had been brought from Wingrove car shed, which lay only a short distance from the "big lamp", but in the opposite direction along Westgate Street.

After changing over, the men who had turned out with the fresh car, proceeded to take 117 to Wingrove shed, but now of course the defective end was in the lead. It was being driven by a fitter from the shed, who had told the acting conductor – a timekeeper – that if he needed the hand brake to be applied, he would nod his head. This scratch crew reached the junction by the "big lamp" without mishap, and prepared to go round the curve which had been specially laid to obviate cars going to the depot having to reverse on the steep hill of Westgate Street.

The driver leaned out of the platform with his point bar to shift the points while the "conductor" got off to change the trolley to the wire for the curve. As the driver got the bar into the points, the car started to roll, but as the points had not been moved, the car ran on to the hill in Westgate Street. His mate did not succeed in putting the trolley on any wire before he fell and could not remount. Thus the vehicle ran down the hill with no hand brake at the leading end and no current to use as a short-circuiting brake[74]. The fitter, who was driving, had not enough experience to deal with the situation.

Here is an interesting reminder that just as nowadays anybody can ride a pedal cycle, in those days anybody could drive any vehicle on the streets without a driving licence,

---

[71] Other systems with tramcars fitted with regenerative equipment included Barnsley, Dewsbury, Gravesend, Halifax, Southport and Wakefield, but in some cases only individual cars were so equipped.

[72] Shunt-wound traction motors were confined to demi-cars, where only one motor was used. Where two (or more) motors were employed, it was necessary, for load-sharing purposes, to have some series turns on the motor field poles. The motors therefore had compound, not shunt, field windings. The phrase "shot away at high speed" (see next paragraph in the text) is entirely compatible with the compound winding described. When the shunt excitation failed, the motors became simple series motors, but in a weak-field condition.

[73] A detailed commentary by J D Markham on Lt-Colonel Druitt's report is to be found at Appendix D *infra*.

[74] The short-circuiting braking technique does *not* require current from the overhead to achieve braking. More probably, the fitter did not know how to apply it. It is reverse power braking that requires current from the overhead supply.

unless it were plying for public hire.   For tram, bus and taxi drivers, the outward and visible sign of a licence was a clumsy enamelled medallion hanging by a leather strap from a button-hole on the man's frontage[75].

Lt-Colonel von Donop carried out the inquiry.   The month of February 1914 was a busy one for Inspecting Officers, but the human damage was relatively light.   Two of the three accidents occurred within the Manchester area network.

Operator: Dublin United Tramways (1896)
Location: Merrion Square, Dublin
Dated: 1 February 1914

The first day of the month was marked by an accident in that portion of Erin now known as the Republic of Ireland, but before partition, the BoT (and later, the Ministry of Transport) was responsible for tramway safety matters throughout the island.   The car involved was no. 295 of the Dublin United Tramways company's fleet, a double-deck covered-top vehicle having Peckham bogies with pony wheels leading, operating on the standard Irish gauge of 5ft 3in.   It was running along the north side of Merrion Square, in an easterly direction, and should have gone straight on into Mont Street on its journey to Dalkey, but it took the sharp turn leading to the east side of the square and, in doing so, turned over.   Two people were severely injured, one woman so badly that she died some days later.   Fortunately for the remaining passengers, all of whom were injured, medical aid was to hand in plenty, as the square was a sort of "enclave" of specialists – a kind of Harley Street – and several doctors were soon on the scene.   One account of the event describes how some passengers got out through the gaps which had been torn in the floor of the overturned vehicle.

The BoT report[76] states that the car weighed 13 tons 18cwt, with seating for 31 inside and 43 outside.   (As most tramcars were symmetrical, it is puzzling how odd numbers like this were accommodated on each deck.)   The item of tramway equipment prominent in this case was an electric point-shifter with the appropriately delightfully Irish-sounding name "Tierney-Malone".   The earliest British point-shifter of which I have a note was installed in Dublin in May 1903 at the Londonbridge Road junction on the Sandymount line, though the system was in use in Detroit in 1898.   This was a Tierney machine, which operated when a car passed over a soft iron plate beneath a non-magnetic lid in the roadway.   If the points needed to be changed, the driver of the car switched on an electro-magnet suspended under the truck.   This entailed heavy equipment on each car, so in June 1905 Tierney-Malone altered the arrangements so that a "short" current was put through the front motor by a contact on the side of the trolley head and corresponding contact bars of sufficient length near to, and parallel with, the overhead wires.   This arrangement had the defect that cars for the diverging routes had to be quite separate, as the contact on the trolley had to be on the side of the head appropriate to the direction in which the points were needed.

To remedy this shortcoming, the point machines were altered so that if the points needed to be altered for an approaching car, the driver *had* to apply power at the place where the trolley wheel rolled along a contact sleeve on the overhead wire (on the LCC, the plough in the conduit rubbed past a similar device).   If the points already lay in the direction required, the driver had to ensure that his trolley passed the contact with *power off*.   An additional refinement, sometimes installed, was a co-acting signal which showed Left or Right. If the pointer went to the middle (or there was no light), it meant the points had stuck in mid-position. The perspicacious reader will be thinking "but what about the car after dark, when its lights will be taking current continuously?". The answer is that things were so designed that the lighting load was insufficient to operate the point machine. On some tramways using these appliances, the points were altered as necessary by each approaching car, but on others the points were kept normally in one position and operated only by a car needing to take the abnormal route. In that event, there was another contact beyond the junction, which reset the points after the passage of the car[77]. This was the way it was done in Merrion Square.

The driver of no. 295 expected the points to be lying for his straight journey and, coming rather faster than he should have done, was almost on them before he realised that they were set, incorrectly, for the sharp curve to the right. He could not check the speed of the car in time to prevent it derailing and rolling over. The inquiry, held by Lt-Colonel von Donop, was unable to establish why the points were so set. There was no discoverable defect in the machine, and the possibility of the previous car having taken the curve and not reset the points was ruled out since that car had taken the straight road. So there were only two other possibilities: it was not improbable that the driver of 295 had inadvertently turned the points by having unthinkingly applied power at the critical place or the points had been maliciously changed by an unknown person. Colonel von Donop inclined to the view that the driver was at fault and it was beyond question that his car had approached the points far in excess of the 2mph prescribed in the Company's rules. At such a crawling pace, even in the darkness of 9.25pm, he could have stopped short. This was an exceptionally low speed limit: as a general rule it was 4mph through facing points. But all of us who remember trams would testify that they quite often went through points at speeds of four or five times the permitted figures.

Operator: Rochdale Corporation
Location: John Street/Smith Street, Rochdale
Date: 14 February 1914

Lt-Colonel von Donop had no sooner finished with Dublin than he was concerned with another car which fell on its left side in Manchester on 25 February. Meanwhile his colleague, Lt-Colonel Druitt, was called to deal with another accident in the Manchester area network, in Smith Street, Rochdale, on 17 February. This gives an opportunity to mention the ten equal-wheel bogie single-deckers in the Rochdale Corporation's fleet, which were built by Brush at Loughborough in 1912.

---

[75] The licence referred to was not a driving licence, and whereas a driving licence is now required in order to drive buses and taxis, this is still not a requirement for tram driving. Since 1992, however, tram drivers have been required to hold a motor vehicle driving licence.

[76] When contributing an account of this accident in the series "Accidents will happen" for *Tramway Review*, published by the Light Railway Transport League, Alan T Newham concluded that there had been no BoT inquiry in this case (see issue no. 35, 1963, at p 72). In the circumstances, it is perhaps understandable that his views as to the causes of the accident differed somewhat from those given in the official report.

[77] On this aspect see the recommendations of Brigadier Langley in his report on the Glasgow Great Western Road accident of 11 July 1955 *infra*.

Trouble started on the 1 in 14.5 gradient down John Street and developed into the pattern now so familiar: the magnetic brake, not previously tested by the driver, failed (or was alleged to have failed); there was no power to reverse current braking because the trolley had left the wire; the hand brake was ineffective when belatedly applied; and so on. The journey came to a sudden end when the car, no. 63, derailed (rear bogie first!) on a properly canted curve ($2\frac{3}{8}$in superelevation), hit a tramway standard and intruded through a shop window.

There was no doubt that the driver had lost control at the outset by starting without proper precautions being taken and Colonel Druitt felt constrained to call attention yet again to the undesirability of keeping a brake for emergency use only. His argument was much the same as it is with radar on ships today – it should be in constant use so that if it gets out-of-order this defect will be known at once. It is apparent that although it was the function of the BoT Inspectors to recommend measures for improving safety, they had no power to insist on their recommendations being adopted. The use of the track magnets at all times, it will be remembered, was recommended as early as 1906 after the crash at the Archway, Highgate (*qv*), yet despite pronouncements from the two professional bodies, the Tramway and Light Railway Association and the Municipal Tramways Association, backing this recommendation many tramways continued to ignore it. Those systems which did use it constantly were able to run to much faster schedules by reason of the rapid deceleration which this brake produced, but it did of course raise track costs as it wore away the rail heads and meant that the motors were for ever under load – when not under power they were acting as generators. The next most powerful brakes were those applied by compressed air, and although such brakes were in being quite early in electric tramway history, their adoption was slow and far from universal. Rheostatic braking for everyday use would have put unacceptable burdens on the car motors and resistors.

In the Rochdale accident, 16 people were injured, five very seriously, including the driver

The messy result of the collision of Rochdale Corporation 11 with a tram standard and a shop front in John Street on 14 February 1914.   *Courtesy: Rochdale Public Library*

who was *hors-de-combat* for seven weeks and the inquiry had to be postponed. The conductor had jumped off. When the driver was well enough to face the inquiry he said, amongst other things, that he had applied sand all the time and indeed "felt the cracking of the clinker pellets" under the wheels. This calls to mind that "sand" was not a standard substance on trams: some used sea sand, some a sort of fine stony gravel, some used crushed furnace slag and similar grits. Sand-drying ovens were often to be found on tramway premises: damp sand clogged in the hoppers and chutes on the cars[78]. On these particular cars, there were six sanders (most trams had only four), two of which were in the middle of the vehicle and were operated from either platform. By this arrangement, sand could, in theory, be ejected on to both rails ahead of each bogie. Not only did the pedals need to be "pumped" continuously to release quite small quantities, but the position of the delivery pipes was so far from the wheels that the sand had every chance of being scattered by the wind before it reached the rails, and on curves it fell wide of the rails. This last failing was not confined to Rochdale, as it happened to some degree on many trams. On a few lines – the MET in north London was one – the sand pipes were flexible and passed through a ring at the leading end of the bogie, so that when the bogie turned, the bottom of the sand pipe was steered towards the rail.

It is in the enormous variety of fitments on trams, and the differences and peculiarities of the cars and their trucks, which made, and still make, the subject so interesting. Each management or township had its own fads and fancies or colour schemes, and doubtless each tried to be seen to be different. Possibly also engineers and managers were, up to a point, "conned" into buying this or that car or gadget by the firm selling it. Basically, commercial methods, like human nature, have not altered over the years.

Operator: **Manchester Corporation**
Location: **High Street/Upper Brook Street, Manchester**
Date: **25 February 1914**

The next accident to come within our purview occurred on a curve in Manchester, so little used that, after the rails had been down for 12 years, they were still in excellent condition. On most tramway systems, it was quite usual to find stretches of track or some junction connection which was not normally used. The reasons were diverse: sometimes traffic had failed to develop, or had dwindled; sometimes the lines were laid in anticipation of a further scheme which was not built; some few lines were laid for strategic reasons – like some railways – to keep other operators out of the territory; and some were laid for use in emergencies.

The car which ran into trouble belonged to the Corporation. It was a covered-top double-decker 26ft 2in long on a four-wheel truck of 5ft 6½in wheelbase. Weighing 8¾ tons, it had seats for 20 inside and 32 outside passengers. Coming from Slade Lane, it would normally have entered Manchester via Plymouth Grove, but because that thoroughfare was closed whilst the lines were being doubled, the service was diverted via High Street and Upper Brook Street. The connecting curve between the former and the latter was a sharp one, with a minimum radius of 40ft. No steep hill – no brake failure – just a case

---

[78] If unprocessed sea sand were to be used, as suggested in the text, the salt associated with it would encourage absorption of moisture, so helping to clog the dispensing mechanism, and the salt would also corrode that mechanism and the hopper itself.

of going too fast for the car to go round without derailing and turning over. It was foggy, so perhaps the driver was at the corner before he knew it.

The wording of the report, by Lt-Colonel von Donop, reminds me of the use in Manchester of the grade "guard". Driving the car was guard Law, who had started tramway work as a trolley boy (we can only conjecture what work that entailed[79]) and had been a guard for six years – seemingly synonymous with being a conductor on other systems. It is interesting to note that guards certified as drivers – Law had a certificate – received a shilling a day whether they drove or not.

For an accident of this sort, the casualty list was unusually light and of the 20 people who were hurt, none was severely so. This was not so in the next accident which happened in the south-west of the country.

Street tramways in Britain were a manifestation (tramophobes would have said infestation) of large population concentrations – permanent as in industrial or commercial centres and seasonal, as in the pleasure resorts. There were some exceptions: the sleepy pleasant Taunton with a small "county" population, and where there were special traffic requirements, as with the Wolverton and Stony Stratford, Wisbech and Upwell and Grimsby and Immingham lines. There were fewer clientele for trams in agricultural and rural areas so there was a paucity in the south generally and in the south-west in particular. But the sea ports of Bristol, Portsmouth, Southampton and Plymouth each had a substantial tramway service. Rather as a coincidence, "Plymouth" came into the last account and the accident we now dissect happened in Devonport, the Siamese-twin town of Plymouth itself.

Operator: Devonport & District Tramways Company
Location: Tamar Terrace, Devonport
Date: 27 November 1914

It was a few minutes after 7.00am on the damp morning of 27 November 1914, that car no. 25, belonging to the Devonport & District Tramways, derailed and overturned on the curve at the bottom of Tamar Terrace causing three people to die and eight to be seriously injured. The company received 72 claims for compensation but, though some were fictitious, the car was undeniably grossly overloaded. The conductor had collected 34 fares inside the car, where there were seats for only 22 people, when the accident occurred, and there were ten or 12 standing upstairs in addition to the 24 seated. The car weighed 7½ tons and the passengers about 4½ tons, and with so many standing upstairs and the narrow-gauge track – 3ft 6in – the car was top heavy and unstable.

The driver who "fell" for this disaster was a stand-in for another, who had failed to arrive for duty. He had been driving the car since 5.30am without bother, and was looking forward to a break after completing the trip which ended so unexpectedly. There was a large exodus of men from the night shift in the dockyard at 7.00am and car no. 25 was scheduled to run as relief to the 7.10am car. As is so usual when two vehicles are provided, whether they be trams, buses or trains, everybody wanted to get on the first and on this occasion many did so to their regret. Only 35 travelled on the second car.

The hill on which the loaded car, 27ft 6in-long on the less usual wheelbase of 7ft 6in,

Car 25 of Devonport & District Tramways overturned at the bottom of Tamar Terrace after running away. The event occurred on 27 November 1914 and three people died as a result. *Courtesy: National Tramway Museum*

came to grief, dropped over a distance of 950 feet, steepening from 1 in 18 to 1 in 11. Before leaving the summit, the driver did what he had done on earlier trips – he applied the slipper brake "as tight as he could". This was not tight enough for such a load on the greasy rails. Finding that putting on the hand brake failed to arrest the car, the driver tried to use the electric emergency brake, but it let him down because its handle overshot its stop on the controller[80]. Possibly given added strength by the desperate situation, he managed to force the handle back into place and got the brake to work just as the car entered the curve. Things then happened very quickly. The sudden harsh onset of the brake locked the wheels, which jumped out of the rails. At the same time, the heavily-laden body of the car surged forward on the suddenly-checked truck and, being on a curve, the top-heavy mass turned over and slid along the road for about 30 feet.

Model makers may care to note that the slipper blocks were of beech wood 18in long, 3in deep and 1⅝in wide when new. They did not last very long, as they wore away in four days or so. The grain ran along the length of the blocks. I have read somewhere that drivers preferred partly worn blocks. Probably this was because they were more effective when bedded down to the profile of the rails.

---

[79] Trolley-boys (as the name suggests) were responsible for turning trolley poles at termini, operating pull frogs (overhead points), changing and resetting manually-operated points, watching over the rear platform, sounding the bell, helping with parcels and luggage. The practice of appointing them was discontinued in 1930. See *The Manchester Tram*, by Ian Yearsley, published by The Advertiser Press, Huddesfield, 1962, at p 89. During World War I trolley girls were also employed by the Corporation.

[80] The car was equipped with Brush HG-2 controllers. The "electric emergency brake" with this type of controller did not have brake notches accessed by advancing the power handle anti-clockwise from the "off" position. Instead the reversing handle had five positions: reverse brake; forward power; off; reverse power; forward brake. The power handle had to be in its "off" position for the reverse handle to be moved. The power handle could only be moved from "off" when the reverse handle was in either of the power positions. The emergency brake was an "all or nothing" affair.

In his report, Lt-Colonel Druitt stated that he considered the primary cause of the accident to be the motorman exceeding the proper speed limit in coming down from Tamar Terrace and, in consequence, being unexpectedly unable to stop the car as he came on to the 1 in 11 gradient. In trying to use the emergency brake in conjunction with the hand brake, the motorman locked the wheels, so that when the car rounded the curve, the wheels got jammed and, with the displacement of the live load and the effect of centrifugal force, this caused the car to overturn. The overcrowding was a considerable contributory cause, but Colonel Druitt accepted that the passengers insisted on getting on the car, overwhelming the conductor.

Operator: **Barnsley & District Electric Traction Company**
Location: **Eldon Street, Barnsley**
Date: **2 December 1914**

Paraphrasing the title of a well-known book on World War II, the serious tram accident towards the end of 1914 could be called "The driver that never was".

At 4.30pm on 2 December, car no. 4 of the Barnsley and District Light Railways started from the Midland Railway station *en route* to the gasworks. It attained a high speed down the 540 yards of gradients varying between 1 in 14 and 1 in 25 and, leaving the rails at a bend, travelled across the road and violently met the wall of a house. The upper portion of this double-deck car was smashed to pieces and the lower parts much damaged. There were only six people on board: they were all seriously injured, two so badly that they died.

What had the driver to say in explanation? Neither he nor his mate could be found in the wreckage. The driver was still at the top of the hill, where his negligence had caused this bad crash.

Driver Tingay and conductor Priestley had made nine trouble-free journeys on the Smithies route from the Midland Railway station to the gasworks and back. Arriving at the railway station at 4.27pm, Tingay stopped and held the car on the rising 1 in 50 gradient by the hand brake behind another car serving the Worsley Dale route. He then took his controller handles to the other end, ready for departure. Conductor Priestley, having seen his passengers disembark, dismounted, walked the trolley round, put it on the appropriate wire and climbed aboard on to what had become the rear platform.

As he entered the car, he heard a gong, the signal that the driver was ready to start. As he was ready himself, he gave the starting signal on the bell and released the hand brake. He straightaway proceeded to collect fares, and it was not until the lights went out when the pole left the wire in passing under a railway bridge 200 yards from the starting point, that he woke up to the fact that the car was travelling unusually fast. Rushing to the back platform, he made a hash of his attempt to apply the hand brake, then seemingly lost his head and, making no attempt to use the slipper brake, jumped off the car.

Unbeknown to his conductor, Tingay had left his car and went to talk to the driver of the Worsley Dale car and was walking back when he saw his own car was going away from him. He couldn't catch up with it. Conductor Priestley most probably mistook the sound of the gong on the Worsley Dale car for that of his own, and Tingay had made the fatal omission of leaving his car without first putting on the hand brake at his end[81], and not telling the conductor he was going away.

The Inspector, Lt-Colonel von Donop, acidly observed that a gradient of 1 in 50 adjacent to 1 in 16 was hardly a suitable situation for a tram terminus, and if it could not be moved there should at least be a rule forbidding the driver leaving his car there and for the hand brake to be applied at both ends. A rule of this purport had been in operation for years in other places where termini lay on steep hills, and the rule relevant to Queens Road, Battersea, is quoted in full in Charles Dunbar's account of the *Tramways of Wandsworth and Battersea*[82].

Operator: Halifax Corporation
Location: Lee Bridge, Halifax
Date: 22 May 1915

There now follows a long gap in the BoT reports. During World War I, as with World War II, many routine activities had to be suspended or curtailed when the nation, with its back to the wall, had more important things to see to. I think it quite likely that the Inspecting Officers who were not recalled to the colours concentrated on mainline railway matters. However there can be little doubt that tramway accidents continued to happen with deteriorating maintenance and as experienced crews became depleted as the war got worse. An example of such an accident, not the subject of an inquiry but simply of an investigation, occurred in 1915[83].   Once again, the system concerned was the unfortunate Halifax.   In May of that year, double-deck open-balcony four-wheel car no. 89 was proceeding along Lee Bridge on the Causeway Foot route when, immediately after negotiating a gentle curve at moderate speed, and on a slight falling gradient, the car left the rails and turned over on its near side.   No fewer than 56 persons were injured, but fortunately no one was killed.

Lt-Colonel von Donop, who conducted the investigation, found the rails to be correct to gauge but that both were considerably worn, and this was especially the case with the outer rail of the curve, against which the flange of the wheel would have pressed when the curve was rounded.   This section of rail was so worn that it would have offered very little resistance to the tendency of the wheel to mount it.   The wheels of the car were in good order, but they were slightly wide to gauge.   The Inspector considered that the derailment must be attributed to the combined effect of these factors.   The concluding words of his report offered the following salutary comments:

> *The lines at Halifax are only 3ft 6in gauge, and on this account the cars are very liable to overturn, as occurred in this instance, immediately that a derailment takes place.   It is essential therefore that both cars and the lines on this system be maintained in a very high state of efficiency.*

[81] Since the car was a four-wheeler, simply putting the brake on at the other end would not have avoided the accident.   The brake would still have had to have been released by the later action of the conductor. In such circumstances, it is necessary to "transfer the brake", achieved by driver and conductor working together: as the driver applies, so the conductor releases.   A different technique applies to bogie cars.

[82] *Tramways of Wandsworth and Battersea,* by Charles S Dunbar, published by the Light Railway Transport League, London, 1971.

[83] Two other tramway accidents occurred in the same year - one in Manchester and one in Birmingham - which resulted in inquiries by the Inspectorate.   Brief details are given in Appendix B *infra*.

The overturning of Halifax Corporation 89 at Lea Bridge on 22 May 1915. The photograph provides a good view of the Spencer slipper brake mechanism, the lifeguard trays and the gong.
Courtesy: National Tramway Museum

Operator:	Dover Corporation
Location:	Crabble Hill, Dover
Date:	19 August 1917

The hiatus in inquiries came to an abrupt end in 1917, when Colonel Pringle held an inquiry into what was, so far as I can discover, the worst ever accident in terms of human suffering to occur on British tramways. This was in Dover on 19 August 1917, when 11 people lost their lives and 59 were injured at the foot of Crabble Hill. The recipe was similar to the other bad accidents that had occurred in dock towns – Chatham in 1902 (*qv*) and Devonport in 1914 (*qv*) – a steep hill, a heavily-overloaded double-deck car without magnet brakes, and the narrow 3ft 6in gauge so prejudicial to stability. As at Chatham, the driver was "raw", but more about that later.

Dover Corporation's car no. 20 – a 27ft-long open-top four-wheeler on a 6ft wheelbase – departed from the Pier to run to River, and picked up passengers so quickly that before reaching Buckland, the conductor told the driver to avoid stopping to pick up any more. At Buckland, near the tram depot, the driver stopped the car quite well on the hand brake. By this time, the car had 69 passengers aboard. The driver then proceeded up the incline to the top of Crabble Hill and, on reaching the summit, shut off power in readiness to bring the car to a stand at the appropriate place for the compulsory stop, some 100 yards further on. Allegedly because the handle turned round and round, the driver could get no response, so he screwed down the slipper blocks, but still without effect. Like the

106

driver at Devonport, he had difficulty getting the reversing lever to the proper position for electric braking. He then jumped off, and two passengers, a soldier and a retired sailor, took his place and tried to bring the car under control, but did not know precisely what to do.

There were two curves bearing left on the way down the descent, which in places was as steep as 1 in 10.5. The car rounded the first curve, which was on the steep part, passed under a railway bridge, near which the driver deserted his post and, about 100

Two views of car 20 after its accident at the foot of Crabble Hill, Dover, on 19 August 1917, when 11 people were killed and 59 injured.

Courtesy: National Tramway Museum

yards further on, met the second curve on which it became derailed and rolled over to the right. The trolley mast snapped off when it struck the wall of the Crabble Paper Mills, followed by the front part of the upper deck rails. The blow broke down the wall and, as the front end of the car slithered "down to road level, the momentum carried the car forward on its side, whilst the rear end swung round to the left, so that, finally, when the car came to rest, it lay on its right side, at right angles to and across the roadway" (to quote from the report). Such was the mix-up from which the passengers had to be extricated.

The line had been in regular use for a few days short of 12 years, with no previous case of a car getting out of control, so what went wrong to bring about a disaster of such magnitude – a death toll greater than many serious railway accidents?

Evidence given at the coroner's inquest contradicted the driver's claim that the brake chain was not on its hook, and people who examined the wrecked car immediately it fell, found the controller set to "ahead", and the power handle at "full parallel". Colonel Pringle made personal tests and found no difficulty in putting the reversing key into the "ahead", "reverse" or "emergency" positions, so the most likely explanation of events was that the driver, with his mind pre-occupied by the conductor's injunction to avoid picking up any more passengers, omitted to shut off power completely as he passed over the summit of the hill. With the motors receiving current, the hand brake could not possibly check the car, and the handle of the power barrel on the controller not being at the "off" position, the driver had inadvertently made the alleged difficulty with the reverse key. The car was running down this steep decline with its motors under power until the pole dewired under the railway bridge. That the controller was found to be set on full power after the spill was probably one abortive result of the efforts of the well-meaning men who went out on to the driver's platform. The car, although very much damaged, "lived to fight another day". It was renovated and worked for several more years.

Elsewhere, I have written about effects which World War I wreaked on Britain's trams. The BoT report on the disaster brought out some facts on the sorry state of tramway staffing at that stage of the war. "The fact must be faced," wrote the Inspector, "that the war has materially reduced safe working conditions on tramways". When the war broke out in August 1914, Dover's trams had 24 drivers, 16 of whom had more than five years' experience, and only four of them had less than one year. In contrast, at the date of this accident, the number had dwindled to only 18, of whom half had less than two *months* service. Of the total of 18, six were boys under 18 years of age.

The driver of no. 20 had been discharged from the army on 1 June 1917 as unfit for further military service, suffering from nervous breakdown. He applied for the position of motorman and was passed out as a driver on 1 August of the same year. In this context, Colonel Pringle wrote:

> *Nerve and experience are necessary qualifications for tram drivers, especially when traffic has to be conducted over severe gradients and in crowded centres. Men discharged as unfit for military duties on account of nervous breakdown are unlikely to prove suitable, two months later, as drivers on difficult routes. At all events, medical opinion should be sought before a candidate of this description is accepted.*

Operator: **Glasgow Corporation**
Location: **Queen's Drive/Victoria Road, Glasgow**
Date: **5 December 1917**

Having met a case of an overturn with two drivers and one with no driver, we now come across an instance of overturning with two conductresses. This occurred on 5 December 1917, when war conditions were at their worst.

Car no. 157 of Glasgow Corporation's magnificent fleet (a car 30ft long on 7ft wheelbase – a covered-top double-decker weighing 13 tons 3cwt) was carrying 68 passengers along Queen's Drive on the Netherlee to Kirklee route, when it turned over on the curve leading into Victoria Road. The result was three dead and 58 injured, besmirching the good name of Glasgow trams. Although they would be considered steep by railway criteria, the gradients, varying from 1 in 160 to 1 in 190 leading down to the corner, were moderate by tramway standards, so the permitted maximum speed was 16mph. The sharpness of the curve is evidenced by the speed limit there of only 4mph.

This accident was obviously the outcome of war conditions alone. Shortage of repair materials and of men to use what materials there were had made the "yearly" overhaul of the car six months overdue, and it had run 58,000 miles since the last one. The rails on the curve were likewise not in prime condition. It was almost pitch dark and the driver was a lad aged 16½ years who had become a fully-qualified motorman only four days previously. Although so young, he must have had a strong personality. He not only gave an honest and coherent account of what had happened, but he had been able to turn a number of standing passengers off the top deck and platforms of his overcrowded car at a previous stop. To quell restive Glaswegians is not usually a simple matter, and it would seem that this boy had done what his duo of conductresses had not been able to accomplish.

Young James Carnegie agreed that the derailment had been caused by the high speed at which his car had entered the curve. He had driven along this road very few times in the dark, and on this occasion was taken by surprise by the nearness of the corner. Belatedly he applied the brakes, but before they could take effect, the car struck the curve so violently that he was thrown off his balance against the stairs. While not absolving the driver from blame, the Inspecting Officer, Colonel Pringle, was more concerned with the absence of street lighting and the parlous state of tramway personnel. "I cannot agree", he wrote, "that over-darkened streets and reduction of tramcar lighting, dictated mainly by nervousness of possible air-raids, is unavoidable".

This gives me an opportunity for a relevant digression. My journeys on other tramways during World War I were made in daylight, so recollections in the dark are confined to the LCC. The street lamps were mainly gas lit, and as there was no way of reducing their intensity – comparable with the use of lower wattage bulbs in electric lamps – the lanterns mostly of the four-sided variety surmounting cast iron standards of the designs so beloved of Sir John Betjeman, were either not lit, or their glasses so heavily painted within that only the dullest glow was emitted. The glass base of the lantern was not painted, so a small area beneath the standard was illuminated. Some 60% of the lamps were out of use, and those lit were mostly on street corners. For convenience, tram stops were usually on corners, and curves were *ipso facto* so, and thus these places had some measure of lighting. Tram drivers welcomed moonlit nights – the black-out taught us town dwellers to appreciate the moon and we watched its waxing and waning with concern.

The lighting on LCC trams was severely dimmed. The headlamp in the dashboard was obscured by a piece of yellowish paper which allowed very little light to shine forward, but enough to enable the oncoming vehicle to be seen. The car's (fleet) number was stencilled on the paper and at night showed up in silhouette. Service numbers and destination indicators were normal; the lower saloons' delicately shaded blue bell-shaped translucent glass shades were removed, never to return and their places taken by black cardboard cubic shades. All four sides of these boxes bore translucent cut-outs advertising Nestle's *café au lait* or cocoa. The bottom was open showing light downwards at three places along each of the longitudinal seats. Upstairs, the bulkhead pattern glass bowls were painted black except for a disc about 2½in in diameter through which a shaft of light shone downwards, one of these lamps being over the head of each stairway. It was noticeable how passengers gravitated to the seats under the lights, and how the conductors edged towards the lamps when giving change or clipping tickets. Doubtless other tramways adopted similar means of dowsing their lights, and must have found fare-collecting to be a near impossibility on the upper decks of open-top cars.

I would like to mention a fact, not recorded elsewhere so far as I know, that all lights on London trams were turned off when crossing the Thames lest the course of the river betrayed to airships lurking above the reflection in the water[84]. It was a ritual at Westminster, to take one example, to switch off all lights at Scotland Yard and turn them on again at Stangate, or *vice-versa* when northbound. On the occasion of a row of bombs being dropped at intervals straddling the main road from Streatham to Kennington, it was said that Lt Matthy, in his silently-drifting Zeppelin L13, took his course from a tram on which the plough was flashing.

Until some form of warning was devised later in the war, the public had no intimation that the enemy was about until bombs began to arrive, the searchlights lit up, or gunfire was heard, but those of us who lived close to tram routes in London knew the approach of the enemy had been detected when we noticed the tram running without lights. How the warning was given to the tram crews is still not known for certain[85]. An anticipatory thrill ran through us boys when a neighbour reported that the trams' lights had gone out.

For Jimmy Carnegie, driving in Glasgow, there had been no street lights for 250 yards, and the lamp at the fatal curve came into view too late to serve as a warning marker. Making a recommendation that compulsory stopping places should be marked by coloured lights, and another that boys under 18 should not be appointed as drivers, the Colonel's report also expatiated on the state of affairs with staff on the Glasgow tramways. Normally employing 1,700 men over 21 as drivers, there were now only 1,558 drivers in all, and of these 266 were women (ten of them under 21) and 46 lads under 21. The heavy work, long hours, black-out and lack of weather protection, had caused no fewer than 534 women to leave after being fully trained as drivers. Many of the men who had been taken on were not up to the medical standards of the forces or had been discharged as unfit. In such circumstances, it is a wonder that there were not a lot more disasters such as this and the one at Dover. But, as I think has been clear, in the absence of able-bodied adult males, the only way the trams in Britain kept going was by the use of substitutes such as those discharged from the Forces, underage lads and females. In due time, the staff position in Glasgow returned to normal, but women drivers and conductors were again employed in World War II, and some remained in the service to the very end of the trams[86].

Operator: **Bradford Corporation**
Location: **Allerton Road/Chapel Lane, Bradford**
Date: **1 February 1918**

After two conductresses, now to a tramcar with two overturnings, and by the long odds of coincidence, the same man was its driver on both occasions. He met his death on the second occasion, which happened on 1 February 1918. Nineteen people on the car were injured. Allerton was an unlucky name for both driver William Gill and his tram. This was car no. 88 of Bradford Corporation tramways, a double-deck, vestibule-type on a single truck with 7ft wheelbase. It was 27ft 8in long and 16ft 8in from rail level to the top of its roof cover. In addition to the normal and rheostatic braking arrangements, there was the unusual Spencer-Dawson track brake. This last-mentioned brake was not only unusual because it was a rarity, but because the brake shoes were pressed on to the rails by powerful springs which were held in the "off" position by compressed air at 350lb per square inch acting on oil in hydraulic cylinders.

The first accident was a pushover, for it was when standing at Allerton terminus on 7 February 1913 that the car was pushed over by wind pressure. (Before we come to the last of these accounts we shall meet another case of a vehicle becoming the victim of Yorkshire wind: Huddersfield on 4 October 1938.) The car was so badly damaged that it had to be practically rebuilt and, whilst in the workshops, it was fitted with 40hp motors, which were not so very common at that date, although tramcar motors had been gradually rising in power as design improvements were made. At the turn of the century, most motors were of 25 or 30hp, and some at 35hp were being introduced[87]. In the early 1920s, 60hp motors began to come into use, followed in a few years by 65hp, and with a tendency for motors to be made smaller in relation to increased power.

Starting from Allerton terminus, within a week of five years after the pushover in the hands of the same driver, the car overturned at the curve at the bottom of Allerton Road. Sixteen years had elapsed since the line on this long slope of some 1,100 yards, on an average gradient of 1 in 14, had been opened and there had been no accident. But, as with most things, there was "always a first time". The car was on an early morning service and at 5.55am it was still dark, black-out to boot, and moreover foggy; it would be easy therefore for a driver to mistake his whereabouts. But, did he?

At the inquiry, held by Colonel Pringle, witnesses agreed that the car seemed to have been going more slowly than usual, no doubt because of the fog. But one averred that she had seen the driver leaning against the bulkhead door just before the accident. Gill was a long-experienced and reliable driver, one not very likely to leave his controls on a

---

[84] The omission referred to in the text was rectified in volume 1 of *London County Council Tramways* by E R Oakley, published by the London Transport History Group, 1989, at p 444.

[85] According to Oakley, the warning was achieved by means of special lamps mounted on feeder pillars and at other key locations, which were illuminated when an air raid was imminent: *ibid* at p 444.

[86] An accident involving a woman driver occurred in Glasgow on 30 March 1953 (*qv*).

[87] British Westinghouse were supplying tramcar motors of 42hp as early as 1907.

Bradford Corporation car 88 in course of being returned to upright after its overturning at Chapel Lane, Allerton, on 1 February 1918. *Courtesy: National Tramway Museum*

steep down slope, so one feasible explanation was that the man had been taken ill, a possibility supported by his controller being found on notch one of power, and by the fact that he was thrown out of and under the car. If he had been in full possession of his faculties, he would no doubt have acted like most drivers in similar circumstances in obeying the natural instinct of self-preservation and clutched on to something. The controller should have been on brake notch two – as prescribed for descending this hill. The driver may have put it on to power to start away from the last stopping place and had then been unable to alter it, and thus the car, accelerating downhill, had no chance of rounding the curve safely.

What one's mind can register in an instant of time is truly astonishing. From derailing, to the car's finishing on its side in a case like this, can have been at most two or three seconds, yet witnesses in several instances spoke of remembering the car travelling for some distance on only two wheels. In many instances wheel marks showed this to have been the case, and it was not unknown for one mark alone to be found – the pitching forward of the car and the centrifugal force of the car would lift the rear end and the wheels from the rail on the inner rail of the curve leaving only the outside left wheel on a rail, where of course it did not remain for long. In this case there were wheel marks for only 14 feet, the equivalent of a fraction of a second in a person's brain, yet it had been remembered amid the other sensations of the instant.

Operator: Bexley Urban District Council
Location: East Hill, Dartford
Date: 5 February 1919

The next event was another sample of the difficulties under which trams had to work towards the end of World War I, or to be a little more precise, in this case the difficulties under which they laboured to restore their services. The armistice was barely 11 weeks old when this runaway occurred on 5 February 1919 yet, in the words of the BoT report by Major Hall[88], "in order to meet the needs of the travelling public" the Bexley Council had already put 80 under-trained drivers into service. This was a large number for so small a tramway, and it was one of these men whose car ran down East Hill, Dartford, and was stopped when its front collided with a tree, damaging the front of the tram severely. Nobody was badly hurt.

This mention of Bexley in the matter of an accident in Dartford may have puzzled the reader. The Dartford Council had lost all its cars in a disastrous fire in August 1917, when they were destroyed inside their blazing depot. The district was one in which there was heavy daily movement of essential munitions workers, who could not be left bereft of a tramway service. The next door neighbour, Bexley, with whose lines there was a physical connection, came to the rescue very quickly with a scratch service and within a few days obtained some spare class B cars from the LCC and took on the working of the Dartford lines on a permanent basis through a joint committee. Thus it came about that a car from London was at work in Dartford, under the aegis of Bexley. The report gives the car as no. 131 (its LCC number) and says it was one of a batch of "about" 16.

In these reports the numbers of passengers are frequently "about", and it is understandable that it was sometimes difficult to know exactly how many were on board at the time. Tickets issued seldom gave a guide – some will have got off after paying their fares, others may not have yet been visited by the conductor, and whenever something untoward happens there are always some people who quickly make themselves scarce. Some wish to avoid getting involved in giving evidence, and some may have good reason not to be there – is there anyone who has not at some time or other been off his beat without the knowledge of his family or his foreman – perhaps even desirous of not being seen by the police? Dubiety in numbers of persons is thus explained, but as tramcars are not counted in fractions, why "about 16" cars?

By 1922, car no. 131 was running again on the LCC tramway system and I have a theory that after this tram/tree collision, the Bexley Council swapped it for another of the same type in order to keep their essential services going. The LCC seem to have had no use (possibly no staff to run them) during the war for their 100 class B cars and in the course of the war had sold an earlier batch to Bexley, ten each to Rotherham and Sheffield, followed by a second group to Sheffield as well as six to Southampton and six to Newport. Most probably the LCC made good the damage sustained by the car in Dartford, which would account for its having a class M upper deck – one of only three to be so treated.

Operator:　　**London County Council**
Location:　　**Pancras Road, Camden, London**
Date:　　　　**16 August 1919**

From its fringe, we will go into the centre of the metropolis for the next case, the subject of which was the overturn of an E/1 class bogie car as it travelled from College Street round the curve into Pancras Road. This type of tramcar, of which the LCC ultimately possessed 1,050, together with 300 class E from which the E/1 was a development, formed the backbone of their fleet (and later that of the London Passenger Transport Board).

---

[88] George Leslie Hall (1882-1947), Inspecting Officer of Railways 1919-27.

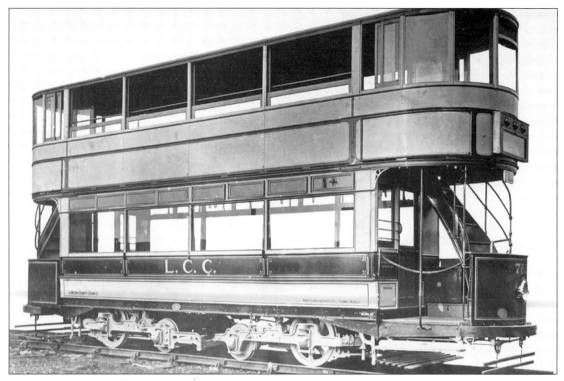

The first of the LCC class E/1 cars, no. 752, on a siding at Hurst, Nelson's works, at Motherwell, in 1907. Over 1,000 cars of this class were built.

Courtesy: National Tramway Museum

The LCC had good reason to be well-satisfied with these sturdy easy-riding cars, which travelled faster than most others. The design was used with minor modifications by several other authorities. I think it will be a worthwhile digression to mention something to which I do not remember having seen reference elsewhere in tramway literature but which could have had widespread effects on tramcar design. Very soon after World War I, the LCC were contemplating ordering some new cars to restore and extend their services, but before doing so launched a competition with a prize of £2,000 (a large sum of money in those days) in an effort to find a better design. It would be more than interesting to see the designs which were submitted, but all we know is that none of the entries received was considered good enough to warrant the award of the prize, so the LCC ordered another 125 of their well-tried E/1's which differed very little from pre-war cars.

A description of this accident, reported on by Colonel Pringle, would probably be tediously like some previous cases, so it will be summed up by saying that the driver, a man of only four months' experience, got the car going too fast to be able to rein it in before entering a curve. This overturn introduced a hazard from which trams rarely suffered – the outbreak of fire. When car no. 908 left the rails at 2.45pm on 16 August 1919, it crossed the road, mounted the pavement and then it struck a section box. As the car rolled over, squashing a hapless pedestrian, it hit and split open another section box when, arcing against the live switchgear, it started a small fire.

Tramway fires, though rare[89], were to the forefront of those responsible for building the trams for the Kingsway Subway, so much so that these vehicles had to be made as far as possible of metal, and the few necessarily wooden parts chemically impregnated against fire. Thus were produced the first all-metal bodies many years earlier than those for railway carriages, on which fire was a much greater hazard [90].

On car no. 908 – which would probably have held to the rails otherwise – the wheel flanges were only half their normal depth due to much running on the bottom of the rail groove, which reveals to what extent rails were worn out during the war.   The report shows a small point of social history.   Although there was at that time, unlike the present day, an urge for women to get back to their natural habitat (their homes), ten months after the end of hostilities, conductresses were still with us.   Books have been written about the railways in two world wars, but for tramways, the effects have gone largely unrecorded, and their praises unsung.   Most of the systems in the industrial towns worked all-out with depleted staffs and minimal maintenance to carry munitions and other essential workers to and fro, and by the end of four years' hostilities, at the end of 1918, they were in a sorry condition.   The lines, worn out, took years to relay and the rough state of the tracks continued to play havoc with car bodies.   For many smaller tramways it was the beginning of the end.   Extension schemes pigeon-holed "for the duration" were never revived, partly because the first task was to try to resuscitate the existing systems, and partly to the boost given to internal-combustion vehicles by the stimulus of military needs.   These factors combined to put British tramways on a "sticky wicket" and they were "run out" one after another.   But some of the stronger ones survived to "play" in fighting World War II to a victorious conclusion.   That war deferred their demise for a few years more: one of the very few benefits of the world conflagration[91].

Operator: Tynemouth & District Electric Traction Company
Location: Borough Road, North Shields
Date: 27 September 1919

The Railway Inspectorate of the BoT had changed their address several times since the Tramways Act of 1870 and, no doubt because of the war, moved their lair from Whitehall to Abingdon Street towards the end of 1917, but a change of a different *genre* overtook these gentlemen when the newly-formed Ministry of Transport (MoT) took them under its wing in 1919 as part of the Public Safety and General Purposes Department.   For

---

[89] The worst example of conflagration affecting a tramcar in traffic was that resulting from the accident at Glasgow, Shettleston, on 28 January 1959 *(qv)*.   Far worse destruction in terms of damage to rolling stock, but not in terms of human life, was occasioned by a number of depot fires, including those at Dartford on 7 August 1917 (loss of entire fleet of 13 cars);   Green Lane, Liverpool, on 6 November 1947 (loss of 67 cars);   and Dalmarnock, Glasgow, on 22 March 1961 (loss of 50 cars).

[90] The reason for requiring tramcars using the Kingsway Subway to be metal-bodied arose from a disastrous fire on what is now line 2 of the Paris Metro, near Couronnes station.   During the evening peak of 10 August 1903, fire from a motor short-circuit occurred in one of the carriages and this spread along the softwood bodywork of that and other carriages.   Passengers had already been transferred to a following train, but this train too became involved and ultimately 84 persons died from suffocation or crushing.   The BoT thereupon issued in May 1904 fire-protection requirements for underground electric railways, which included the stipulation requiring all-metal construction of carriages, while seats, panels and other fittings had to be made of non-flammable materials, and cables had also to be covered with non-flammable materials.   See *Rails Through the Clay*, by Alan A Jackson and Desmond F Croome, published by George Allen & Unwin, London, 1962, at pp 92 and 93.

[91] Contrariwise, concentrated aerial bombardment in World War II resulted in the closure of Coventry tramways in 1940 and Bristol tramways in 1941.   Other systems suffered major damage as a result of air raids during World War II, most notably that operated by the London Passenger Transport Board which, apart from damage to the tramway infrastructure, sustained the loss of 68 cars and significant damage to 13 depots (some more than once).   Air raids during World War I occasioned less damage, but an unusual feature was the shelling of Hartlepool tram depot by an enemy warship on 16 December 1914.

tramways, it was just a case of "a rose by any other name", so the only noticeable sign of change in Major Hall's report on a turnover in Borough Road, Tynemouth, on 27 September in the time-honoured protocol of the opening sentence – "I have the honour to report for the information of the Board of Trade the result of my Inquiry…" became "I have the honour to report for the information of the Minister of Transport…" a form which has been retained ever since, save for the change of title of the addressee.

As in so many other incidents of this sort, the driver of the tramcar allowed it to get going too fast and in trying to regain control on a hill as steep as 1 in 11, he locked the wheels and skidded the car. Seventeen people were injured.

There is said to be something unlucky about the figure 13, but it is the first time it has cropped up among the unfortunate cars in this saga. The car, no. 13, was an open-top four-wheeler belonging to the Tynemouth and District Light Railway – another 3ft 6in-gauge line. On a 6ft wheelbase, the car was 27ft 5in long and had motors of 22.5hp (not very adequate one would think for steep hills) with the usual hand brake, oak-shod slippers and emergency short circuiting of the motors actuated by the controller reverser. This accident led to an immediate alteration in the rules[92], but this action did not prevent an accident happening all over again in the same place, but with far worse results, on 31 July 1921 (*qv*).

Operator: **Midland Railway Company**
Location: **Bearwood Hill, Burton-upon-Trent**
Dated: **8 October 1919**

Thirteen comes into another of these stories. In the enabling Acts or Orders tramways were listed by numbers, and tramway no. 13 was one of the numbered sections of the Burton-upon-Trent Corporation's system, and it was on here that a car operated by the Midland Railway and belonging to the Burton and Ashby Light Railway came to grief. It was a wider car than most which ran on 3ft 6in lines, but was electrically and mechanically complete with "all mod cons" for its day and age. It had 40hp motors; hand brakes with double purchase gear applying blocks on all four wheels; magnetic track brakes operating two pairs of track shoes between the wheels and blocks on the sides of the wheels opposite to the blocks operated by the hand brake; and automatic electric run-back brakes.

The car was no. 19, being 28ft long, 6ft 3½in wide over the side-pillars, and 13ft 5in to the top of the railings of its open upper deck. It was proceeding quite normally up the Bearwood Hill with about a dozen passengers on each deck, and had reached the steepest part of the hill, which was in a cutting some 25ft deep and overhung by trees, and was on a gradient of 1 in 11.65, when the wheels lost adhesion and started to spin. Losing momentum, the car soon came to a stand, and then started to run backwards with the wheels still revolving forwards. The date was 8 October 1919, in the "fall", and most certainly fallen leaves were the main cause of the wheels slipping, but it was another of those simple mechanical failings which prevented the driver from stopping the car from a rapidly accelerating flight which finished in derailment and overturning on the 59ft-radius curve at the foot of the hill, resulting in two people losing their lives and in 12 being injured, some very seriously.

The coming to a stand was an emergency equivalent to a power failure, and the driver

Two views of overturned car 19 of the Burton and Ashby Light Railway at the foot of Bearwood Hill, Burton-upon-Trent, on 8 October 1919, as a result of the driver losing control. *Courtesy: National Tramway Museum*

tried all the permutations of his brakes that he would have tried in these circumstances, but to no avail. (The driver averred that his sanding gear failed when he tried to use it at the moment the wheels began to slip.) It is obvious that once the car had ceased to move forward, sand would be no further use at the front but would need to be put down very quickly at the back. With this object in view, many undertakings had a rule that the conductor should be on his platform when the car was on a hill in order to be instantly ready to carry out the tasks as set out in the extract from the Tynemouth instructions, but this was not always possible if the conductor's job of collecting fares from short-distance travellers was to be done. The luckless conductress on this car was upstairs at the time

---

[92] The revised instructions to conductors are set out in Appendix E *infra*.

the car started its headlong runback, but she was quickly down and not only dealt with passengers but made a valiant effort to apply sand. She was not there at the vital moment of runback, but this was of no account as the sand gear at her end had the self-same defect as that at the driver's end.

Another tramwayman, wheeling his bicycle up the hill, did some useful detective work. After the accident, he noticed sand which had not been run over near the top of the hill, and a short length of sand lower down, over which tram wheels had passed. He observed that the sand in both places was of the colour and consistency of that used by the light railway's cars, which was quite different from that used by the Corporation's trams. These patches of sand proved that the driver had managed to get sand flowing briefly at his end but, as he said, not in time for the wheels to reach it; the second patch being the small ineffective amount the conductress had been able to eject before the apparatus failed. This unfortunate lady did not survive to tell what she had done.

Now to the sanding gear. In the days of electric traction, it was almost universal practice for sand to be dropped by treading on a pedal (sometimes two pedals) set in the floor of the platform. Each pedal was mushroom-shaped and, when in the operative position, its head stood above the surface of the floor. To put a pedal out of use, it was lifted a little, turned through a right-angle and allowed to drop through a slot in the sand lever below the platform. In this position, the head of the pedal was flush with the platform floor and the conductor or passengers could not unintentionally drop sand on to the track. When changing ends, it was part of the driver's duties to alter the pedals accordingly, and the driver at Burton was quite sure that his pedal had been set in the correct position. However, it was a well-known fact that on these cars the pedals had the bad habit of dropping into the "off" position on the slightest provocation. When he most needed sand, the pedal fell and, by the time it was restored, it was too late. At the rear end, the conductress had to spend time raising the pedal before she could apply sand; the pedal was found after the accident to be "down", so it had to be presumed that after the brief application of sand at her end the pedal had again retracted. It was obvious that not only must the design be improved, but at all times the pedal at the rear end must be ready for use to deal with emergencies, as the Inspector, Major Hall, called for in his report.

Operator: **Burnley Corporation**
Location: **Briercliffe New Road, Burnley**
Date: **28 November 1919**

Every motorist knows, many have experienced it – that he can be taken by surprise when suddenly, without the slightest warning, his foot brake may fail to act because of a rupture or leakage in the hydraulic tubing. In a not dissimilar way, a tram driver could lose his electric braking by the sudden parting of a cable, and it was just this which caused Burnley Corporation car no. 10[93] to arrive at the bottom of Briercliffe New Road on its side at 12.55pm on 28 November 1919. The track gauge of this remarkably accident-free system was four feet. The car, 33ft 10in long and 6ft 6in wide, with a covered upper deck was mounted on two maximum-traction bogie trucks, each having a wheelbase of 4ft; the total wheelbase being 14ft 6in. The customary hand and rheostatic brakes were present, and by way of contrast to other tramways so far encountered in this book, the slippers were of cast iron.

A later accident to that described in the text to car 10 of Burnley Corporation.   The tram was hit by a lorry and then ran backwards into houses at Lane End on 21 December 1923.
Courtesy: Lancashire Library

The mention of maximum-traction bogies seems an apt opportunity to interject a few words about bogies.   They appeared in several forms and of many designs, but the twofold object was the same, although they had an advantage in giving a much better ride, lessening the stresses and strains to the bodywork.   They made it possible to convey more people for a given number of cars and frequency of service and enabled passengers to be carried as economically as possible.   In the larger townships, both criteria applied – large crowds had to be lifted, hence large cars – and it was desirable to carry as many as practicable with one pair of tramway crew.   The capital cost was not proportionately greater, nor did it consume proportionately greater power than a smaller car.   There were limits, of course, and they were not always technical ones.   I once asked the manager of Sheffield Corporation's tramways why, in view of the numbers of people requiring to be moved during the peak periods, they did not employ bogie cars.   His reply was that it was difficult enough to collect fares on a crowded four-wheeler on the short stages, and he was sure that on bigger cars there would be a loss of revenue because fare-dodging would become even greater than it was.

Tramcars started as four-wheelers and had to remain so while horses pulled them, but the advent of mechanical traction in the form of steam opened up possibilities of heavier, more capacious and, consequently, longer cars.   In order to support greater length, not only bogies but Bissel trucks (pairs of wheels on independent pivoted frames) were used, and furthermore, an articulated tramcar (pre-dating Gresley's Great Northern Railway and London and North Eastern Railway trains, and Continental buses and trams, by many years) was patented in 1882.

The 30in – more or less – wheel which had been a standard from the very earliest days

---

[93] The same car was to be involved in a further accident, at Lane Head on 21 December 1923, when it was hit by a lorry.   That accident resulted in the deaths of two and injuries to seven persons.   No copy of the Inspector's report has come to light.

of tramways, was carried into electric practice and remained so through the lifetime of most British tramways. It was however too big to pass under the side sills of car bodies which was necessary when the length of cars postulated using bogies, which could negotiate sharp curves. Hence the smaller, or pony, wheels came to be adopted enabling the bogie to swivel freely to adjust themselves to curves. It was not desired, nor was it needed, that more power in the form of additional motors should be installed. With bogies, there were twice as many wheels to share the weight of the car, so in order to retain sufficient adhesive weight for the driving (larger) wheels, it was arranged that they should carry the greatest possible share whilst leaving enough on the pony (smaller) wheels to ensure that they stayed on the rails and to be of value in braking. This result was achieved in the maximum-traction truck in which between 60 and 80 per cent of the weight was on the driving wheels. Bogie trucks on this principle appeared in numerous designs, and those with swinging bolsters would take up many words of explanation, with its sideways floating movement independent of the bogie frames. As we have seen, it was a practice on some tramways to place the pony wheels towards the platforms (there were said to be some technical virtues in doing so), instead of the normal position towards the centre of a car[94].

There were equal-wheel bogies in specialised cases, and perhaps the best known were the HR/2 class of the LCC designed to work on steep hills with all axles motorised, but by then electric designers had produced a more compact motor which allowed the use of smaller wheels.

When driver Fairclough of Burnley relieved driver Sheppard only a few minutes before the car was wrecked, the latter described it as in A1 condition with all three of its brakes working well and a plentiful supply of sand running freely. Why then did it so very soon get into serious trouble? We shall see.

Car no. 10 was climbing the 1 in 12.2 rise quite normally until "about 4 pole intervals up" (this can be taken as a distance of some 450 feet because it was a statutory requirement that the trolley wires should be supported at intervals of not greater than 120 feet), when the wheels began to slip and the car to lose speed. In order to stop the spinning of the wheels, the driver shut off power and, as the car came promptly to a standstill, he applied power again, but the car did not respond and immediately began to roll back. According to driver Fairclough's account, he did the correct thing by putting the controller to reverse, with its main handle to the last notch of the electric brake. This, also, failing to have any effect, he tried the other expedient – generally regarded as a "last ditch" measure – controller at full parallel forward with the canopy switch "off". Still there was not the slightest effect on the increasing speed. The car, in running back, eventually overturned on the curve at the bottom of the incline. Fortunately, there were only four passengers on the car at the time. All were injured, one seriously. A boy standing on the pavement near where the car overturned was also seriously hurt. Neither the driver nor the conductor was injured.

Like cars on many other tramways, these Burnley cars had destination boards inside the lower-deck windows and the conductor was busy altering one of these when his driver called for his help with the brake. It took him some seconds to realise what was wanted of him and valuable time was lost: he should of course have been on his platform in case of trouble. Breach of the regulation laying down that the conductor should remain there on steep hills seems to have been commonplace: doubtless it was a matter of familiarity breeding contempt – so many thousands of uneventful hill journeys lulled them into a sense of false security. Another interesting and related instruction, seemingly not often carried out, was that, before ascending hills, the slippers should be lowered close to the track in order to avoid wasting time if an emergency should arise, in which case they could be quickly applied. The wheel for operating the slippers is shown in fig 5. It turned co-axially with the ordinary hand brake spindle and was below the handle of the latter. In this position, it had to be operated in the same way as a motor car steering wheel. Not exactly a rapid job to do in its entirety in emergency, when it is remembered that on this typical Burnley car it took 15 turns of the wheel to apply the slippers.

Why could the driver not stop his car with its electric brake? The inquiry, conducted by Major Hall, found that at some time prior to the accident, strands of cable to a motor had broken due to fatigue fracture from constant bending, and when the hill climb began, there were too few of them intact to carry the high current at this point. These few strands consequently burnt out through fusing and isolated the motor. The sequence of events was: one motor cuts out by fusing of cable: second motor, unable to lift car on its own, slips; driver shuts off power and re-applies series notch; no result as there is no circuit due to isolated motor; short-circuiting brake does not work because there is no live motor to pit against the good one; the good one on its own is not man enough to check the car when used as a rheostatic brake. QED.

Operator: **Yorkshire (West Riding) Electric Tramways Company**
Location: **Kirkgate, Wakefield**
Date: **29 January 1920**

No tramcar was involved in this accident, but it gives an opportunity to describe an important part of tramway equipment not often mentioned, and of which many ardent tramway students are not aware – the guard wires which the BoT had commanded should be placed above the overhead wires. Couched in the quasi-legal language of such dictates, the regulation required that "If and whenever telegraph, telephone, or other wires unprotected with a permanent insulating covering, cross above or are liable to fall upon or be blown onto, the overhead conductors of the tramway or trolley vehicle routes, efficient guard wires shall be erected and maintained at all such places." These wires are details of construction which not even the most meticulous of model makers has put into his sophisticated layout. As the years went by, more and more General Post Office (GPO) lines were put underground, so the need for guard wires decreased until it became a rarity to see them.

It was on the Yorkshire (West Riding) Electric Tramway Company's route that this accident happened in Wakefield. In the small hours of the morning in January 1920, a

---

[94] Mention should be made in this context of the "Burnley bogie". This was a bogie developed from a Simpson & Park radial truck, one of which was delivered to Burnley in 1907. The design was a failure, but Burnley Corporation (acting through Henry Mozley (1854-1942), its eminent manager), in partnership with the industry, worked to transform the truck, which was rebuilt with a tailframe and pony axle. Compared with other maximum-traction bogies, it had a far higher percentage of the adhesive weight on the driving axle, with the pivotal point immediately above the driving axle and providing a weight distribution of over 80% on that axle. The weight of the car was carried by side-bearing pads, borne by sprung pillars, and located on the underframe of the car by quadrant angleplates. In this form, the bogie was extremely successful.

raging gale and thunderstorm blew down a large number of GPO wires in the area. Among the wires down were two of a line of 12 which, following the Lancashire and Yorkshire Railway, crossed the tramway almost at right-angles by the railway bridge near Kirkgate station. The telephone wires fell on to the tram wires which were usually "dead" at such an early hour, but on this day they had been made "live" in preparation for running snow-ploughs.

A railway guard, walking unsuspectingly to work along the path by the bridge, got his feet entangled in the loose coils of the fallen telephone wire which, being in contact with the tram wire, was energised at 550 volts. Another railwayman came to his assistance but, as is so often the case with bathers who get into difficulties, when it is the would-be rescuer who gets drowned, it was the man who tried to extricate his mate who died. Grasping the wires, the second man received a shock so severe that he fell on his face dead[95]. A policeman who then tried to help had to desist owing to shocks, and the first man was ultimately freed by using a broomstick.

The Inspector, Major Hall, blamed the absence of guard wires and held the tram company responsible for the railwayman's death. Their guard-wires were in a poor state on the system generally, and this was only one of the places where they were non-existent. The tramway was still suffering from the shortage of materials and a big backlog of maintenance resulting from World War I (the peace treaty had been signed barely six months earlier). In addition to age and weather deterioration, they were being damaged and pulled down by the trolley heads of their own cars by consistent dewirements due to the atrocious condition of their trolley wheels.

Operator: **Pontypridd Urban District Council**
Location: **High Street/Market Street, Pontypridd**
Date: **22 March 1920**

Major Hall was soon on his way to his next inquiry, which took him to Wales and to Pontypridd, the town at the confluence of the Rhondda and Taff rivers, where the Urban District Council operated a small 3ft 6in-gauge system. An accident occurred at about 9.30am on 22 March 1920 which involved a runaway and subsequent derailment. The car concerned, no. 16, was a top-covered double decker on maximum-traction bogies. There were no fatalities, but five persons complained of injury, of whom two were passengers.

Driver Albert Brangwynne had taken the car out of the depot at 8.15am, after checking that it was in good order. He arrived without incident at a compulsory stop in Station Square, where he pulled up the car. He then applied sufficient power to start away, and applied four notches of magnetic brake when the gradient became about 1 in 28 This first application was normal and the car travelled at its usual speed to the north end of the square, where the gradient was about 1 in 20. At this point, the driver noticed a motor van fouling the track ahead and so put his brake on to the fifth notch. However, the speed increased and so Brangwynne applied another notch of brake, again without effect. By this time the car had probably reached the steepest gradient of 1 in 14. He shut off the brake and reapplied it to the fourth notch. Finding that this failed to check the car, he reversed the controller and applied two notches of power, but immediately afterwards the car collided with the van.

The impact bent the dash panel and knocked the controller on to the driver's legs. As a result, he no longer had electrical control and the car and the obstruction caused by the displaced controller prevented him from using the hand brake. In any event, it was subsequently proved that the hand brake had also been damaged by the collision and was not serviceable. The car, being out of control, continued on its way, subsequently colliding with a lorry and a milk van, on or just beyond the bridge over the river Rhondda. The car finally reached the curve leading into Market Street, by which time its speed was estimated at between 10 and 12mph. Shortly afterwards it derailed, tilting over against the Old Bank Chambers building (the front of which was about ten feet from the nearest rail). Apart from the initial collision damage, the car was not badly affected.

Major Hall found nothing amiss with the motors or magnets, and the controller was found to be satisfactory when later tested. He attributed the problem to greasy

Car 66 belonging to Pontypridd Council leaning drunkenly against a building at the corner of Market Street in that town after the car had skidded out of control. The date was 22 March 1920.

Courtesy: Pontypridd Public Library

rails (owing apparently to greasy water being thrown on the track from adjoining buildings) and to lack of sand. For some two or three weeks previously, the council had been compelled to fill the hoppers of the cars with crushed clinker because they could not obtain a wagon to deliver sand. The crushed clinker was greatly inferior to sand as a retardant and it was made worse by its propensity to cake on the rail. The Inspector had no hesitation in ascribing the driver's failure to make the initial stop to this combination of poor rail and inefficient sand substitute. The later events were directly caused by the damage to the equipment arising from the first collision. He therefore absolved the driver from all blame. The conductress appears to have been fully occupied in preventing passengers from leaving the car. The council was pressed to sort out its delivery problems over the sand.

---

[95] Fatalities from electric shock can take very little electrical energy. The effect of shock depends much on the path taken by the electricity through the body: the greatest risk is where its route is in proximity to the heart. A current of 30 milli-amps for a duration of 30 seconds can be sufficient to give a high probability of death. It is possible that the feeder circuit breaker would be set to trip around 600 amps, a value 20,000 times greater than that which could cause loss of life.

Operator: Lancaster Corporation
Location: Pointer Junction, Lancaster
Date: 27 September 1920

We now pay a solitary visit to Lancaster where, at about 7.20am on 27 September, car no. 2 of the Corporation's tramcar fleet, ran out of control down Bowerham Road hill, to derail at Pointer Junction, where it proceeded straight across to the opposite pavement and crashed into the wall of gardens in Springbank. A person was trapped between the car and the wall and died shortly afterwards from his injuries. Thirteen passengers received various injuries and suffered from shock. The driver remained at his post and was severely shaken.

Car no. 2 was a double-deck, open-balcony, single-truck car and its braking equipment consisted of a hand brake operating on all wheels and a Westinghouse magnetic track brake operating two pairs of track shoes between the wheels. As a result of the derailment and collision, the whole front platform of the car was demolished and the controller and brake lever were "carried away". The relevant part of Bowerham Road started on a falling gradient of 1 in 60, followed by successive falls of 1 in 17, 1 in 14, 1 in 12, 1 in 14, 1 in 20 and 1 in 38. At the Pointer, there was a double track junction with the Scotforth route, which came in from the left. The car derailed when leaving the diamond crossing at this junction. The maximum permitted speed along Bowerham Road to its junction with St Oswald Street, where there was a compulsory stop, was 6mph. Thereafter it was 4mph to the Pointer.

According to evidence given by the motorman (Hayes), he left the car shed at 6.55am after testing the hand brake and both sanders. Along Bowerham Road the rails were greasy and with a smattering of leaves. He reached the terminus at Williamson Park without incident and left it at 7.13am. At an intervening passing loop, he tested the magnetic brake, which acted satisfactorily. He then proceeded to the compulsory stop at St Oswald Street, and by applying five notches of the magnetic brake, the car reduced speed and he was able to hold the car on the hand brake. Hayes stated that he had been applying sand up to this point. In starting away from the stop, he released the hand brake and allowed the car to run forward on four notches of magnetic brake. He did not, however, feel the brake pick up. He accordingly proceeded to apply sand and found that the sanders were not working. He was aware of this because "the sand pedal was working easily, and it usually works somewhat stiffly when we are letting out sand". He applied the fifth notch of brake. This did not appear to have any effect, the car gaining speed all the time.

In passing Dale Street, he reversed and applied power notch by notch. This had no effect. He continued to work the sand pedal, but did not think that any sand was released. After finding the reversing was ineffectual, he cut off the current, replaced the controller handle to the forward position, and applied the magnetic brake. Again this was useless, and he went through the reversing process twice again, to no effect. By this time, the car had reached the junction at the bottom of the hill, when it derailed. He did not think that the wheels skidded at any stage.

With regard to the sanding arrangements, Hayes said that he had had no previous trouble with the pedals, but he had occasionally experienced failure due to tickets, which had fallen through the seats, blocking the exit aperture. The Inspector, Major Mount[96],

124

examined the sanding arrangements on the car. He found it difficult to consider how failure of both hoppers could occur simultaneously, but since the connecting rods at the driver's end had been "carried away", he could not offer a definitive opinion. The Inspector asked Hayes why he had not attempted to use the hand brake, to which the latter responded that he feared that this would lock the wheels. The Inspector also tested the magnetic track brake and found it in order from the conductor's end. He examined the controller at the driver's end, which had been separated from the car, but could find no evidence one way or the other. In the circumstances, the Inspector accepted Hayes' version of events, but suggested he made an error in not using his hand brake at once.

In the course of his inquiry, Major Mount ascertained that the Corporation had no rules regarding the use of brakes for the guidance of drivers and Hayes said that he did not "know of any particular speed restrictions". The Inspector said that the 4mph speed limit must be strictly observed and that a further compulsory stop (at Dale Street) be instituted. He also said that simple requirements should be drawn up to guide drivers and conductors in the case of runaways and run backs. He also recommended covers be fitted over the sand hoppers to prevent tickets falling into them. A further suggestion was that the rails should be swept every morning during autumn before the first car operated, to avoid accumulations of leaves: an onerous task, perhaps of little value on a windy day.

The Inspector stated that it had been suggested that the fitter responsible for maintaining the cars had not been keeping the complaint book properly signed up. He had therefore examined the book, particularly in respect of complaints concerning car no. 2 prior to the accident and commented that he could find no real indication that the necessary attention had not been paid to running repairs to the car. At the same time, he found the book was being kept in a dilatory manner. This seemed to be due to the fact that, with few staff, no one was responsible for the book. Nor was there anyone immediately in charge of the shed and running staff. The Inspector said the advisability should be considered of introducing a better means of coordination, so that one official was directly responsible to the manager, including control of the complaint book. He thought it not unlikely that the Corporation might find the present staff to be inadequate.

As a passing comment, the Inspector concluded his report by mentioning that those cars of the Corporation's fleet of 12, which were of open- or covered-top type, were gradually being converted to single deck and one-man operation. In actuality only six cars were so converted and they were all open toppers, so that car no. 2 was not among them.

Operator:　　**Halifax Corporation**
Location:　　**Bull Green, Halifax**
Date:　　　　**23 November 1920**

From Lancashire we cross to Yorkshire, for our final visit to Halifax. This concerns yet another runaway which ended in a collision. The accident occurred at about 4.50pm on 23 November 1920, at Bull Green, near the centre of the town. Car no. 12 was descending the road when the motorman lost control and the car collided with a motor wagon which was standing obliquely across the track. Prior to the accident, there were

---

[96] Sir Alan Henry Lawrence Mount (1881-1955), Inspecting Officer 1920-29, Chief Inspecting Officer of Railways 1929-49.

some 40 passengers on board the car, of whom a dozen or so jumped off before the collision. Of the remainder, two were injured, and a pedestrian, who was standing near the stationary motor wagon, was killed. The front end of the car was extensively damaged, the controller and brake spindles being torn away, and a number of windows on the car were broken.

No. 12 was a single-truck double-deck open-top car, equipped with hand, rheostatic and mechanical slipper brakes. It was also fitted with double-ended sanders, operated by two pedals, enabling both the motorman and the conductor to apply sand at will in front of and behind the wheels. The car was proceeding inwards on the Triangle route and the track at this point was double line. From Perkins Lane, the gradient fell consecutively at 1 in 23 for 310 yards, 1 in 21 for 430 yards and at 1 in 14.29 for 110 yards. The weather at the time was damp and foggy. Before leaving the outer terminus, the motorman, Baines, ensured that both sand hoppers were completely full.

On leaving the Perkins Lane stop, Baines applied two or three notches of power, after which he allowed the car to coast down the slope. Before the next stop, he applied the hand brake, but according to him the wheels picked up and there was no drop of speed. He then applied sand, three or four times, but there was no response. He then let the hand brake go and applied the slipper brake. As the car approached the 1 in 14 gradient, he tried the hand brake again, but the wheels appeared to be locked. Four notches of the electric brake were then applied, without effect, after which he tried to reverse. At that juncture, he called on the conductor to activate the rear sander. The conductor, McMahon, did so and also sought to apply the slipper brake, but he was hindered in this by a succession of passengers rapidly leaving the car. The trolley pole then dewired at a section insulator, so that the car was plunged into darkness. As Baines was trying to put more sand in a hopper, the collision occurred.

Major Hall, who took the inquiry, found the evidence left little room for doubt that the brake gear was correctly adjusted and in good working order: a finding strengthened by the fact that Baines had driven the car all day without the gear showing any signs of defect. He considered that the car was travelling too fast and that the initial braking had been tardily applied. There were no signs of flats on the wheels, as would almost certainly have been the case had the wheels been locked. According to the Inspector, Baines's own evidence, taken with that of fitters who had examined the car afterwards, demonstrated that his unskilful manipulation of the brakes and sand gear were the chief causes of the accident. Baines's then current period of service with the Corporation dated back only some six or seven weeks.

The Major had no criticism of the brake and sanding equipment. He found the dimensions of the slipper brake (three feet) particularly generous. However, he recommended that gradients which required the application of this brake should be indicated by a sign and that the procedure for applying this brake be clarified. He dismissed suggestions that "sprinklers" should be added for gradients such as this, to keep the track clean, complimenting the Corporation on having already installed them on more severe gradients. Although it was not entirely clear, it would appear that the deceased pedestrian had not been saved by the car's lifeguard since he had fallen, or been thrown, at a sideways angle, where no side guard had been fitted. The Inspector accordingly recommended that side guards at least on the nearside should be fitted "as are now required in the case of new or comprehensively reconstructed cars"[97].

126

Operator: Dudley, Stourbridge & District Electric Traction Company
Location: Castle Hill, Dudley
Date: 29 November 1920

Six days after the previous accident, a runaway occurred in Dudley, then forming an enclave of Worcestershire. In this incident, car no. 77 of Dudley, Stourbridge & District Tramways ran out of control down Castle Hill. At the bottom of the hill, the car collided with a lorry and then derailed, travelling a considerable distance until it mounted the pavement and came to rest on the edge of the top of the cutting of the Great Western Railway bridge approach. There were 14 passengers in the car at the time, four of whom received shock and minor injuries. The body of the car was slightly damaged and both sides of the lorry were smashed. At the time, the road surface was damp and the rails were very greasy.

The car was a single decker on a Brill four-wheel truck. It had a hand brake operating on each wheel, a rheostatic brake and a hand-wheel "Halifax-type" slipper brake operating hardwood blocks on each rail. Castle Hill descends from Dudley to the railway station and is practically straight. The track was double throughout and of 3ft 6in gauge. There was a compulsory stop at the top of the hill and from that point it was some 400 yards to where the collision took place. After leaving the track, the car followed a course between the tracks before turning left and on to the pavement, as already described. This movement occupied a further 70 yards. From the compulsory stop, the gradient falls at 1 in 16.5 for 85 yards, then 1 in 12 for a further 25 yards, thence 1 in 13 and 1 in 16.5 for a further 180 yards, and 1 in 19 and 1 in 30 for the remainder.

Motorman Frank Richards' evidence was to the effect that he had started work at 5.10am. Car no. 77 was a replacement car, which he tested before proceeding on his journey. In starting down the hill, he released the hand brake and allowed the car to run down the gradient. After travelling five to ten yards, he applied one notch of the electric brake. After travelling a further distance of 100 yards, his wheels picked up. He had not applied sand before, but he then did so and continued working the sand pedal. He said that it seemed to work normally, but without effect. The speed of the car reaching 20mph, he applied the track brake while retaining the electric brake in the one notch position. This appeared to have no effect, so he then applied three notches of the electric brake. He then reversed and applied two notches of power, which blew the circuit breaker. He then short-circuited the motors, but the car continued to gain speed. He estimated that he struck the lorry at 35mph, although the Inspector, Major Mount, thought it more likely to have been about 20mph.

An inspector who had passed Richards as a qualified driver and considered him to be a good motorman, suggested that the sand had "blogged" in both hoppers and so had not passed down the pipes. On the other hand, when inspected after the accident, he found the sand to be dry. The traffic superintendent had found no signs of flats on the wheels

---

[97] Given the sad series of accidents on Halifax tramways described in these pages, it is worthwhile recording that "Halifax-designed cars built after 1924 encountered none of the problems revealed by these accidents because their overall height, and therefore their centre of gravity, was significantly reduced, and the post-1928 'De Luxe' cars embodied so many quick-acting brakes that a driver would have needed a special determination in order to achieve a runaway!" This passage is quoted from a letter to the Editor from Councillor J Stanley King, during the course of his offering helpful observations on the texts of the Halifax accidents. See further *Halifax Corporation Tramways*, by E Thornton and J S King, published by the Light Rail Transit Association, Scarborough, 2005, at p 89.

at a subsequent inspection. When asked why he had not applied the slipper brake, Richards said that double deck cars running regularly on the main line were not fitted with track brakes, so he thought it unnecessary to use this brake on car no. 77. But the company's regulations made it quite clear that this brake should have been applied. Major Mount found no evidence of clogging in the hoppers.

In the circumstances, the Inspector thought the case was one of the driver losing control due, primarily, to failure to observe regulations. He took the hill too fast, apparently unaware of the speed limit of 5mph. However, he paid tribute to Richards' staying at his post and his war service, which included participating in, and being wounded at, the battle of Ypres.

Operator: **Bradford Corporation**
Location: **Five Lane Ends, Bradford**
Date: **3 February 1921**

Now and again, despite all precautions, trams became "unstuck" in fog. One such occasion occurred at about 10.55pm on 3 February 1921 at Five Lane Ends, on the Bradford system. The tramcar in question was proceeding fully-loaded along Idle Road in a thick fog and was derailed at the facing junction between the Thackley and Idle routes. Of some 60 passengers on the car, 50 complained of shock or injuries. The injuries, in the case of three or four of the passengers, were of a serious nature.

The car, no. 56, was of the double-deck, Bailey-roof[98] type, with a single truck of 6ft wheelbase. It was equipped with hand, rheostatic and mechanical slipper (wood block) brakes. As a result of the accident, the top deck of the car was practically demolished, but the car sustained no other extensive damage beyond broken glass, and was towed to the depot on its own wheels.

The tramway along Idle Road branched off Bolton Road in a northerly direction at Bolton tram depot. It was laid in double track and the Idle route branched off to the right at a double junction at Five Lane Ends, with facing points on the outward bound line. The points were of the double-tongue type. The total distance from Bolton depot to the junction was half a mile. The fairly gentle gradients rose and fell, and then rose and fell again before reaching the junction.

Motorman Benson, the driver of the car, came on duty at 2.35pm, and at 5.30pm he took over the car in question. He left Bolton depot with a full load and proceeded without incident for about 330 yards, where he appeared to have recognised his locality without difficulty. But after that he seemed to have lost his bearings in the fog. He stated that he was looking for the usual landmark, Norman Bank (a house some 180 yards from the junction) and was still looking for it when he reached the points. He said at that time he was running without power and "might have had his hand brake slightly applied".

The marks of the wheels on the setts indicated that the nearside leading wheel of the car derailed about ten feet from the point of the left-hand switch rail, the trailing wheel at that side being derailed about 15 feet further on. The car then travelled slightly skewed to the left, off, and roughly parallel to, the rails of the straight Thackley route for a distance of 76 feet from the original point of derailment. It was then deflected to the left

128

and, crossing the northbound straight line of rails, struck the kerb on the left of the road, 135 feet from the points, and turned over with the body approximately at right angles to the track. Benson realised the derailment probably as soon as it occurred and applied both hand and electric brakes.

Major Hall, who took the inquiry, reported that there could be no doubt that the original derailment was due to the fact that, as the points were lying at the turn-out, the speed was too great to allow the car to negotiate the curve, and the flanges in consequence mounted the rail. The subsequent overturning was due to the impact on the kerb of the leading wheel.

Benson was unable to give an estimate of his speed, but the Inspector calculated that it was probably not less than 15mph. Given that the car was approaching a facing junction of whose exact position he was uncertain, the Inspector considered that Benson could not be absolved of responsibility in the matter. Apart from this aspect, the Inspector asked the Corporation to consider installing a special light signal at an appropriate distance in advance of the junction to act as a warning to motormen.

Fog has been the enemy of transport since the dawn of history, and man has done his best to overcome it and keep moving. Bellbuoys, gunfire, sirens, radio and radar all take their places with ships and/or aircraft, but little can be done for surface transport. Railed transport has come off best by reason of its inherent dirigibility. Detonators and train-stop devices assist the railways, whilst growlers, hansom cabs with other horsed vehicles and later motor buses groped their way through city fogs led by flares until eventually they gave up, the trams kept going. I well remember the much-maligned LCC trams giving a public service running through fog long after the vaunted London General Omnibus Company's buses had packed up.

The rails guided the cars, but the drivers still needed to know where they were, especially with regard to hills, curves and tram junctions, but most men seemed to know almost to a few yards where they were. It goes without saying that speed was very much reduced, for although a driver might know well enough his whereabouts, he could not know how near he was to the car ahead until he could see or hear it. In later years, the LCC fitted their cars with white tail lights (it may have been done in other towns), switched on only during fog to minimise cars being run into from behind. Running at low speed for any length of time meant frequent switching power on and off and running with the resistances in circuit. In absorbing current not being taken by the motors, the resistances became hot and, on protracted journeys, became overheated, sometimes starting fires. This difficulty could be minimised by installing "fog resistances" – additional resistances brought into use only during fog.

Operator: **Tynemouth & District Electric Traction Company**
Location: **Borough Road, North Shields**
Date: **31 July 1921**

Almost two years after the accident involving car no. 13 of the Tynemouth & District

---

[98] This type of top cover took the form of a totally-enclosed centre section, with the end balconies left uncanopied. It was named after its designer, Albert Bailey (1857-1934), foreman at Bradford's Thornbury works. Top covers of similar design on other systems also took their names from their respective designers: Bellamy, Magrini and Kennington.

Company in Borough Road, North Shields (*qv*), a similar accident occurred at the same place involving sister car no. 12. The sole technical difference between the cars was that the latter had ash brake slipper shoes. This tramway had 17 cars of this type and there had been no trouble on this hill since it was opened in 1906, until these accidents occurred within 22 months of each other. On this occasion, the effect was more serious, with five persons killed and 72 injured. The driver of the car lost control during the descent of the hill in Borough Road, known as Borough Bank, with the result that it overturned at the sharp right-hand curve at the foot of the hill. The rails were wet after a shower.

Major Hall opined that the electric short-circuiting arrangements were "not now accepted….as an adequate brake" and thought the slippers could be doubled in length to be 36in. He nevertheless found that the driver, Thomas Hill, could not be "acquitted of insufficient care and unskilled manipulation of the brake". He therefore concluded that Hill must bear the main responsibility for the accident. In the wake of the previous accident in Borough Road, the company had issued new instructions for motormen and conductors. Those for conductors are particularly enlightening and are reproduced at Appendix E below. Perhaps also worthy of note is the invention of the onomatopoeic word "sissing" for the sound of skidding wheels. It is a word which might equally well be used to describe the sound of the trolley wheel of a tramcar, although the latter had a "thinner" higher pitch.

As to the conductor, James Park, he had been passed out as a conductor only three weeks before the accident. Although Park had recently received his certificate of proficiency from the Chief Inspector and he, Park, had acknowledged in writing that he had been thoroughly instructed in his duties and had carefully studied the applicable rules on which he had been questioned and examined, in his evidence to the inquiry it became apparent that he had a very imperfect acquaintance with the rules in cases of emergency and did not remember the relevant instruction which appears in Appendix E. No action to apply the brakes had been taken by him during the descent. The Inspector concluded that Park's training was insufficient and that he had taken his obligation to read the rules very lightly. Accordingly, he too had some responsibility for the accident.

Operator: Burton-upon-Trent Corporation
Location: Station Street, Burton-upon-Trent
Date: 3 November 1921

We now come to a trio of accidents in the Midlands. In the first of these, car no. 22, a single-truck, double-deck, top-covered car of Burton-upon-Trent Corporation, operating on the 3ft 6in gauge, was proceeding along Station Street, Burton, when, at the facing points leading from single to double track opposite the Stafford Knot hotel, the leading wheels took the left-hand track and the trailing wheels followed the right-hand track. This caused the rear of the car to swing round and a sideways motion ensued, with the result that all wheels left the rails. The car then skidded for a few feet on wood block paving and overturned. The car came to rest about 18 yards beyond the toe of the points, assuming a position at right angles to the road.

The track was practically level and in first class condition. It had been raining hard and the rails and paving were wet, but clean. There were ten passengers in the lower saloon and eight on the top deck. All suffered from shock or minor injuries, and the motorman was also shaken. The body of the car and its frame and truck were not seriously damaged, but the trailing axle was found to be broken. The car was one of four which had been built by the English Electric Company and had been put into service on 22 December 1919. Since then it had run some 38,000 miles.

According to the records, the trailing axle had fractured at an earlier stage after 17,000 miles and the current failure had taken place after a further 21,000 miles. The other axle had failed in November 1920 after 18,000 miles. The current fracture had occurred at the seat, flush with the inside edge of the running wheel on the gear side. This was the right-hand side in the direction of travel, namely the switch-rail side.

The Inspector, Major Mount, found the car to be in good order. The driver said that he had approached the points at a speed "near four or five miles an hour", which the Inspector concluded was a slight underestimate, although he did not attach any significance to this. About one car length beyond the points, the driver had felt the rear of the car turning round. An application of the hand brake appeared to have stopped the forward motion, but the rear of the car continued to swing across the road until it finally overturned.

The cause of the accident was clearly the failure of the axle. Major Mount came to the conclusion that the axle had failed at, or just before, the car had reached the points. He examined the records of other cars in the fleet and found that axle failures in these cases were equally unsatisfactory, fractures occurring between 9,000 and 26,000 miles. Of three of the new cars, eight axles had broken in the previous two years. New axles provided by the same manufacturer had shown no improved life, whereas axles of older cars in the fleet had lives on average of 76,000 miles. The Inspector concluded, after an analysis had been carried out, that the quality of the steel in the recent axles was satisfactory, but that it was probably the heat or mechanical treatment received during the manufacture which had given rise to the problem.

Primary causes of axle failures on the system were attributed to the sharp curves and the many railway level crossings. The Inspector also thought that the setting of the gear wheels was a significant factor, since the chief strain occurred on that side of the axle, particularly when a car took a curve. The running of these gears on their true pitch circles was therefore a matter of importance.

Operator: **Potteries Electric Traction Company**
Location: **Shelton New Road/Brickkiln Lane, Newcastle-under-Lyme**
Date: **6 September 1922**

Panicked passengers. This alliterative epithet sums up the reasons why car no. 43 *en route* from Newcastle-under-Lyme to Hanley on the 4ft gauge of the Potteries Electric Traction Company's system turned over on to its *left* side after it derailed from a *left* hand curve at the corner of Shelton New Road on 6 September 1922. Obviously the centrifugal force of a moving car would turn it over towards the outside of a curve, and this has been a consistent feature of the accidents so far recorded here. This car however turned almost completely round before it rolled over.

Vehicular traffic on the streets in the days of these tram accidents was nothing like its

21st September, 1922.

Sir,

I have the honour to report for the information
of the Minister of Transport, in accordance with the Minute
of the 12th September, the result of my Inquiry into the
circumstances of a tramcar accident, which occurred at about
8.30 a.m. on the 6th September, between Newcastle and
Hanley on the Potteries Electric Traction Company's system.

As the tramcar in question was leaving Victoria
Road an electrical fault became manifest, which resulted in
arcing at the controller and fusing under the right-hand
seat in about the centre of the car. The motorman in
endeavouring to open the canopy switch at his end of the car,
missed his footing and fell into the road. The conductor,
as soon as he observed that this had occurred, endeavoured
to apply the hand brake at the rear end of the car, and had
begun to do so when he was crowded away from the brake by a
rush of passengers; with the result that the car continued
to descend the gradient with gradually increasing speed,
and after running a distance of about a quarter of a mile,
left the rails at the left-hand curve at the foot of the
hill, and travelling at a tangent, eventually struck the kerb
on the right-hand side of the road and over-turned. On its
way down the hill it collided with and damaged a two-wheeled
coal cart and a Ford wagon. As a result of the over-turning
15 passengers were injured, one suffering from a fractured
thigh. The motorman and conductor were unhurt.

The damage to the car included a broken platform
bearer, considerable damage to the front end dash-plate and
controller, mainly caused by the collision with the coal cart
and Ford wagon, and a number of broken windows.

The car concerned, No:43, was of the single deck
single truck type, the overall dimensions and equipment
being as follows:-

Gauge	-	4ft.8½ins.
Length	-	26ft.
Overall width	-	6ft.6ins.
Seating Capacity		24
Wheel diameter	-	New 31ins.
		Present 29½ins.
Wheel Case	-	6 feet.

Electrical Equipment:

2 Walker 33N Motors.
2 B.T.H.K2 Controllers.

Brake Equipment:

Hand brakes operating blocks upon all 4 wheels.
"Short circuit" electric brake.

The/

The Secretary,
   Ministry of Transport,
      London.

The scene of the accident was Shelton New Road which runs approximately from west to east in the Newcastle to Hanley direction. Victoria Street loop is situated at the summit of a continuously falling gradient which varies between 1 in 17 and 1 in 28.2, the average inclination being 1 in 20. From the Victoria Street loop to a point about 242 yards east of the loop points the line is single. Thereafter in an easterly direction the line is double, and at the foot of the gradient this double line turns from Shelton New Road into Brickkiln Lane by a curve northward with a radius of 90 ft. and a superelevation of 3 ins. on the east-bound track. The car appears to have left the rail in about the centre of this curve, and struck the kerb of Shelton New Road at a point approximately 70 ft. south-east of the centre of the curve. After striking the kerb the end of the car slewed in an easterly direction and it finally turned over on the left-hand side of its original direction of travel, in a position approximately at right angles to the kerb and with the body lying roughly north and south.

The car concerned was in charge of motorman Edward Frost who has had rather under three years' service with the Company and has been a motorman for 6½ months. Frost took over this car in time to make the first trip in the morning at 5.54 a.m. from Newcastle to Hanley, and continued driving on the regular service to and from these places, leaving Newcastle at intervals of 45 minutes. His evidence is that the behaviour of the car was normal on these runs. The trip which terminated in the accident was that leaving Newcastle at 8.9 a.m., and Frost stated that there was nothing unusual in the running of the car as far as the Victoria Street loop. When starting away from this loop he found it necessary to apply power, which he did by moving the controller handle on to the first series notch, and, after leaving it there for a few seconds, switched it off again. After the car had run about 12 yards out of the loop Frost heard a loud report which seemed to him to have been caused by some collision with the rear of his car. This report he said he heard some two or three seconds after he had switched the power off. Immediately after hearing this report he saw flames issuing from the controller and at once jumped back intending to open the canopy switch. In doing so, however, he missed the switch, and, losing his balance, fell into the roadway. The car at the time appeared to him to be moving at about 3 miles an hour. Frost then picked himself up and shouted to the conductor to pull down the trolley and to apply the rear hand brake. He saw the conductor catch hold of the trolley rope and also put his hand on the brake which he appeared to apply about half a turn. He noticed also that the back platform was crowded with passengers, two of them being on the step. Frost then ran after the car and endeavoured to board it again but failed to do so, and eventually heard the crash of the over-turning car when he himself had reached the commencement of the double line, rather more than half-way down the hill.

Richard Hennesey, the conductor, who has had about 12 months' service with the Company, stated in his evidence that five or six passengers boarded the car at the Victoria Street loop, there being already 17 or 18 others inside, so that he left the loop with a full load. He signalled to the motorman to start and stood with his back to the car looking into the direction of Newcastle. After it had run 50 or 60 yards Hennesey heard a loud report from the inside of the car,

and /

and turning round, saw a flash of flame from the right-hand
seat. The passengers immediately rushed outside on the
platform and Hennesey reached for the trolley rope and pulled
the trolley off the overhead conductor. He advised the
passengers not to get off and at the same time saw his
motorman in the road running after the car: realising then
for the first time that there was no driver on the front
platform. He at once attempted to apply the hand brake but
was unable to give the handle more than half a turn when he
was jammed against the dash board by the rush of passengers
to such an extent that he was thereafter unable to exercise
any brake control over the car at all; with the result that
it proceeded down the incline with gradually increasing speed
to the curve at the bottom where it left the rails.

James Malkin, one of the passengers in the car,
was seated at the rear end of the right-hand seat. His
attention was first attracted by fire in front of the car where
the driver was. After seeing this fire he heard a loud
noise and saw smoke inside the car, which then began to run
away down hill. There was at once, he said, a stampede for
the back platform, and he was forced on to the step, where
he remained until the car overturned. The conductor, he
said, was so wedged in by the passengers on the platform that
he was quite unable to apply the brake.

2. It will be observed from the foregoing evidence
that the cause of the runaway and the eventual derailment
is clear, and was due primarily to the driver slipping off
the front platform as he was endeavouring to open the cut-out;
and secondly, to the rush of passengers on to the back
platform preventing the conductor from exercising any control
over the car. The gradient is not particularly severe, but
is of sufficient inclination and length to allow a considerable
speed to be reached, which would be quite enough to cause
derailment on a curve of this radius. The permanent way
was in good condition and the superelevation well maintained.
Derailment was due to excessive speed and not in any way to
the condition of the permanent way or of the car.

I do not attribute any responsibility either to the
driver or conductor for the accident. Motorman Frost did
not strike me as being at all the type of man to lose his
nerve and leave his post in an emergency, and I am satisfied
as to the correctness of his statement that he missed his
footing and fell off the platform. Hennesey, the conductor,
was evidently rendered helpless by the crowding of the
passengers, but he had already done what he could by cutting
off the current and suppressing the arc; action which
probably prevented an outbreak of fire. In the circumstances
the rush of passengers from the inside of the car is hardly
to be wondered at, but it is to be regretted that they did
not subsequently realise that the arcing had ceased, and by
returning to the car, enable the conductor to regain control.

3. The initial factor which led to the events narrated
above was the electrical failure manifested in the firing of
the controller and the explosion under the right-hand seat of
the car.

The latter trouble originated in the series control
resistance which is in these cars of the cylindrical type
mounted upon pedestal brackets at each end secured to the
flooring underneath the seat. This resistance has two
intermediate tappings and two end connections, being thus
divided into three sections and having four cables running

to/

to the controller. Connection between these cables and the resistance unit is made by lugs into which the cable ends are secured by set screws. An examination of the car after the accident shewed that both the cables to the intermediate tappings had been pulled out of the lugs, the ends of both cables being fused as far back as the insulation adjacent to the bare ends. A vertical iron strap forming part of the car body construction behind the resistance unit was partially burnt away, as was also one of the frame bolts immediately underneath it. There was, however, no sign of any fusing in the lugs on the resistance unit from which these cable ends had pulled out. It is therefore clear -

(a) That both these cables had parted from the lugs at some time when they were not carrying current.

(b) That subsequently the bare ends of these cables must have touched the vertical strap behind the resistance unit, with which they were in contact when electrical pressure was applied to them by the movement of the controller handle, so that a short circuit to earth was set up via the bolt under the strap.

An examination of the controller shewed a hole some 3 or 4 ins. in diameter burnt through the vertical casing opposite the top contact finger, the whole of which was burnt away. This was evidently due to an arc struck between the finger and the casing, the former being at the full trolley line potential and the latter earthed.

There can be little doubt that one of these two failures was the result of the other. It is probable that the primary cause was the contact between the loose resistance unit cables and the frame of the car. There is a somewhat remarkable discrepancy between the evidence of motorman Frost and of Malkin, the passenger, in regard to the sequence in which the electrical manifestations occurred. Frost's attention was first arrested by the report inside the car, which undoubtedly came from the arc underneath the seat between the cable ends and the frame, and it was only after he had heard this that he noticed the firing of the controller. Malkin, on the other hand, is quite sure that the report inside the car followed and did not precede the firing of the controller. The probability is, in fact, that they were nearly simultaneous and it is also probable that the short circuit underneath the seat had been established prior to the subsequent explosion. My own opinion of what actually occurred is as follows. At the time when the car was standing in the loop both the resistance leads were loose and either close to or actually touching the iron strap on the side of the car. It is impossible to say when these leads came adrift, but it is probable that the disconnection of one of them at least occurred quite a short time previously, since with both these leads disconnected, the main circuit would be broken as the handle travelled over the controller notches, and the result on the action of the motors can hardly have escaped the driver's attention. In these circumstances, therefore, when the motorman applied power he must, I think, though he is confident that he did not pass the first notch, have moved the handle sufficiently far for the segmental contact to touch the second finger, and so to complete the short circuit to earth via one of these two free leads. Almost immediately afterwards he swung the controller handle back to the neutral position, thus tending to break an abnormally heavy current. The result would be, particularly with a rapid movement of the handle, a sufficiently high induced pressure to break down the gap, which is somewhat small with this type of controller, between the trolley wire finger and the casing, and so perpetuate the short circuit current to earth in the form of an arc between these two points. This arc was subsequently suppressed by the removal

of/

135

of the trolley wheel from the overhead wire by conductor Hennesey.

4. The possibility of electrical failures of one kind or another must always be recognised in any system of electric traction. Assuming that the apparatus is well designed and the quality of manufacture good, immunity from electrical accident can best be secured by careful attention to the assembly of the various component parts (particularly the securing and protecting of cable runs and connections) and by systematic inspection to discover latent defects or weakness.

In the case of these cars I recommend for the Company's consideration the following action:

(1) The installation of at least one automatic cut-out. Neither of the canopy switches in these cars is of the automatic type, the only cut-out provided being a copper fuse of 12 S.W.G. No form of cut-out can be definitely relied upon to break the circuit when an arc has formed, since the current may not in many cases be sufficiently in excess of the maximum traction current. On the other hand, a mechanical form of cut-out is more likely to be effective than is a fuse, owing to the high over-load capacity of the latter for a short space of time.

(2) Shielding the cable runs behind the resistance unit from possibility of contact with the metal work of the car body or frame.

(3) Cleating the cable runs inside the car to prevent movement and abrasion as far as possible.

(4) The use of lock-nuts on the cable lug set-screws.

(5) The insertion of micanite or similar material between the metal casing of the controller and the asbestos lining, where the former is in close proximity to the live contact fingers of the controller.

I also recommend that the whole of the cable runs and connections should be periodically tested and examined after a Car has run a certain number of miles, based upon its normal use over a period not exceeding a month.

5. Some question has been raised in the local press as to the adequacy of the braking equipment of this car, and it has been suggested that had it been equipped with an air power brake the conductor would, in spite of the obstruction of passengers, have been able to stop the car. This is probably but by no means certainly, correct. In any case, however, though the use of air brakes on tramcars has been encouraged and their value recognised, this type of brake has never been definitely called for in the case of any tramway undertaking. As a matter of fact, the Potteries Electric Traction Company has gone further in this respect than the majority of tramway undertakings. Of 117 cars in service, 86 are fitted with air track brakes, 7 with magnetic track brakes and 4 with hand operated slipper brakes. Of the remaining 20, 10 are now being fitted with hand operated slippers and 10 are to be fitted with air track brakes. All these classes of equipment are acceptable for use under any conditions of gradient.

The car concerned in this case is one of the 10 to which hand operated slippers are being fitted, the presence of which on the car at the time of the accident under report would have had no effect upon the result.

I/

I do not, therefore, attribute the accident in any
way to inadequacy of braking equipment, the brakes fitted
being sufficient to control the car in the circumstances.
The fact that the brakes were not used was due to a very
unusual combination of circumstances which is unlikely to
recur.

> I have the honour to be
> Sir,
> Your obedient Servant,
>
> (Signed)   G. L. HALL
>   Major.

present-day volume, but nevertheless it seems very remarkable that so few runaway trams collided with other vehicles. This Potteries car was not so lucky, for more of the damage it sustained was caused by hitting a two-wheel coal cart and a Ford wagon than by hitting the road.

Major Hall's copious report, this time from Whitehall Gardens, is another which gives a sidelight on running schedules. The car left Newcastle at 45-minute intervals revealing that the journey time was about 20 minutes each way. The car's first trip had been 5.54am from Newcastle, and its fourth – which proved to be its last – at 8.9am, and so far nothing out of the ordinary had occurred.

A call was made at Victoria Road loop at the top of the hill, which had an average inclination of 1 in 20. The car picked up seven or eight people and then had its full complement of 24. The car was equipped with only hand and rheostatic brakes, but if it had possessed the most elaborate possible braking system it would not have saved the car after the driver had released the hand brake and applied a touch of power to give it a start. At once there was an "explosion" accompanied by flames underneath the centre of the right-side longitudinal seat and startled passengers jumped from their seats. A split-second later, as the driver, who had heard the report shut off power, his controller took fire. Reacting quickly, he turned and reached for the canopy switch to cut off the line power supply, but in his haste missed his footing and fell out into the road. Fortunately the man was not injured. He picked himself up and ran after the car shouting to the conductor to remove the trolley pole from the wire. Unable to outpace his car, he was forced to watch it running away and soon afterwards heard its crash. Fifteen people were injured.

The conductor gave the signal to start and stood with his back to the door of the saloon where, after the car had travelled only a few yards, he heard a loud report from within. Turning round, he saw a flash of flame from under the seat and passengers at once commenced to rush to his platform. He acted quickly and reaching for the trolley rope got the pole off the wire. Then trying to restrain his passengers, he espied his driver in the road and running behind the car. Then, for the first time, realising that nobody was on the front platform, he made a frantic effort to apply the hand brake, but was prevented from doing so by being jostled and jammed against the dashboard by the rush of passengers. So the tram ran down the hill completely unchecked.

A distant view of overturned car 43 of the Potteries Electric Traction Co after its runaway at Shelton New Road corner, Newcastle-under-Lyme, on 6 September 1922.

Courtesy: Newcastle-under-Lyme Public Library

By now the reader will have come across the terms "circuit breaker" and "canopy switch" several times, and perhaps an explanation of these "musts" of tramway equipment is overdue. It was essential that there should be some means, on each platform, of cutting off power in emergency, and when repairs were being made to the electrical equipment. For the latter, it was of course possible to remove the trolley from the wire, but inconvenient because it robbed the car of its lighting. These very necessary cut-out switches were mounted, more often than not, on the ceiling of the platform canopy (hence their name) to the left of the entrance to the lower saloon and were operated by a sideways movement of the handle. In this position, the switches were easily accessible to driver or conductor. It could be noted here that in the interests of safety, trams stabled in depots were always left with canopy switches in the "off" position whether or not the trolley was left on the wire. (In London conduit depots reliance had to be placed on the use of these switches as a car was alive the whole time it had a plough.)

The least technically-minded person nowadays knows that his household electric circuits are protected from overload by fuses – simple devices which cut off the current should it rise above a safe level. A similar safeguard was desirable on trams, and it took the form of a spring-loaded switch actuated by an electro-magnet which operated when the current reached a pre-determined value. The usual arrangement was to put a canopy switch at one end and a circuit breaker at the other end of a car[99]. They were very similar in appearance and their manual operation identical. If the automatic breaker "blew", it had to be reset by hand. Breakers often blew – "tripped" perhaps is a better word – if a driver notched up too quickly when starting a heavily-loaded tramcar. Then it was an even chance that it would be the one at the rear end, which was additionally inconvenient if the conductor was upstairs.

The exact date eludes me, but an accident involving a fatality did indeed result from this

138

very cause.   LCC car no. 478 – class E – was climbing the short sharp hill in Cedars Road, Clapham, at about 6.30 one evening in the winter of 1919/20, when the rear-end breaker tripped.   Of course the driver should have kept command of the situation, but he didn't, nor did the conductor have time to get downstairs in time to reset the breaker.   I missed seeing it happen by only five minutes.   The car which had derailed, but not turned over, looked eerie standing without lights and with some windows broken, on the granite setts in the mellow gaslight of those days.

Before returning to the panic of the Potteries passengers, a few words about resistances – often called rheostats and more properly referred to as resistors – will not be amiss.   These devices were usually iron grids positioned beneath the platforms[100] where they were exposed to the slip-stream of the moving car and were thus able to dissipate the heat generated by their action.   On starting, a car had all the resistances connected in the circuit with the motors in series and, as speed rose, the resistances were progressively cut out by the controller contacts changing the tappings as the driver turned the handle until all resistance was removed.   After quickly passing over what were known as transition notches (the function of which was to change the motors from series to parallel with one another without a jerk), resistances were reinserted in the circuit and cut out again step by step as speed increased until all were out at top-notch, *i.e.* full speed in parallel.

For braking electrically, the motors served as generators and again resistances were inserted in the circuit to absorb and dissipate the current not being used by the brakes, *e.g.* the track magnets.

On some trams, the resistances were placed on the platforms or even under the seats where they possessed some value in heating the saloon in cold weather.   This is where they were on the Potteries car, fixed to the floor.   There were four leads to the tappings on the rheostat, and two of them had come adrift and shaken by vibration into contact with a steel bracing strip in the bodywork (a few words about this later).

When the driver placed the controller on to a power notch in order to give the car a start, his action made all the rheostats "live", and the loose leads, touching the metal strip, made a direct connection – a short circuit – to the rails.   The arcing of this lead against the iron strip caused the alarming bang or flash under the seat, and as the driver moved the controller handle to "off", the abnormally high current created an arc which the controller could not suppress, and the arc short-circuited to "earth" via the casing of the controller, where it burnt a 3in hole.   As the driver's efforts to throw the canopy switch had failed, the arcing and burning went on until the conductor dewired the trolley.

Assuming that what I have written in a previous paragraph is understandable, you will be asking: "What about the automatic circuit breaker?"   The answer is simple – the car hadn't got one.   It had only manual canopy switches: a truly astonishing state of affairs as automatics had been standard tramcar equipment for well over 30 years[101].   It is

---

[99] In later years, Dick, Kerr & Co and English Electric routinely supplied cars equipped with two circuit breakers, one for each end feeding the local controller only.

[100] Under-platform resistors were a feature of London tramways.   Elsewhere, they were usually accommodated in a cabinet on one of the platforms (under the stairs in the case of double-deck cars); occasionally they were located under seats, as described later in the text.

[101] It was usual for tramcars without circuit breakers to be fitted with some form of traction fuse.   Drivers were issued with lengths of fuse wire for use in the event of the fuse needing to be rewired.

noteworthy that the power-station breakers did not trip – they must have been set for a higher current even than the "dead short" produced by this car[102].

Until comparatively recently, and with the notable exception of the Kingsway Subway in London (for the reason already explained in the LCC accident of 16 August 1919), tramcar bodies were made of seasoned hardwoods, mainly ash and oak with some beach and teak. Morticed, tenoned and screwed, their structure was preponderantly rectangular and lacking the cross bar principle of triangulated bracing of which the most familiar is seen in the five-barred farm gate. Tram body angles were strengthened by steel "knees", as were prevalent in railway coaches of the period. The latter, it will be remembered, had truss bars beneath the solebars (the main frame longitudinals) adjustable by turnbuckles to keep the body straight and to prevent it from sagging or bowing under the weight of passengers. It is not generally realised that tramcars had similar truss-bars, but instead of hanging downwards they went upwards and were concealed behind the seats. It was also not unusual to incorporate unseen tie-rods from end to end of the woodwork of the lower saloon just below the main window sills and between the large and small windows. As bodies became weakened by age and stresses, skilfully-concealed cross-braces and gusset plates were added.

When trams were built, things were made to last, and "built-in" obsolescence was unheard of (anything built on such lines would have been regarded as shoddy and inferior and unworkmanlike), and it was the general rule to keep rolling stock in good repair in contradistinction to the methods, so wasteful in material and effort, and so productive of unsightly scrap-heaps and of litter, of internal combustion-engine vehicles which are discarded after a very short life.

Operator: **South Staffordshire Tramways (Lessee) Company**
Location: **Holyhead Road, Birmingham**
Date: **10 December 1922**

The last of the trio of Midlands' accidents occurred on 10 December 1922 within the city of Birmingham but involving the derailment and overturning of a tramcar belonging to the South Staffordshire Tramways Company, operating over the 3ft 6in gauge metals of Birmingham Corporation. The tramcar in question, no. 47, was a four-wheel, top-covered, double decker equipped with a hand brake, a run-back brake and a magnetic track brake which could also be applied mechanically.

The car had started off from Handsworth depot, proceeding along Holyhead Road, Handsworth, towards the city. It had stopped at the New Inns public house to pick up passengers and then, at 9.42am, about 120 yards later, all four wheels became derailed and the car, after proceeding diagonally across the adjoining (outward) track, overturned on its nearside in a position about 70 yards beyond the point of derailment. All five passengers on board the car were injured, mostly from broken glass. The motorman was more seriously injured and unable to attend the inquiry. The conductor suffered from shock and a slight cut. The damage to the car was not serious and consisted for the most part of broken windows.

The tramway in the locality consisted of a double line of track, on a curve of one-mile radius and with a continuously falling gradient varying from 1 in 36 to 1 in 49. The

An earlier view of a South Staffordshire Co car (no. 46) which came to grief further along the same road as that involved in the accident to no. 47 described in the text: Soho Road railway station, Birmingham, on 26 June 1916.

Courtesy: National Tramway Museum

motorman stated that on leaving the New Inns stop, he had applied series notches, shortly afterwards cutting off power to allow the car to proceed by gravity, with the hand brake slightly applied. The car then suddenly left the track at an angle to the right, crossing the other track and then overturning. He had applied the electric brake and attempted to apply sand, but was thrown off balance by the swerve of the car.

An examination of the track revealed that the derailment originated at a point where the check rail was missing from the left-hand rail for a length of about four feet. Both that section of rail and the corresponding rail on the right-hand side showed a considerable amount of wear. This latter rail had its check intact, but a considerable step had been worn in the rail head, varying in width from $^3/_{16}$in at the ends to $^{11}/_{16}$in in the centre, opposite where the left-hand check rail was missing. The depth of this step was about $^3/_8$in, so that the total vertical wear of the rail head immediately adjacent to the groove was about $^3/_{16}$in. The condition of the track suggested that it was *prima facie* the cause of the derailment.

The Inspector, Major Hall, considered whether there were other causes of the derailment. One possibility was excessive speed. The Inspector observed that the motorman appeared to be a steady and reliable man, who calculated that his speed was considerably less than the 14mph permitted speed. His assessment was supported by passengers and a pedestrian. So that factor was ruled out. A second possibility was a defect in the car. Its condition appeared to be satisfactory, having only two days before left Tividale works after undergoing repairs. The car was then driven to Handsworth depot (about eight

---

[102] There would only have been a "dead short" if it was the trolley lead that came into contact with the frame. In the case of a resistance lead, there might well have been some resistance still in circuit which would have limited the current to a value less than that needed to trip the feeder circuit breaker.

miles from the works) without giving any trouble. The fitter at the depot noted that the car wheels were unworn.

The Inspector concluded that the cause of the accident was the missing length of check rail combined with pronounced wear of the other rail. The fact that the car's flanges were unworn would also have assisted in the derailment, in that immediately prior to the derailment, the flanges would have been resting on the step of the right-hand rail, without any contact between tread and rail head. He also took the opportunity of mentioning that the whole tramway between the Colmore Row terminus in the city and the West Bromwich boundary was under repair and at the date of the accident, the reconstruction work had progressed to within a short distance of the scene of the accident. No other section of track awaiting repair exhibited the peculiar nature of wear found at this point, nor was it clear how long the check rail had been missing, although some small pieces of it might have been broken off by the car itself. Major Hall stressed the importance of the check even with so slight a curve as was to be found in this instance.

Operator: **Leeds Corporation**
Location: **Elland Road (Churwell Hill), Morley**
Date: **12 May 1923**

The city of Leeds, with its fair-sized tramway, sustained only two accidents to be examined in the course of this review and these events occurred some 30 years apart. But unfortunately they were both very serious. This is an account of the first. Referring to the locale of this case, Lt-Colonel Mount's report records that nearly half-a-million descents had been made "successfully" down Churwell Hill. However, as seems inevitable in the course of time – like the journey of the biblical earthenware to the well – when a problem did occur it was severe. Seven people died and 44 were injured from a complement of about 60 on the tram concerned. There were, at the time, 360 cars on this busy municipal tramway.

Car no. 191 had a body length of 16ft 4in, a maximum width of 7ft 0½in and a height of 15ft 8in. Like so many hundreds of others in the country, it had been very much reconstructed. Built in 1900, it had been subsequently equipped with new platforms, staircases, an added top-cover and improved motors of 40hp each.

In addition, like 82 others in the fleet, it had a very sophisticated system of brakes which gives the opportunity to introduce the Maley track brake, named after its designer, Alfred Maley. The brake had two applications. One took the form of a mechanical track brake, which consisted of four corrugated cast-iron track shoes riding normally ¼in above rail level and applied by hand by a wheel on the platform hand-brake pillar. Each shoe began life 8½in long, but increased to 12½in, as the bottoms (paradoxically at the top) of the corrugations came nearer the rails in the course of wear. There were two such shoes between each pair of wheels. Secondly, there was a magnetic track brake, with its own track shoes, one magnetic brake shoe being located in the middle of the distance from one mechanical shoe to the other; the magnets being energised in the usual way through the controllers by current generated by the motors when braking. Several times we have come across the arrangement in which the magnet shoes were linked to the wheel brake blocks, but these Leeds cars had a quite different linkage. Their magnets, when applied, were linked to the mechanical brake shoes, so as either to

142

add to their downward pressure, if they had already been applied by hand, or to apply them without prior application of the mechanical brake. Then there was the usual hand brake, applied by means of a handle with a ratchet head actuating a 13in cast-iron block on each wheel. Lastly, there were the two electric brakes – applying reverse power – and the "last resort" of putting the controller to "full parallel" at "reverse" with the car running forwards.

Since as far back as 1906 (Highgate Archway) the BoT reports had been hammering away on the desirability of using all brakes for routine working, to keep them in order and to make the drivers thoroughly conversant with and confident in their use, whereas Leeds were in 1923 still regarding the magnets as emergency brakes. When the emergency arose on this Leeds car, the brake failed in its purpose: it had a serious defect which regular use would have revealed. This defect was reminiscent of the equally-bad accident in Bournemouth on 1 May 1908 (*qv*) with which it had another similarity – the dilution of responsibility for repairs resulting from frequent transfers from depot to depot, though not so promiscuously as in the seaside town.

There were nine tram depots in Leeds, and Maley-equipped cars operated from five of them, cars being moved about as necessary for economical working. In the six weeks before the accident, car no. 191 had, omitting a few days at Kirkstall works, transferred seven times between Swinegate and Chapeltown, with one night at Morley. On the fatal day, the driver of car no. 191, George Knight, reported for duty at 5.20am at Chapeltown depot, obtained his time board from the office, went to the car and made static tests of the controllers, brakes and other equipment before leaving the shed at 5.40am. Before following driver Knight's progress, let us spare a few lines in explanation of the time board just mentioned.

Whilst they are not necessarily published, there are always working schedules or timetables in being for the organised operation of any regular transport service. Even on the smallest undertaking, there must obviously be some basis for providing vehicles and for arranging the duties of the staff. On a system such as that at Leeds, the schedules will have been of considerable complication to cater for varying demands during the course of a day and from route to route, fitting in meal breaks for tram crews, also for rostering car repairs and cleaning. Quite a "jigsaw" in fact. On some tramways – it is still a practice on the Continent – the movements of men and cars are set out on display boards in the depots, and men have to study these schedules when they clock on. Other tramways – Leeds and London were good examples – the information was handed to the driver and handed on to relief drivers so that full details of their working was available to all men who handled the car[103]. A scheme of this sort generally needed four sets of boards – Mondays to Fridays, Saturdays, Sundays, and Specials *e.g.* Bank Holidays, Sports Fixtures, etc.

---

[103] I knew the LCC time boards best. They were about 8in square, with a printed form filled in in ink by hand, stuck on one side and varnished over. The driver took the board with him when he changed ends, but very rarely placed it in the slot provided on the underside of one of the stair treads. Instead, it was usually laid face upwards on one of the steps where he could glance at it or, more frequently, it was tucked behind the bars of the grille protecting the bulkhead window. Tantalising as it was to me, it was generally turned with the blank side towards the passengers, but now and then it was placed so that my avid eyes got a glimpse of its contents. In London, the route number (trammen pronounced it 'rowt' – as in shout) was carried on both sides of each car, and was essential to enable inspectors and regulators to identify cars when there could be as many as 85 (each with a different timetable) on one service in peak hours.

The scattered remains of car 191 of Leeds Corporation after its runaway down Churwell Hill, Morley, on 12 May 1923. *Courtesy: I. M. Dougill*

Leaving the depot at 5.40am, the car was driven safely to Bruntcliffe, Morley, negotiating ascents and descents, and after three minutes' turn-round time set out at 6.45am *en route* to Leeds. It was a busy journey, the car having to call at all stopping places, and when full, with some passenger standees, came down Scatchard Hill (1 in 10) without trouble on the Maley brake. The line then descended the Churwell Hill section, first at a gradient of 1 in 18, which inclined to 1 in 14 at the Victoria Street loop. Here the car was brought to a stand to let an ascending car pass. When it had gone by, driver Knight eased the brake of no. 191 and let the car start by gravity. After a few yards there was a sudden jump, such as Knight had never experienced before. He tried to stop the car at once and managed to squeeze a fraction of a turn on the Maley brake, which was already hard on, and then tried to apply the hand brake, but he was the victim of something we have not met before. The handle would not bite and commenced to slip "like something grinding and giving way". The magnetic brake was next "applied", but failed to check the rapidly-growing speed as the gradient inclined to 1 in 13 and then 1 in 11. Knight, at this stage, neglected to try the electric emergency brake. Instead, he then deserted his platform and went to the rear, where he found that the brakes had already been applied by a conductor who had been travelling as a passenger but, as was often their wont, was helping the official conductor by looking after the platform and giving bell signals while the latter was upstairs collecting fares. Both Knight and this man jumped off before the car crashed.

The regular conductor, named Herbert Littlewood, rose to the occasion and heroically went to the front platform of the runaway, joined by a passenger (a regular soldier) called

144

Herbert Smith, where between them they tried in vain to bring the car under control. Nothing could stop the tram and, travelling at a speed estimated at over 40mph, it left the rails on an easy right-hand curve, swerved across the left-side footpath and plunged into a boundary wall from which it rebounded, swung completely round and turned over on to its right flank.

What was the cause of all this human and material damage? The rear axle was found to be broken, but was this cause or effect? It could have been the bad jolt the driver felt at the top of the hill, or it could have been done by the wrench of derailment at speed One should be forgiven for thinking that with no fewer than five members of the artisan staff making their respective examinations with the specific object of ensuring the fitness of the equipment, a car would be in perfect working order – but this one wasn't. The leads to one of the magnet shoes were disconnected (shades of the Bournemouth disaster again) so at best the car could have had only 50% braking capability and this unbalanced on one side. To cap all this, the teeth in the ratchet in the top of the hand brake pillar had worn to such an extent that they would not mesh. The crank handle just swung round and round, as the helpful passenger, who rushed forward to use, was able to testify. The simplest way of describing this sort of handle is to liken it to the winder on one's watch, which winds one way and free-wheels the other. The dog-tooth pawl engaging in teeth in the cog on the floor, and controlled by the driver's foot, prevented the pillar from unwinding, as necessary. The ratchet-type of handle enabled the driver to use his greatest strength, always in a pulling motion – the other, steering-wheel handle, was of smaller diameter, requiring a two-handed motion during which the controller could not be manipulated.

Colonel Mount's report is a long one: it occupies 13 foolscap-size closely-printed pages, stuffed with tramway interest and perhaps it is not out of place to quote some excerpts from it.

First as to the state of the car at the scene of the crash. The Inspector did not see the car *in situ* and he reports the verbal accounts given by the Rolling Stock Engineer and the Works Superintendent:

> *The upper saloon, roof, sides, end frames and seats were lying on the ground entirely separated from the lower portion, of which some side and corner pillars were broken and all the glass shattered. The leading end (which was facing Morley), was badly damaged. The dash and hand rails were torn off and the brake pillar bent through an angle of about 45 degrees, The controller was hanging by its leads upside down. The reversing handle was in the forward position and the power handle in the off position. Neither was damaged nor marked in any way. The rheostat was broken in two parts, the platform woodwork splintered, and the buffer beam grazed and bent. The brake chains and rods were intact and attached to the brake spindles. The track brake chain was partially wound on the cone of the spindle and held in this position owing to the fact that the brake pillar had been bent, thus preventing the rotation of the spindle. The wheel brake chain was slack.*

The Colonel then betrays a slight irritation as to what had been done in his absence:

> *Owing to the car being on its side, the whole of the mechanism was exposed, and*

appeared to be in good order. One mechanical track brake shoe had been torn off and was lying in the roadway. Unfortunately, however, a minute examination was not made then, and to add to the subsequent difficulties of investigation, the front controller leads were cut where they passed through the platform. This was done in order to release the controller, though the necessity for this is not apparent.

After raising and re-railing the car, the operation of towing it to Swinegate depot, nearly three miles, was commenced. It was then discovered that the rear axle was broken at a point about ¾in inside the boss of the gear wheel, viz., near the off side running wheel. . . . The wheel at the short end became fixed at an angle and continued to skid for most of the remainder of the journey to the depot.

As to the routine checks made to the car before it left Chapeltown depot on the morning of the incident:

[Foreman Oliver, wheel brakesman Hall, mechanical track brakesman Smith, electrical leads and motor mechanism examiner Nichols and controller examiner Furniss] *all stated that they remembered the car and their various inspections; possibly this was so, having regard to the fact that the car had not been in this depot for some time. On the other hand, the evidence generally was indefinite, and as no defect was reported, I gather that nothing more than the "regulation" of the brakes was carried out or thought to be required, viz., Hall took up the wheel brake half a turn, his inspection lasting 15 minutes; and Smith adjusted three of the four mechanical brake shoes. It transpired, however, in the course of the evidence, that Smith, who had no electrical knowledge, and in fact had to be prompted as to the number of cables leading to each track magnet, while being responsible for the examination and replacement of the magnet shoes, also carried out the examination under the car of the cables leading to the magnets. Nichols apparently left this matter in Smith's hands – an old standing practice – as his (Nichols') duties did not take him under the car.*

As to the failure of the magnet shoe:

In regard to the magnetic track brake, I carried out trials with other cars to ascertain the effect of the failure of one magnet, and I discussed the subject at much length with Mr Maley, the inventor and manufacturer of this brake. By calculation, the reduction in effect is only some 10 per cent, of the total braking efficiency, and in practice it would not be noticeable. . . . At higher speeds than 20 miles an hour, the loss of the second magnet might make some difference, in that the car would not be brought under control again so quickly. There is, however, not the slightest doubt that at such speeds the emergency effect of a single magnet could not be mistaken, though it might not have the effect of bringing the car to a dead stand on a heavy gradient.

As to the hand brake ratchet:

The defective ratchet was an entirely unforeseen and unexpected feature. As the handle had not been removed during the straightening of the pillar, it was only discovered by Messrs Maley and Allan [the Works Superintendent] *during their* *endeavours to ascertain whether the gears below the platform were not meshing properly. . . . I found on the 31st May that great force was not required to make the teeth ride. They were of insufficient depth (5/32nd of an inch instead of 5/16th of an inch), and evidently the case-hardening can only have been skin deep to have permitted the large amount of wear that had taken place. All the working surfaces were of the same shape, worn to angles of about 45 degrees instead of being vertical. It is remarkable that the ratchet had stood up to its work for so long.*

As to the driver:

Knight is a man of 42 years of age. . . . He joined the Corporation's service as a conductor on the 26th July 1914. . . . In March 1917, he joined the R.F.A. and proceeded to France in the following June. He was unfortunately gassed on the 19th March 1918, and as a result 17 teeth were extracted shortly afterwards. . . . After rejoining his unit in June 1918, he was wounded on the 30th September in the left forearm, causing a compound fracture of the ulna. He was demobilised on the 11th February 1919, and a week later was re-engaged as a conductor without medical examination. Twenty months afterwards, on the 25th October 1920, he was medically examined and passed fit to act as motorman. . . . He did not take up the work until the 28th June 1922. . . . during the interval, I understand that the wound gave trouble and 16 pieces of bone were removed. . . At times he suffered from headache and eye trouble as a result of the gas. . . . He stated that he thought he could not make the application [of the mechanical track brake] *to the extent that other motormen did.*

Finally, a glimpse of the frenzied state of affairs on the tram as it careered to its fate:

Littlewood, a man of 26 years of age, had been working as a conductor for only one week (once previously on this particular route) after a course of instruction lasting ten days. The work was therefore new to him, and he was evidently taking longer than usual to collect fares on the top deck. For this reason, contrary to regulations, he was not on the rear platform . . . I gather that shortly after leaving Victoria Street, one of the passengers on the top of the car got up and said "It's away". Littlewood endeavoured to persuade him to sit down and for a few moments did not realise that the speed was excessive or that anything was wrong. However, the man, followed by others, quickly moved towards the stairs. Someone climbed over the side and slid down the handrail in rear. Littlewood also got down as quickly as he could and arrived on the crowded back platform just before the car passed under the bridge. Passengers were jumping or being pushed off the car from the rear platform. He hurried through the lower saloon, which then contained only a few people, and found another passenger (Smith) just in front of him opening the front door. He followed Smith on to the front platform. The car was then travelling on the straight at high speed with wheels rotating. Smith apparently grasped the top of the controller case with his left hand to steady himself and endeavoured to operate the wheel brake. Littlewood devoted all his strength to the track brake. . . He remembered no noise like ratchet failure when Smith was operating the wheel brake handle. . . . Both Smith and Littlewood evidently remained on the front platform till the collision took place, and I think they deserve much credit. Clearly they did their best to stop the car, and even if

Littlewood had been a more experienced man and had used the electric brake, he would probably have been too late.

Earlier on in his report, Colonel Mount refers to the "gallantry" of the two men who, while they had remarkable escapes, were both seriously injured and shaken.

So the accident was brought about by a succession of failures: failure by the depot staff adequately to check the car before it left on service; failure of one magnet; failure of the hand brake ratchet; failure of the driver to use other forms of braking at his disposal; failure of management adequately to train and monitor staff. Car no. 191 was scrapped after the accident.

On that sad note, we leave for Scotland, after making a passing reference to an accident in Dover four months later. Crabble Hill, in Dover, was again the scenario but luckily the casualty list this time was short. On this occasion, it was car no. 23 on 21 September which ran away, primarily because of a hand brake defect: the car got out of control as a result of the driver bungling the electric brake, so that the tram collided with no. 24 at the foot of the hill.[104]

Operator: **Edinburgh Corporation**
Location: **North Bridge Street, Edinburgh**
Date: **26 February 1925**

Edinburgh is distinguished not only by its historical and tourist features, its castle and all that, but by the extensive and efficient cable tramways which it retained until after World War I. It was the last city in Britain to electrify its tramways (in 1922) and was able therefore to start with the best-tried equipment, but this did not give freedom from accidents caused by men not doing their work competently. It was at 10.22am on 25 February 1925 that car no. 123, a modern vehicle on a Peckham "pendulum" truck, with the long wheelbase of 8ft 6in, with wheels only 25½in in diameter and equipped with 40hp motors and with magnetic track brakes, got out of control. For the first time, we come across a car on which the magnetic brake could be applied by the controller, equally effective in either direction irrespective of the position of the reversing key. There were very few injuries to the passengers or the staff when the car crashed at a fair speed into two stationary tramcars opposite the General Post Office. (An interjection here to mention that at this point a few feet of the cable track has been preserved *in situ*.) All three trams were extensively damaged and, as was the rule in such triple events, the one in the middle came off worst.

I can only summon up the word "astonishing" when, on studying the report, which Major Hall submitted, that at so late a date in tramway history this modern line, despite the experience of other cities that a powerful reliable brake was needed not only for safety, but to attain fast-running schedules as an antidote to unbridled bus competition, Edinburgh still kept the magnetic brake for emergencies. As so often happened over the many years, the emergency brake was no good when it was most needed. The hill was not steep – as tram hills went – it was 1 in 27 – but there were 340 yards of it, giving a tram a splendid opportunity to gather speed if not checked. The driver had had the car for three-and-a-half hours before trouble supervened. In the meantime, he had tried the magnetic brake twice and on both occasions its behaviour was such that nothing happened until the last notch was reached on the controller, at which point the braking was, to quote the driver "the same as you would get in the ordinary way from the first notch".   Nevertheless, such was the nonchalance with which the emergency brake was treated, that the driver took no action to have the car taken out of service as the rules commanded.   Having stopped at High Street, the car started down the hill and was nearing the *Scotsman* office when the driver made an attempt to apply the hand brake which apparently jammed. Without wasting too much time with this brake, he turned on the magnets which, as might be expected, had almost no effect.   Reverting to his hand brake, the driver succeeded with a "vicious shake" (in getting it to "spring off and revolve"), but it was too late.

The freak operation of the magnets had been brought about by the complete severing of all their leads by chafing against the metal truck frame and burning through by short-circuiting to earth.   This had been developing over several days during which the depot men had failed to see it at their inspections, and the weak braking, which appeared on the last notch, was a vestige of the rheostatic effect.

Operator:	**London County Council**
Location:	**Dog Kennel Hill, East Dulwich, London**
Date:	**31 July 1925**

Now from the Scottish capital to the English.   The county of London is relatively flat, lying as it does in the Thames basin, and although there were a few hills on the tramways, they were not in any way comparable with places bordering the Pennines.   There were however two hills of special significance, and the one to the north – Highgate – has figured earlier in this account.   To the south, after running almost level to Camberwell, there was a gradual rise up Denmark Hill and, on attaining the summit at Champion Hill, there was a very sudden drop down into Dulwich.   This was Dog Kennel Hill, well-known to tramway students because of its unique quadruple tramtracks[105].   Originally laid with two tracks, it was soon found that the regulation which specified one car only being on the hill at a time, prevented the running of a service adequate for the demand. In order to overcome this bottleneck, each line was duplicated, enabling one car to start down the hill while another was still descending on the alternative track.   Likewise with going up.   In this way, the capacity of the hill was doubled without sacrificing safety. The cars plying on this hill were equipped with magnetic brakes (a standard on all LCC cars), the track shoes of which were applied by hand also (slipper brakes).   After years during which nothing serious occurred, calamity came on 31st July 1925.   One lives and learns – it was not until reading the report, submitted by Major Hall, that I added the word "lunters" to my extensive tramway vocabulary, but I have yet to find its meaning in a dictionary[106].

---

[104] This accident does not appear to have been the subject of a Railway Inspectorate report, but full details of it appear in *Dover Corporation Tramways, 1897-1936,* by J V Horn, published by the Light Railway Transport League, London, 1955, at p 56.

[105] Through-running quadruple, even quintuple, tracks existed elsewhere (*e.g.* Birmingham (The Hawthorns), Liverpool (Old Haymarket) and Oldham (Hollinwood), but the unique feature of the Dog Kennel Hill layout was that it was devised so that trams (both when proceeding uphill and downhill) could take alternate tracks and so greatly reduce the possibility of collision in the event of a runaway, as explained in more detail in the text.

[106] The complete (20-volume) edition of the *Oxford English Dictionary* contains no entry for "lunters".

The car which met trouble could be likened to George Washington's hatchet or to the repeatedly renewed stairs up which Anne Hathaway climbed. From the report, "constructed in 1904, [the car] has been rebuilt and reconstructed in details so many times that little of the original car remains". Like several others we have met in these pages, it was mechanically practically new, having run only 44 days since its last complete overhaul – a very thorough job carried out at Charlton central repair depot. Consequently, it could be expected to be in tip-top condition, as it was indeed found to be afterwards, allowing for damage sustained in the collision. The miles it had run until this unfortunate day reveal that cars on these Dulwich services averaged 130 a day – the equivalent of Kings Cross to Retford or Paddington to Taunton.

Class B no. 226 was climbing the hill on its second journey from Catford to Victoria – the first one had been uneventful, but the driver noted that a little sand had been needed on the hill as the weather was wet – after leaving the last stop at East Dulwich Station, fully-loaded with five standing passengers. The car went up without difficulty (although to an onlooker this type of car often looked as though it would give up the ghost on the 193 yards of 1 in 11.16 – the steepest part), but when it reached the flatter stretch near the summit the current from the power station was cut off. Trams and their foibles were no strangers to Albert James who, after driving horse cars for seven years, had been handling the Council's electric cars for 20 years, of which the last 18 had been taken very frequently up and down Dog Kennel Hill. He had previously had to counter power cuts on this hill, so he was not perturbed on this occasion, and according to his version of what happened, he correctly reversed and applied the magnetic brake. It was patent from the burning on some of the fingers of the controller that he was mistaken and forgot to reverse, when his car commenced to roll back. He took other recognised steps, but could not check the car which soon reached the steep part of the hill where it quickly gained speed.

No. 1704 – a class M car – had arrived at the foot of the hill just short of the points giving access to the alternative "up" lines, and its driver saw 226 bearing down on him at a distance of about 50 yards. His first inclination was to start his car on to the other track, but he decided he would not be able to clear the fouling point before the descending car got there. He thereupon decided to reverse away from the oncoming menace, but was unable to do so before collision occurred, forcing his car backwards 78 yards. It was extraordinarily lucky that no traffic was behind 1704.

Both cars were extensively damaged, but not so the passengers amongst whom nobody was seriously hurt, although 38 had to receive first-aid treatment. It was on 226 that "platform boards were broken and crushed, and the lunters driven back". I assume them to have been what were usually called platform bearers, the equivalent of joists under a house floor. It was to these members that the gate, the gong, sand levers and so on were fixed.

The accident raised yet again the old discussion about the prevention of runbacks, of which so few drivers had actual experience (fortunately), so when it happened their reflexes were not automatic. The LCC were always alive in matters of this sort and took steps to see that their drivers were given some practice, and I had it as hearsay that, after this occurrence, it became the custom for a posse of drivers to be assembled on Sunday mornings to practice runbacks on Dog Kennel Hill before the day's traffic began.

On the evening before the deepened Kingsway Subway was reopened, several cars were shuttling between Aldwych and Bloomsbury to familiarise drivers with the place and its conduit-contact-operated signals and, as these cars climbed the steep exit at Southampton Row, an official on the back platform would open the canopy switch and an inspector riding with the driver would observe the latter's actions to this unexpected loss of power. I watched, secretly hoping something exciting would go wrong. So, six years after the affair at Dulwich, the LCC had not relaxed their vigilance in this matter; they were taking no chances on their drivers getting bewildered when the emergency arose.

Operator: **Scarborough Tramways Company**
Location: **Vernon Road/Valley Road, Scarborough**
Date: **16 September 1925**

Major Hall had barely finished his report on the London collision, when his colleague Colonel Mount was called on to inquire into another interesting runback, this time on the Yorkshire coast. So we turn our attention to Scarborough, a popular seaside resort, the last resting place of one of the Brontë sisters, the home of the Sitwell family, the town where the loquacious hold forth at seemingly interminable conferences, and the one-time location of an efficient compact company-owned 3ft 6in-gauge electric tramway, worked by four-wheel open-top cars painted reddish chocolate and cream. The trams and their rails disappeared before I visited the town, but some overhead work was still in place and the pattern in the granite setts still showed in locations where the lines had lain. On my walks between hotels and Spa Conferences, I tried to picture trams spiralling round the steeply-rising curve from the Spa, varying from 1 in 9 to 1 in 11, and marvelling on how they climbed the hill on which the accident happened. The replacement bus service avoided negotiating that hill.

This was the only major accident to befall the system and no one was severely injured. As may be supposed, the accident was a runaway, involving car no. 21. This was no power cut, or blown breaker. The car just slipped to a stand on a "greasy" rail, with its wheels spinning unable to get a grip. There was perhaps the presence of fallen leaves to make things worse. The driver was an experienced man, who claimed to have done all the right things, but whatever he did, he failed to prevent the car gaining speed backwards. It failed to round the curve at the bottom of the hill and crashed through the wall of a basement ballroom and landed on the floor in a nose-dive entangled in bunting. The conductor had "deserted the sinking ship", having jumped off quite early along with the three passengers, and the driver had to be cut down from the wreckage without much harm. He was found wedged between the seats and was extricated at some hazard since the tram had not then settled into its final position. There was some doubt whether the driver had allowed his attention to wander, as when going up the hill he was alleged to have exchanged some badinage with the driver of a car going the other way – possibly a racing tip for that day's horses.

The conductor was only a relief and he claimed that he had not been instructed in how to apply the brakes in an emergency. He had also been completing his waybill in the saloon at the time, instead of occupying the back platform as the regulations required. Colonel Mount, in his report, recommended that all staff (including relief and temporary staff) should be instructed in their duties in the event of an emergency, and the requirement to occupy the back platform on gradients was reinforced by him. After the accident, the car was examined and its equipment was found to be in proper working order, so that the

The spectacular descent of Scarborough 21 through the roof of the Aquarium ballroom in Valley Road on 16 September 1925. The driver had lost control of the car on the steep Vernon Road gradient. *Courtesy: National Tramway Museum*

Inspector was unable to pin-point the precise cause of the runaway. Although the trolley was stated to have dewired at a late stage, this should not, of course, have compounded the problem.

The Scarborough cars were equipped with slipper brakes, and this the driver had said he had used without effect. Some of the cars had at one time been fitted with regenerative brakes about which comment has earlier been made.

Operator: **Darwen Corporation**
Location: **Sudell Road/Bridge Street, Darwen**
Date: **20 September 1926**

From the north-east to the north-west, on to the 4ft-gauge line of the Darwen Corporation, which had a branch to Hoddleston by way of Sudell Hill, an incline of 260 yards at 1 in 10.5. Four cars were kept for this route and were equipped with 11in hardwood slippers, hand brakes and the usual rheostatic arrangements. Coming down Sudell Hill at 6.25am on Monday 20 September 1926, in a severe thunderstorm, car no. 11 ran away and, derailing at the 46ft-radius curve into Bridge Street at the foot of the hill, was almost completely wrecked when it collided with buildings. Of its passengers, two died and seven were injured. The driver failed to make due allowance for the state of the rails – water, albeit a poor one, is nevertheless a lubricant. The holding power of the brakes was lessened.

Major Hall's report might almost have been entitled "Twenty Years After" (apologies to Alexandre Dumas), as his recommendations were so similar to those of his predecessor whose words of profound wisdom seem to have fallen on stony ground, especially on the smaller tramways. Yet again the report emphasised that the slipper brake was of little value in stopping a runaway – its function was to hold the speed in check from the outset,

First of two views of Darwen 11 after its flight down Sudell Hill on 20 September 1926, resulting in severe impact damage.
Courtesy: Alan Brotchie

Another view of Darwen 11.   *Courtesy: National Tramway Museum*

preventing the car from accelerating.   Once again the futility of having the sand delivery pipes 3½ft ahead of the wheels – curvature of the line, the wind and the slipstream all contributed to minimising the amount of sand which got under the wheels.   One new feature appeared – a recommendation that air brakes should be considered for this route. British tramways had been loath to adopt, or to develop, air brakes, but by this time a few authorities had them in use to a limited extent.   Sheffield Corporation was one of the first, and some of their cars were so arranged that this new brake was regulated by normal movements of the controller handle.   The first few brake notches applied the air progressively, and the last few the magnetic brake, so once again the magnetic brake had been relegated to being the stand-by with all the risks its demotion implied.   Some pages below, we shall make the acquaintance of two air-braked runaways in different contexts: one at Eltham and the other at Leeds.

Operator: **Metropolitan Electric Tramways**
Location: **Southbury Road, Ponders End, Enfield**
Date: **11 December 1929**

Tramcars on busy streets often had minor collisions, not only within the family but on an increasing scale as the density of traffic grew.   In its earlier days, the electric tram, by reason of its weight, speed, power and passenger capacity, could perhaps have been called the king of the road (although I was in one which met its match in the form of a steam-roller – *i.e.* the tram came off second best, the impact having made a large dent in the dash-plate and uprooted the staircase).   The interloping motor bus became a nuisance to tramway activity on an ever-increasing scale, but there seems to have been no instance of a bus knocking a tram over until the end of 1929, when an insignificant single-decker bus submitted a proud double-decker tram to this indignity.   No doubt some of my readers will recollect "revenge" when a magnificent London HR/2 of the withered ex-

LCC fleet, in full cry on the Embankment, came upon a flimsy modern double-deck bus which had usurped the Kingsway service and "knocked it for six" on to its side.

MET car no. 53, an open-top bogie vehicle of type B in that company's stock, was travelling westwards along Southbury Road towards Enfield. On its tail was a motor bus, no. AD11, one of 39 of the same design owned by the National Omnibus Co. The tram had stopped to pick up a passenger, and the bus had closed to within about 15 yards of it with its offside wheels on the centre line of the track. It was well clear of the opposite tram track, the centre lines of the two tracks being 8ft 2in apart. It can be noted here, by way of a digression, that tram track centres were by no means alike. Whatever the gauge, the closer the tracks, the narrower the roadway which the tramway had to maintain, but of course the closeness of the tracks dictated the maximum width of the cars. The choice of track centres in some cases prevented development of wider, more comfortable, cars in later years. Track centres were not necessarily the same throughout a system, and in any case had to be increased in the immediate vicinity of junctions to allow for the greater clearance of the overhang of cars on curves. As just mentioned, the track-centre dimension at this point on the MET was 8ft 2in, in the Leeds case above it was 8ft 3in. On the LCC conduit lines, the standard was 8ft 6in, increased to 9ft at junctions. Having mentioned the LCC again, it is worth noting that, on the original 1903 electrification, the centres were only 8ft 0½in apart (Clapham to Tooting) for a considerable way, and passengers were very soon being injured at such a rate that the wire side grilles on the upper decks of the open top cars were heightened, and a notice placed at intervals warning people not to lean over the side, and for many years afterwards these notices were standard on all cars on the system, although the covered cars had no side one could lean over, and one needed a "rubber neck" to put one's head out of the windows.

To return to Southbury Road in Ponders End; the evening of 11 December 1929 was dark and clear, the road and rails were dry, and a strong wind was blowing. Tram no. 53 had overtaken a man on a push bike, and the bus was about to do so having got within two or three yards of him, when the cyclist riding in the middle of the space betwixt tram and kerb suddenly swerved to his right, possibly because of a gust of wind. Rather than hit him with the left front wheel (no grandmotherly legislation had seen to it that buses should have frontal protection similar to lifeguards on trams – there is no protection on the largest juggernauts on the roads even to this day), the bus driver swerved to his right which took his vehicle foul of the opposite tram track. This pin-points one of the chief differences between driving trams and driving dirigible vehicles; a tram driver had to be alert and prepared to stop short of any obstruction, which in my opinion required more skill and judgement than turning away. Had the bus driver been using tram technique, he would not have got in the path of oncoming MET car no. 118. The two met at a relative speed of about 30 mph, and both were very considerably damaged, the bus, a lightly-built box, by the impact, the tram from the effects of overturning. Nearly all the windows were smashed. Safety glass was not then in widespread use, and Lt-Colonel Anderson's[107] report notes that "in accordance with normal practice", it was not used anywhere in either vehicle.

For those readers interested in omnibus dimensions, the following may be of value. Length 25ft, height 9ft 3in (single deck seating 30 people), width 7ft 2¾in, weight loaded 5 tons 18cwt, tyres 38ft x 7in front single, rear double, maximum speed on level 35 mph,

---

[107] Edward Philip Anderson (1883-1934), Inspecting Officer of Railways 1929-34.

wheelbase 16ft, minimum turning circle 58ft diameter, maximum steering lock 45ft, either side of centre, and full movement needing two-and-a-half turns of the steering wheel.

The tram it hit was of the same type as that in the Highgate Archway disaster in 1906. This time it was no. 118, and was another of those cases in which much effort had been spent only a few weeks earlier on a major overhaul. In those days, when artisans had a greater interest, and, it must be admitted, a greater incentive to personal pride and interest in the vehicles on which they worked, it will have been to some degree disheartening for one's handiwork to have been wrecked so soon.

The tram rolled over on to its left side and diagonally across the road most likely because its bogies "spreadeagled" – but MET cars were well-known for their tendency to be top-heavy.   Ten of its passengers were injured or shocked, but the bus, which remained upright, had a very heavy casualty list – eight died and 20 were injured. Several versions of the accident cropped up. The swerve to avoid the cyclist did not have an independent witness, although one upper-deck passenger on no. 53 said he remembered the tram overtaking a cyclist, so the possibility that the cyclist had been invented by the bus driver to cover his misjudged attempt to overtake no. 53 on the offside received a slight challenge. There was also the counter-allegation that no. 118 had derailed and suddenly veered towards the bus. This unlikely possibility was prompted by the finding of a broken brake shackle after the overturn – a fracture most likely to have been a result of the strains of the roll-over.

Both tram drivers were "shellbacks" with 25 years experience of electric cars, and one of them had eight years previous horse-tram driving to his credit.

Operator: **Great Orme Tramways Company**
Location: **Old Road, Llandudno**
Date: **23 August 1932**

Three years elapse before there is another report of this nature, no doubt because tramways were being uprooted at a growing pace – some abandoned and some converted to trolleybus operation making use of the overhead installations, generating resources and distribution networks of tramways.   The tramways which survived longest being the "gilt-edged" systems of the larger towns.   That some of them disappeared prematurely could perhaps be explained by a theory, of which I heard, that oil and rubber interests "got into the pockets" of town councillors and such ilk: a theory on which one can do no more than speculate. It is not until mid-1933 that there is record of another of the so-typical runaways on a hill, but in the meantime an outstanding accident of a very different *genre* occurred on 23 August 1932 on the lower section of the quaint cable-hauled Great Orme Tramway at Llandudno, in North Wales.

The tramway operates in two independent sections and it was on the lower section that the accident occurred.   The undertaking has four cars, of which two work the lower section, one car ascending as the other descends, and passing one another in a loop at the mid-point of the section.   Each car was hauled by an individual cable on separate winding drums on the same engine.   There were no grippers as on other cable lines, as for instance at Brixton or Edinburgh, and the cable was permanently fixed to the plough-like drawbar projecting from the bogie down (in the street sections of the tramway) into a conduit through a slot in the road surface.

In all, the line climbed to about 680 feet above sea-level in just over one mile, but the portion on which car no. 4 broke loose was steeper, the climb from the terminus to the engine-house being 390 feet. The car, a single-deck bogie vehicle, was roofed, but the sides were open above the level of the seat-backs. It weighed 6½ tons when empty and 9½ tons when full. It was equipped with hand and slipper brakes of standard tramway types, operated from each platform in the normal manner except that the brakes were worked by wheels on separate staffs. Additionally, the design included an emergency brake of the type believed to have been adopted on the Highgate Hill cable line after its disasters – a clutch brought into action by a powerful spring whenever the tension in the cable slackened (the principle used on lifts, where the operating parts can often be seen on lifts working in mesh-wired shafts). The general arrangement of this clutch is depicted in the accompanying illustration. When tension in the drawbar eased, the powerful spring took charge and thrust the cam bar along, forcing the jaws against the inner sides of the slot rails. The track and conduit were most unusual in construction. The running track of 3ft 6in-gauge consisted of 60lb/yard flat-bottomed rails bolted to longitudinal timbers set in concrete. The check rail was formed by angle irons bolted to the sleepers. Unlike the conduits of the electric lines in Bournemouth and London, or the cable conduits in Edinburgh, London and Birmingham, the Great Orme line had no metallic yokes. The conduit was of concrete only (5in wide), surmounted by Z rails face-to-face giving a slot opening of 1¼in at the top, which at road level was 18in from the bottom. Pulley pits were frequent, but had to be spaced very irregularly owing to the constantly changing gradients and curves, it being essential to site the wheels so that the cables did not chafe against the concrete. With speed restricted to 4mph, no superelevation was needed on even the sharpest curves.

The simultaneous speed of the two cars on this funicular (so named because of the comparison of its cable with the funiculus, or umbilical, cord) line, was controlled by the winchman in the engine-house at the top of the section, using a band brake between the

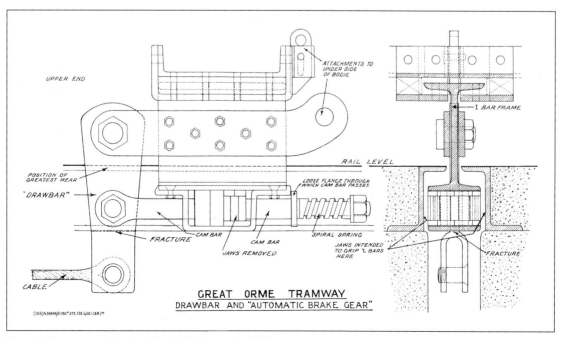

Great Orme accident dated 23 August 1932.

winding drums (one for each car) and by the throttle valve on the steam engine which drove the cable. Normally he could stop the cars within a very few feet. This man arranged the speed according to electric bell signals received from the man on the leading platform of a car. The cars were fitted with trolley poles and a casual observer could get the impression that the cars were being worked electrically, but the trolleys were merely the means of bell and telephone conversation.

It is of more than passing interest that the first application of an overhead wire to rail traction was for the purpose of communication. As early as 1855, telegraphic contact with a moving train had become possible through a bare overhead wire. The illustration of the appliance patented for making the continuous contact shows a pair of rollers mounted on the roof of the vehicle. These rollers rotating parallel to one another sloped downwards, the centre forming a shallow V in the angle of which the wire rode. The rollers, at right angles to the direction of motion, were hinged at the upper (outer) ends, and pressed upwards by springs at their inner ends. In view of such a promising start, it is unfortunate that current collection did not develop on similar principles. Instead there was the cumbersome four-wheel trolley which rode on the top of twin wires, and later a single wheel pressed up to a wire by a long pole with a spring at its base: the conventional device to which the name "trolley" adhered, and still adheres.

It became standard to mount the wheel in two different ways – one in which the wheel could swivel so that it could follow a wire whose course varied many feet either side of the line of the track[108], and the other, the rigid type which dictated that the wire must keep in line with the car[109]. The wheel, a pulley with a flared V-shaped groove and usually of brass or hard copper or bronze, was housed in a trolley head which, in later years, was cleverly designed so that in the event of dewirement none of the wiring could get caught up in it. As an additional precaution to prevent a trolley head pulling the wiring down, the head was in later years fitted to the pole only tightly enough to secure it under normal conditions. If the head did get entangled in the wiring, it would be pulled off the pole. In the event of this occurring, to safeguard it from falling on to the road, and possibly injuring somebody, a short piece of rope or chain was inserted.

Some authorities used rigid trolley heads for most of their history, a notable example being the Manx Electric Railway and (until converted to bow collectors) Glasgow tramways. Sheffield, Birmingham and Bristol were firm devotees of the swivelling head. From time to time trials were made in substituting skids for wheels, notably in Edinburgh, but little success seems to have attended this change until the days of the trolleybus. Apart from instances where cars were equipped with two trolley poles (one for each direction of travel), it was necessary to rotate the pole when the car reversed direction. Whatever the design of wheel and head, there were three ways of achieving this. The simplest was on open-top cars, on which the pole could be manhandled by the conductor[110]. On covered-top cars, either a rope was tied to the head and its loose end slip-knotted to the staircase rails or to a special mooring, or a metal ring was provided on the head and a long bamboo cane used to manipulate the trolley pole. On systems using bamboo canes, each car usually carried one on hooks along the lower edge of the bodyside. On the "rope" tramways, it was customary to keep a bamboo handy at junctions where trolleys were wont to dewire, because quite often a car's rope shot upwards out of reach. Whether by rope or bamboo reversal at termini, or at intermediate crossovers, the procedure entailed a man walking a semi-circle, which in later days became an increasingly difficult and dangerous task as street traffic grew. The principle of the trolley reverser, whereby the wheel described the same trajectory as a motor car backing into a gateway to reverse, was applied quite early in tramway history. Many tramways used them with various degrees of enthusiasm, but Sheffield installed a reverser at practically every crossover, although nevertheless a bamboo was slung on each car.

The use of grooved trolley wheels also made necessary complications in the overhead wiring system. Facing points with moveable tongues, coupled in one way or another, so as to coincide with the lay of track points and grooved trailing points and crossings, had to be provided and maintained. There had to be greater care in aligning the wire to the geometric "path of pursuit" of the trolley if fast running were to be achieved. All these interesting complications would have been obviated if sliding contacts had developed, instead of wheels. They did develop later[111], especially on the Continent where many may be seen in use today. The only British town to start with them was Sheerness in 1903[112], which also had the distinction of being the first British tramway system to be abandoned. Some systems made jabs with experiments, but retained wheels. However some, Glasgow, Leeds, Aberdeen and Dundee being fair examples, did change to the use of bow collectors and reaped their attendant advantages. It is my opinion that the inventor of the trolley wheel did tramways a disservice[113].

The first application of overhead wires to feed power to a moving vehicle (other than, possibly, demonstrations) would seem to have been the Bessbrook and Newry line in Northern Ireland, as early as 1885. There it was an expedient to bridge the gap in the third rail made necessary at a level crossing over a public road. In this primitive installation, which was devised by one of the Hopkinson brothers[114] – who as clever engineers seem not to have received the acclaim they deserved – the wires were slung loosely from crossbars straddling the track. Two wires, on different catenaries, were slung so that at their ends they were 5½in above the collector mounted on the roof of the car. The sag in the wires came into contact with the collector about five feet from the point of suspension, and by gravity remained in contact until, by the rise in the sag at the far end, the wire left the collector[115]. The collector was a lubricated steel bar, mounted

---

108 The first application of the swivel-head was on South Staffordshire tramways in 1893, designed by Alfred Dickinson (1856-1941).

109 The first application of the fixed-head was in Richmond, Virginia, USA, in 1888, perfected by Frank Julian Sprague (1857-1934). The first application in Britain was on the Roundhay Park line, Leeds, in 1891.

110 This procedure has been used on the Eastbourne and Seaton small-scale systems, but its use elsewhere has not been verified.

111 In point of fact they did develop earlier: as narrated later in the text, the Bessbrook & Newry line used a sliding contact from its commencement in 1885: one of the vehicles (rebodied but with original equipment), no. 2, is preserved in the Ulster Folk and Transport Museum, Cultra, Co. Down. The Manx Electric Railway employed sliding contacts at the outset, in 1893, and the Snaefell Mountain Railway, starting in 1895, has always used them.

112 The apparatus took the form of the Siemens bow collector, familiar on the Continent, but which caused the company some trouble in having to adapt it for double-deck open-top operation.

113 All modern British tramway, or light rail, systems employ pantographs as the mode of overhead collector.

114 The designer of the installation was Dr John Hopkinson (1849-1898).

115 It should be further noted that each overhead wire was in contact with the collector over only half of the crossing: at the midway point, the collector ceased contact with the one wire and transferred its contact to the other.

at right-angles to the wire: a good beginning and a practical method over the short distance involved – at most 150 feet – but a flexible collector on a more or less horizontal wire were obvious improvements.

Back to the Great Orme; car no. 4, with seating for 48 passengers, but not at this time carrying anything like so many, was descending the hill and had reached the steepest part (1 in 3.6), when the lower portion of the drawbar to which the cable was fixed, snapped off. No longer tethered to the cable, which had been holding the car at the speed at which it was being unwound from the engine drum, the car immediately ran away. The brakesman – he could not properly be called driver although he was on the front platform – promptly applied both brakes, but these had no effect on the headlong flight. Reverse curves a little lower down were too much for the car's speed, so it departed from the rails and crashed left-side-on into the ten-foot high stone wall of a cutting. A portion of the conduit rail was torn out as the remains of the drawbar dragged its way out of the slot.

The derailment of car 4 of the Great Orme Tramway in Old Road, Llandudno, on 23 August 1932. The accident was caused by the snapping of the drawbar, which connected the tram to its cable.

Courtesy: National Tramway Museum

The conductor on the rear platform, and 14 of his passengers, were injured. There was no rule against passengers travelling on the platforms. There was a child on the front platform, and probably thinking to save its life, the brakesman jumped off with it in his arms, but both were crushed against the wall and died.

The next day, a searching MoT inquiry began and resulted nearly three months later in Lt-Colonel Anderson's very informative report: a most absorbing read for tramway students. Replete with recommendations, it contained the findings of the National Physical Laboratory after exhaustive mechanical, physical, chemical, macroscopic and microscopic tests, analyses or examinations respectively made on the broken drawbar. In the meantime, the Inspector had closed the line pending his recommendations being put into effect.

I have noted earlier that men, even those who should appreciate the reasons for regulations, and understand the risks attached to ignoring them, will remove or isolate equipment prescribed for safety, if it causes bother. This had happened in double measure on the Great Orme. The speed regulator had been removed from the steam winding engine, and the gripping jaws had been taken away from the slot brakes[116]. The excuse for removing the latter was that they were too sensitive. They were constantly coming into operation, because there were so many changes in speed brought about by the rapid succession of alteration of curvature and/or gradient changing the tension in the cable. Whenever tension eased, the brakes and governor came into action.

In the event, absence of the governor from the engine could not have affected the accident. Not so in the conduit – when the drawbar parted, the jawless brakes might as well not have been there at all. Brakes or no brakes, the "$64,000 question" was why did one of these drawbars break after the design had been in use without incident for over 30 years? The bars themselves however had a short working life as they were quickly worn away by abrasion against the sides of the slot rails, and the management, seeking to reduce the number of renewals, ordered them to be made of a harder steel than the usual carbon steel. The very reputable steel company concerned supplied bars of a good quality chrome-nickel-molybdenum steel, but did not know the purpose for which they were to be used or they might have advised a different alloy. A seemingly innocuous change had the most unfortunate results. The metal successfully resisted wear but was not "tough" enough to survive the tugs and snatches of a heavy cable tram.

In his report, Colonel Anderson inevitably criticised the decision to remove the emergency brake, which was a statutory condition of operation, without attempting to substitute a new system which was at least as effective. He recommended that the line should not be reopened until such a brake had been designed and tested. He also recommended that when such a brake had been installed, it and other parts of the equipment should be periodically tested formally. In the light of these recommendations, a new braking system was devised which did not suffer from the inherent problems (variation of cable tension whilst running and integrity of the towbar coupling cable to car) that the original slot brake system had displayed[117]. It was approved by Colonel Trench[118] on behalf of the MoT on 11 May 1934 and thereafter a procedure was put in place to ensure that the braking system was tested annually. The line was reopened for public traffic on 17 May 1934.

In not far short of 50 years actively associated with public transport, I have often

---

[116] This action was taken in 1908.

[117] The new brake was (and is) unique to the British Isles (and possibly to the world). It is best described as a sledge brake (not to be confused with the brake described in the account of the Highgate Hill accident of 31 July 1884). There are two methods of initiating it: each platform has an emergency brake lever which can be pulled by the driver and there is also a speed-sensitive governor device which will operate the brake if a speed of 6mph is exceeded. The brake is only effective in the downhill direction.
The brake itself comprises two cast steel plates on each truck, one either side of the slot, which are suspended parallel to, but clear of, the concrete paving between running rails and slot rails. The paving is ridged and the plates have a number of ground-breaking teeth cast into their undersides. The plates are suspended by links so that, when released, they swing down while remaining parallel to the road surface until they come into contact with it. They then dig in slightly, and then go "over-centre" on their links. This transfers the entire weight of the car from the wheels on to the toothed plates, but the geometry is such that the wheel flanges are still within their grooves and directional control is not lost. The retardation achieved, even on the steepest gradient, is severe.

[118] Arthur Henry Chenevix-Trench (1884-1968), Inspecting Officer of Railways 1927-49.

cogitated after accidents about the element of criminal liability. Although death, personal injury and material damage have resulted from negligent or deliberate breaches of regulations – by tram and train drivers, signalmen, platelayers, artisans for example – there have been few prosecutions at law. In all this long list of tram accidents, only one has mentioned court proceedings. This was in respect of the bus driver involved in the tram overturn at Ponders End – he was charged with dangerous driving and dismissed. In the Great Orme case, the manager, Henry Sutcliffe, who had been responsible for the removal, without replacement, of the automatic emergency brake and for the change of specification of the steel for the broken drawbar, without informing the supplier of its intended purpose, remained in his post despite these failings until retirement in 1945.

The Great Orme tramway has been described in the past tense, but the line fundamentally unchanged still plies. Worked by the Llandudno Urban District Council it carries thousands of summer holiday-makers[119]. One of my earliest tram journeys outside London was from Old Colwyn to Llandudno and then up the Great Orme line – but we walked down as pennies were not squandered so lavishly as they are today.

After a gap of more than a quarter of a century, we come upon Sunderland again, but this time the trouble-free Corporation tramway experienced the seemingly inescapable "first time". It came on 15 June 1933, when car no. 70 suffered the indignity of being pushed over by a brewer's lorry which reversed into its path. Overturning broke a lot of glass, but fortunately without injuring any passengers seriously. Incidentally Sunderland trams made use of pantographs as well as bow collectors, after beginning with the usual trolley pole.

Operator: **Bath Electric Tramways**
Location: **Wells Road, Bath**
Date: **3 July 1933**

Lest the reader's interest is beginning to wane, it may be as well to state now that there are still four more tramway hill runaways on which to dilate. This one, reported on by Colonel Anderson, occurred in Bath, on the not-much-heard-of company-owned line of 4ft 8½in-gauge, which had about 19 miles of track serving some 14.8 route miles. The Combe Down route left the town by Wells Road and ascended steadily for 3,000 yards, in which it climbed some 450 feet. The car, no. 6, a conventional open-top four-wheeler, built 30 years earlier by the British Westinghouse Company, ran backwards for 530 yards along Wells Road, which had gradients varying between 1 in 11.6 and 1 in 26.7. Like so many other trams, this one had hand brakes and the magnetic brake which interworked with the blocks on the wheels. After the car started to run back, the driver never really lost some degree of control, although he could not stop its flight. This was checked by impact with car no. 18 standing on the same track. The two, locked together, ran for 150 yards, and would have gone further had not the conductor of no. 18 stopped the pair with his hand brake at the rear. Neither car was derailed and neither trolley left the wire.

Car no. 18 was climbing steadily when its driver saw no. 6 coming backwards towards him. It was then about 150 yards away and he had to make a quick decision. His first thought was to reverse, but not being sure whether the road behind was clear, he decided to stop and apply the hand brake, get quickly to the other end, and drive the car downhill, but he found himself hemmed in by a perambulator. He could not remove it, but managed to move it sufficiently to enable him to jump before collision occurred. The

A scene after the collision of cars 6 and 18 of Bath Electric Tramways in which the former had run back down Wells Road into the latter on 3 July 1933.

Courtesy: National Tramway Museum

conductor of no. 18 reacted well. On the top deck collecting fares, he saw the other car bearing down on his car only just in time tell the passengers to "hold tight" before he was thrown to the floor by the impact. Recovering himself, he hastened to the back platform and applied the brake, which though put on by the driver, had been knocked out of action by the collision.

There were about 40 passengers on car no. 6, and car no. 18 was also well-loaded. Two passengers on the former sustained injuries which proved fatal: in one case this was due to the passenger jumping or falling from the car before the collision. Thirty-seven other passengers were injured or suffered shock. Neither of the drivers was injured and the conductors escaped with a few bruises.

Car no. 6 was well-maintained, with brakes in good order, and their use not muddled as was so often the case in accidents like this. Speaking of brakes, this car had a refinement not frequently met with – application of the magnets started a flow of sand – but, because it was operative at the forward end, was unavailing at the back, so had no effect on this runaway[120]. The day was one of those all-too-rare in the alleged summers we experience in these islands. A fine, hot afternoon and the borough engineer logged a temperature of 84.5 degrees F shortly after this accident.

---

[119] The line is still in operation and under municipal control (now Conwy County Borough Council), but with substantial changes of equipment. It survived a further serious accident, this time on the upper section, on 30 April 2000 (*qv*).

[120] The need to sand at rear automatically in the event of a backwards runaway was appreciated by Liverpool at the design stage of their single-truck streamline cars (the "baby grands"). Their controllers were adapted for automatic sanding, *but only when running in the reverse direction to the controller setting*. This was to ensure sanding at the correct end when running back, while the driver was at the front intending to go forward. It employed a special form of connection on the English Electric run-back circuit, which is thought to have been unique to this class of car.

In the days before the modern elephantine internal-combustion vehicles displaced horse-drawn drays and bled the railways of traffic, there were considerable numbers of steam wagons on the roads. It was one of these steam lorries which, travelling up the hill more slowly than car no. 6, caused the tram driver to shut off power when he was unable to overtake it. The tram came to a halt where a patch of tar, softened by the heat, had spread over the nearside rail. When current was applied again, the wheels slipped on the tar and, although sand was dropped, the car did not move ahead the few inches needed to reach it, and instead rolled backwards. There were other patches of tar intermittently on the hill and these must have acted as a form of lubricant, and so vitiated the applications of the brakes.

The road surface at the site of the tram accident was a sort of tarmacadam rather than a true asphalt, and it was the characteristic wearing of the tram rail which had lowered its head, added to the raising of the road by successive tarrings, which allowed the melted tar on this hot day to run under the car wheels. In common with all other tramways, the Bath concern had the statutory liability to maintain a generous width of the roadway, but there the unusual arrangement had been made of the municipality being paid by the tramway to do it – so, it could be argued, that the accident was not caused by the tramway undertaking.

Operator: **Liverpool Corporation**
Location: **Paddington/Crown Street, Liverpool**
Date: **3 January 1934**

Now to the next hill runaway. In his report, the Inspector, Lt-Colonel Anderson, wrote of the excellent record of the system, which had not experienced an overturn for many

Two views of the accident at Paddington, Liverpool, on 3 January 1934, when car 181 overturned as the result of a runaway. *Harper & Taylor*

years (the Leece Street case mentioned much earlier), since which the Corporation's service had carried 4,750,000,000 passengers on over 385,000,000 car miles. The car concerned was an old one, no. 181, a double-deck, with a Bellamy[121] top cover, four-wheeler on a 6ft wheelbase. It still relied on the long-established rheostatic brake for emergencies, using the hand brake for service stops. Although quite irrelevant to the accident, it may be noted that this car had the unusual feature of sand being applied electrically from the third brake notch upwards.

The accident introduces no new aspect of tramway operation or equipment, but it is the first mention of a parked motor car, a pest which we now accept as a sort of incurable proliferating cancer.

The 4ft 8½in-line along Paddington, fell on an average gradient of 1 in 19, and at the bottom was a left-hand curve on which the runaway derailed. A passing pedestrian was pinned beneath the left side of the car as it fell over, and a woman was crushed between the car and the shop into which it crashed. These two unfortunates and a passenger died, and about 30 were injured. The runaway was due to mishandling the brakes, which was surprising in the view of the driver's long experience. In its downhill rush, during which the driver "resigned himself" to the consequences, the car caught up with a milk cart, which had been compelled to go on to the tram track to get past the parked car. The milkman was seriously injured.

---

[121] The top cover took its name from its designer, Charles Revill Bellamy (1856-1905), former general manager of the Liverpool transport undertaking. A car of this general type (Wallasey Corporation no. 78) forms part of the collection of the Wirral Heritage Tramway, Birkenhead. See also footnote no. 98 *supra*.

Operator: London Passenger Transport Board
Location: Westhorne Avenue, Eltham, London
Date: 25 March 1934

We now come to the antepenultimate instance in the Inspectorate's records of a tram overturning – not a runaway or a runback, as so many were, but what might be called a "snatchaway" at the end of a long, but steep, descent, the last 560 yards averaging 1 in 100. The LCC tramways stand out in the minds of most people – not only tram students – as the slot system, but it also had miles of overhead line, more than quite a few total overhead systems. At the outset, it had built 950 cars capable of working on the conduit system only, but towards the end there were only a few cars which could not work on overhead lines as well. The accident occurred on one of the overhead lines to one of the well-known E/1-class cars on Sunday 25 March 1934. By this date the ex-LCC tramways had got into the clutches of the London Passenger Transport Board (which progressively strangled them).

All LCC cars were equipped with highly-efficient magnetic brakes (including their novelty blue no. 1, which also had air brakes), and the LCC had kept aloof from frequent suggestions that magnetic brakes should derive their power from the traction supply but, in their unwisdom, the LPTB had decided to equip a car with air brakes and make its magnets mechanically-dependent on the mains, as indeed was its air compressor. This was not their first venture into disaster with air brakes – the Bluebell runaway afforded an earlier example[122]. There was nothing wrong mechanically or electrically with the car, no. 1103, when it departed from its depot at New Cross Gate. It had successfully worked from there to Southwark, and thence to Woolwich via Lewisham, a trip of some 14 miles. Trams on this route did not reverse at Beresford Square, but continued round a loop on to their return journey. Doing this, the car set out again for Southwark. A few minutes later, when negotiating the points at the junction at Well Hall roundabout to enter Westhorne Avenue (the last new line to be laid by the LCC), its trolley became dewired, its head being dragged off by entanglement in a span wire. The position of frogs (points), in the overhead line was often indicated by a simple signal on the adjacent standard – it was generally a pointer turned to left or right and co-acting with the pull wire which operated the frog on the overhead wire. The driver of 1103 was sure the points were properly set, and the signal showing the frog was set for his route, and the cause of the dewirement remained obscure but, as Colonel Trench, the Inspector, was content to record in his report "such unexplained dewirements do occur from time to time". Using the bamboo cane kept at the roundabout for this very purpose, the driver cleared the trolley fittings from the wires and stowed the trolley pole under the hook provided at each end of all LCC cars for housing the pole when running on conduit lines.

An inspector had by then arrived at the roundabout and instructed the driver of the following car (E/1 no. 988) to couple to 1103 and push it to Lee Green, at which point was a change pit, where it could pick up a plough and proceed normally on the conduit under its own power.

Technically, the inspector was wrong to give this order – practically, he was right. He was wrong because Lee Green was one-and-three-quarter miles away and the regulations said a disabled car "may be pushed to the nearest crossover but no further". But how was it possible to run round a disabled car at a single crossover so as to get in front to tow it? The only solution would be to indulge in fly shunting – a practice banned on the railways as being too dangerous. How very much worse to do it on a public road.

166

The two cars were joined by inserting and pinning a steel-stranded tow rope in the fenders (LCC tow ropes were tested to ten tons' strain) and 988 commenced to propel 1103 down the slope in Westhorne Avenue towards Eltham Road. For such operations, speed was limited to 6mph, with the leading driver responsible for braking, keeping in touch with the other driver by means of bell (or whistle) signals. The code was: emergency stop – 1; ordinary stop – 2; shut off power – 3; line clear – 4; (any signal not understood to be treated as danger). In addition, all passengers were to leave the defective car. On 1103, they were asked to do so, but four "awkward" ones would not budge – they paid for their obduracy when injured in the subsequent crash.

All started well, but possibly because men on these cars were so confident in the equipment, coupled with the anxiety of transport men not to cause delays, the pair ran with a sort of *laisser-faire* attitude. There is no need to go into detail; it will suffice to say that they were going too fast, and when the time came to make the compulsory stop before entering Eltham Road, the leading driver found that neither the air nor magnetic brakes would work. The rear driver then braked somewhat too heavily with his magnets. The snatch snapped the tow-rope and 1103 ran forward on its own, left the rails when it encountered the 100ft-radius curve of the junction, struck the kerb and overturned. All "the eggs were in one basket" so to speak, both power brakes being dependent on line current, which they were denied by the absent trolley head. Even at the very unwise speed of these cars – 20 to 25mph – and heavy as they were, they could have been stopped on their hand brakes alone, but reliance was placed, until too late, on the power equipment.

Operator: **Birmingham Corporation**
Location: **Saltley Road, Birmingham**
Date: **12 December 1935**

Now for a tram accident which was a triple collision at Saltley in Birmingham, at the entrance to a temporary single line on 12 December 1935. The other line was interrupted by sewer excavations, and car no. 791 was coming from the city on the single track while no. 782 waited for it in Nechells Place. While stationary no. 782 was run into from behind by no. 776, which forced 782 into collision with no. 791. Sixty-five people complained of injury and shock. Much glass was broken and the platforms of 776 and 782 wrecked, the driver of 776 being seriously injured. This unfortunate man had remained at his post, but was unaware of it. His mind was a blank, and he seems to have had slight epileptic seizures[123], so there is little to be gained by stating any further detail, but, apart from the tram point of view, there is just one small point in the report which will bear amplification.

According to the report, submitted by Lt-Colonel Woodhouse[124], the driver had a hazy recollection of "shutting off power and reapplying it when passing under a section

---

[122] As explained in Part I *supra*, the Inspectorate's report of this accident has not come to light. The accident occurred in 1927, under MET auspices and before the establishment of the LPTB, but the Author no doubt had in mind the carry-over in managerial thinking which was a feature of the transition.

[123] One wonders whether a similar affliction beset the driver for the otherwise seemingly inexplicable disaster at London Transport's Moorgate station, when on 28 February 1975 an underground passenger train on the Northern City line was driven at speed into a blank wall at the end of the station platform, killing 43 persons (including the driver).

[124] Ernest Woodhouse (1884-1972), Inspecting Officer of Railways 1930-49.

insulator at Crawford Street". This was a recognised part of driving – to shut off power at a section insulator, on the conduit system at other dead places in addition – and was desirable to avoid arcing damage to the collector gear and conductor wires or rails. Controllers were designed to break the arcs formed when heavy currents were suddenly broken and, by shutting off, the arc was dealt with in the controller, and not where it could harm equipment.

Operator: Huddersfield Corporation
Location: Leech's Hill, Outlane
Date: 4 October 1938

It was mentioned many pages ago, that the Railway Inspectorate – which by now had flitted to Northumberland Avenue – extended their responsibilities to trolley vehicles, so this record takes the opportunity of including the two Inspectorate reports into trolleybus accidents which have been traced. The first is concerned with an accident that occurred on 4 October 1938 in Huddersfield, at Leech's Hill, Outlane, on a former Corporation tram route. Trolleybus no. 12, a double-deck six-wheeler, was working between Waterloo, some two miles east of Kirkgate in the town centre, to Outlane, about four miles away to the west. Colonel Trench, in a ten-page report, gives a wealth of information about the technical features of the vehicle, which would be apt in a work on trolleybuses, but not here.

The event has some of the features that we have encountered on tramways – a defect develops; the crew do their best to rectify it; they report to a supervisor who ought to replace the defective vehicle; but he has no spare; the crew agree, or are cajoled into, making another trip while a substitute is found – transport men do not like to delay or inconvenience the passengers or the schedules on a wet day – so the tramcar or bus goes on and meets disaster. This time it was the air compressor which would not work, and the bus left on a hilly journey with its brakes very unlikely to function[125].

Having breasted the summit of Leech's Hill, and in view of the "dicey" brakes, the bus made only a perfunctory halt at the "All cars stop" post before the descent, and went on to the 1 in 14.7 gradient. The weather was very bad and, after a few yards, the bus left the shelter of houses and was on an open stretch of road. A strong gust of cross wind caught the front end and slewed the vehicle off course. Without an effective brake[126], the driver could not control it, so it veered across the road, struck the kerb, ran up a low bank and overturned. One passenger received a slight cut. The only other casualty was the driver, who suffered severely from shock.

Operator: Maidstone Corporation
Location: Upper Stone Street/Knightrider Street, Maidstone
Date: 7 August 1939

The other trolleybus accident in the Inspectorate's records occurred at the bottom of the gradient in Upper Stone Street, Maidstone, at about 1.15pm on bank holiday Monday, 7 August 1939, after a shower of rain. Trolley vehicle no. 39 of Maidstone Corporation ran out of control and overturned on its right-hand side. When descending the 1 in 15.5 to 1 in 17.5 gradient at moderate speed, the vehicle got out of control as a result of a rear wheel skid. There were about 30 persons on board the vehicle, of whom 17 suffered cuts, bruises and shock: two were detained in hospital. The chassis was only superficially damaged, but the right-hand side of the body suffered extensively: the body pillars of the upper saloon under the trolley base were broken and the panels of the upper saloon were considerably distorted and the windows shattered.

The trolley vehicle was built by the English Electric Company in 1930. It was a double-deck six-wheeler, fitted with an air (foot) brake operating on all six wheels, and a hand brake operating independent sets of shoes on the four rear brake drums only. No electrical braking was fitted. The vehicle was found to be in first class condition, save for its tyres. The tyres on the front wheels were nearly new, but the rearmost tyres were quite smooth and the centres of the treads of the tyres on the wheels of the intermediate axle were also smooth.

The Inspector, Major Wilson[127], attributed the accident to (a) an exceptionally slippery road surface for which the weather conditions were mainly responsible; (b) mishandling of the vehicle by the driver, F D Anderson; and (c) unduly smooth tyres, having regard to the condition of the road surface. Anderson's failure was due to his using only the hand brake and not applying the foot brake. He said that he was afraid to use the latter in case it caused the front wheels to skid, but the Inspector said that this risk would have been minimised since it would have distributed the braking effect over all six wheels.

The report tells us that the driver had worked as a conductor until the previous February. He had received a fortnight's driving instruction (about three hours every evening) but had had no practical training in the control of a skidding trolley vehicle. In these circumstances, the Inspector considered that Anderson was insufficiently trained to handle a vehicle of this size and weight safely under adverse conditions.

Operator: **Darwen Corporation**
Location: **Bolton Road/Kidder Street, Blackburn**
Date: **20 September 1941**

We now come to a rare report during the course of World War II, which is addressed to the Minister of War Transport at Berkeley Square House, London, the Inspectorate's final administrative headquarters so far as these accounts are concerned. The report related to an accident that occurred in Blackburn on 20 September 1941 when a Darwen tramcar,

---

[125] The reader may, perhaps, have been misled by the Author's final comment. It was the air-operated wheelbrake, actuated by a foot pedal, that did not work. The entire fleet at that time used regenerative brakes to slow speeds down to 13-14mph, and then a two-notch stabilised rheostatic brake to reduce speed to 5-6mph, with the air brake for the final stop. Also all the trolleybuses had hand brakes, and all starting was achieved by applying power whilst held stationary on that brake. The trolleybuses were also fitted with an electric coasting brake, which was used on some of the town's routes that had a fairly long steep section (*e.g.* Elland, West Vale).

[126] Notwithstanding what has been written in the previous footnote, if the vehicle had dewired then this would have rendered both the regenerative and rheostatic brakes inoperative, causing the driver to be totally dependent on the hand brake.

[127] George Robert Stewart Wilson (1896-1958), Inspecting Officer 1935-49, Chief Inspecting Officer of Railways 1949-58.

Photographs showing the partial derailment and overturning of Darwen 17, caused by incorrect point setting at Kidder Street siding, Blackburn, on 20 September 1941.

Courtesy: National Tramway Museum

operating on the jointly-worked through route between the two towns, overturned. At about 1.0pm on that day, car no. 17, a double-deck, totally-enclosed, Brush-built car of 1924, mounted on Burnley bogies, was travelling along Bolton Road, Blackburn, when it was wrongly diverted through facing points leading from the main road to a siding in Kidder Street, installed to handle traffic serving the nearby Ewood Park football ground. The car derailed on the sharp left-hand curve immediately following the points. Its body left its bogies and overturned on its right-hand side.

The motorman was pinned under the overturned body and was killed instantly. There were 24 passengers on the car, distributed about equally between the upper and lower saloons. Of these, 13 were taken to hospital with cuts from broken glass and bruises, but only eight were detained. Three or four others were treated locally for minor injuries. The body of the car was not crushed, but suffered considerable damage on the right-hand side, and the upper deck had partially split from the lower. The bogie check chains and hand brake chains were broken, but the bogies themselves remained on their wheels in the roadway and were practically undamaged.

The track along Bolton Road was double, with a single facing point on the left-hand side for cars approaching from Blackburn, the point leading at right angles to a single-track siding in Kidder Street. It had a single switch on the left-hand side with a dummy with diverging flangeways on the other. The siding had last been used in May of that year for special football traffic. The curve following the points was of 150ft radius gradually increasing to a 25ft radius about 32ft from the toe of the points. The points had been laid new in 1934 and appeared to be in good condition, although wear was noticeable. The tracks in both thoroughfares were laid in granite setts.

The switch tongue was electrically operated by a solenoid controlled from a box on an adjacent pole. When the siding was not in use, as on this occasion, power was cut off from the solenoid and the control box was locked. The switch tongue was then quite free to be moved either way and so, to secure it for the straight road, a hard rubber block about 3¼in by 2in by 1¼in, roughly cut from an old solid tyre, was jammed between the switch and the check rail. This block was recessed at the side to fit over the head of the stop bolt which limited the travel of the switch in its open position. The rubber block which was in place when the Inspector, Major Wilson, examined the points fitted tightly, and had to be prised up with a point iron to dislodge it.

After describing the bogies in some detail[128], the Inspector made the point in his report that apart from the bogie check chains, which were provided for another purpose and were broken, there was no positive anchorage between the body and the trucks, which would have accounted for the former overturning independently of the latter. However, comparison of cars on comparable systems, in relation to the various centres of gravity, indicated that stability of an unanchored body was substantially the same as that of a car in which the trucks and body were positively connected. It also appeared from theoretical calculation that the critical overturning speed of the car on a curve of 25ft radius would be about 13mph.

Immediately after the accident, the points were found to be undamaged and fully open for the siding: the rubber securing block was missing and had not been found subsequently. Marks on the setts indicated that derailment to the outside of the curve commenced after the leading wheels of the car had travelled 42ft from the toe of the points. It appeared that the leading (small) wheels of the rear bogie were the first to derail, probably by the centrifugal force acting on the body. After the car had travelled a further 5ft 6in the leading wheels of the front bogie became derailed, and derailment of the remaining wheels followed. It appeared that the body commenced to overturn as the result of centrifugal force before any of the wheels were derailed.

---

[128] Information on the Burnley bogie has been given in footnote no. 94 *supra*.

According to the conductor of the car, it was travelling at about 6 or 7mph when traversing the points, although passengers and a bystander thought the speed to be somewhat higher. The conductor went on to say that during his 20 years' experience as a conductor, cars on which he was working had been unexpectedly diverted into the siding on about four or five occasions, fortunately without untoward results. The driver of the car which had immediately preceded no. 17 (another Darwen car) said that the points were not in the correct position but "slightly open". He could not recollect whether the rubber block was in place. On the other hand, another driver on the route – a Blackburn driver – found nothing wrong with the points and said that if the rubber block was missing, or the points slightly open, he would have stopped his car and reset the points with a point iron. The Inspector, travelling on the driver's platform of a car, said that he had no difficulty in seeing the setting of the points and the rubber block from a distance of about ten yards.

The latest direct evidence that the rubber block was in position was that of point cleaner F Holt, who attended to the points between 2.30 and 3.30pm on the previous day. It was Holt's duty to examine, oil and clean all the points on the Blackburn system: each set received this attention daily from Monday to Friday, and on alternate Saturdays. On the day of the accident, a Saturday, the points were not dealt with. According to Holt, on the preceding Friday he removed the rubber block with his point iron, worked the points to and fro, saw a car go over, and replaced the block, which he said was a good tight fit. He was unable to suggest how the rubber came to be missing.

Major Wilson concluded that the accident was primarily due to the open position of the switch tongue and that, on balance, the rubber block was not in place during the morning and that the vibration of passing trams and other road vehicles had caused the tongue gradually to open.   What had caused the rubber block to be dislodged or removed remained a matter of speculation, but he had no reason to disbelieve that Holt had properly replaced the rubber the previous afternoon.   The Inspector considered the practice of securing facing points by this method to be inadequate and recommended that some positive mechanical arrangement should be put in place both at Kidder Street and at all other places on the system where there were facing points not in regular use.   The Corporation should be asked to report what action they proposed taking in this respect.

Operator: **Leeds Corporation**
Location: **Oakwood, Leeds**
Date: **4 September 1952**

The staged demise of tramway operation in London following World War II resulted in almost a production line of tram scrapping at a purpose-built facility in Charlton. While few London trams escaped this fate, the significant batch that did were the surviving "Feltham"[129] or UCC cars, some 90 in total, sold to Leeds Corporation in 1950/51. Following overhaul and adaptation in Leeds, all but a few entered service there to become major players in what, not so long afterwards, became the twilight years of Leeds tramways. The cars were double deck, 40ft 6in long and weighing 18 tons 6cwt unladen, of steel-frame construction with steel exterior panels. The bodies were mounted on a pair of maximum-traction trucks.

The braking equipment of the cars consisted of: (a) an electro-magnetic track brake, which was applied through four track magnets; (b) an air-wheel brake, operating shoes on each of the eight wheels; (c) a hand brake, which was applied by means of a vertical wheel and was normally intended for parking purposes only; and (d) an emergency air-wheel brake, which was provided in the conductor's vestibule at each end of the car. It was fixed on a panel to the left of the driver's doorway, painted red with a plaque alongside saying "EMERGENCY USE ONLY". This brake was applied by pulling down a horizontal handle to a vertical position, thereby opening a valve on the air-brake system which connected the air reservoirs directly to the brake cylinders irrespective of the position of the brake control handle.

Having set the scene, we now come to our final account of a runaway. On 4 September 1952, UCC car no. 507 had entered service from Swinegate depot at 7.40am. Motorman Norris took over the car at 3.32pm. Up to that time there had been no problem with the car, nor did Norris have any until his arrival at Roundhay Park gates at 5.38pm, where he had to reverse the car for its return to the city. He was on the point of changing ends, having removed the air-brake handle from the cab which he had just vacated, when his conductor, Cunningham, called for his assistance in reversing the bow collector. Norris obliged, and then went to a nearby lavatory for about two to three minutes, taking the air-brake handle with him. He had not applied the hand brake before leaving the car, as the rules required him to do, given the propensity for air brakes to leak off.

On his return, he was surprised to see his tram going over the crossover and assumed that Cunningham was moving it down to the loading point where several passengers were waiting. Only when it did not stop did Norris realise that the car was running away on the 1 in 21 gradient towards Leeds. He gave chase, but was outpaced by the tram. On board, conductor Cunningham came to realise that Norris was not on the car. He went to the then rear of the car, where he expected to find the air-brake handle, but since it was not there, he went to the leading end to see if Norris had put it there, only to discover it was missing from that place too. He tried to apply the hand brake, but to no avail. Then, in a selfless act of self-preservation, probably prompted by panic, he jumped off the tram, leaving it to its fate.

The tram continued to run forward unchecked on the falling gradient, along the reserved track which bordered Princes Avenue for a distance of over three quarters of a mile. At Oakwood, where another tramcar, no. 92, had just set off from the stop, a collision of considerable violence occurred between the two vehicles. No. 92 was a double-deck, wooden-framed, steel-panelled car of the Chamberlain class[130], mounted on a P35 four-wheel truck. It was 31ft 3in long and weighed 13½ tons. Upon impact, conductor Ingram on no. 92, was thrown into the road as the rear platform, on which he had been standing, was demolished as far as the stairs by the collision. The leading cab and upper deck end of no. 507 were driven back to the lower saloon bulkhead.

No. 507 became derailed and veered into the left-hand kerb of the road where it came to rest, while its momentum was imparted to no. 92, which held to the rails and was forcibly propelled on to the next section of reserved track. Its motorman, Mason, was knocked

---

[129] The name "Feltham" was derived from the location of the works of the Union Construction & Finance Company (UCC), at Feltham, Middlesex, where these cars were built.

[130] This was a large class of cars named after its designer, William (later Sir William) Chamberlain (1877-1944), a former general manager of the Leeds transport undertaking.

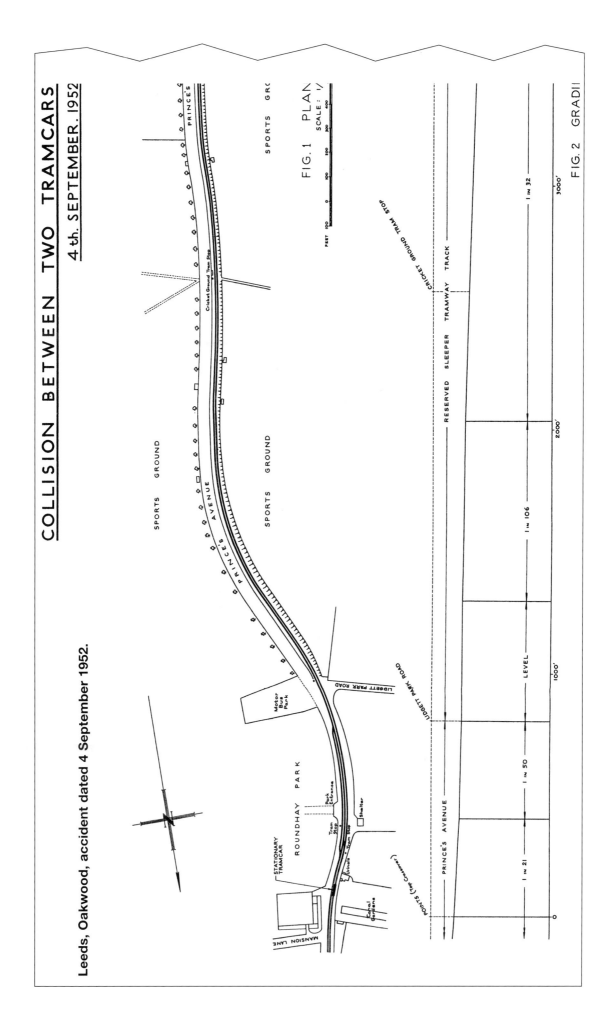

COLLISION BETWEEN TWO TRAMCARS
4th. SEPTEMBER. 1952

Leeds, Oakwood, accident dated 4 September 1952.

FIG. 1 PLAN

SCALE: 1/

FIG. 2 GRADII

PRINCE'S

SPORTS GROUND

SPORTS GRO

SPORTS GROUND

SPORTS GROUND

PRINCE'S AVENUE

Cricket Ground Tram Stop

ROUNDHAY PARK

Motor Bus Park

LIDGETT PARK ROAD

LIDGETT PARK ROAD

STATIONARY TRAMCAR

Park Entrance

Tram Stop

Tram Stop

Shelter

Urinals

Central Gardens

POINTS (1st Crossover)

MANSION LANE

CRICKET GROUND TRAM STOP

RESERVED SLEEPER TRAMWAY TRACK

PRINCE'S AVENUE

1 IN 32

1 IN 106

LEVEL

1 IN 50

1 IN 21

3000'

2000'

1000'

0

FEET 100 0 100 200 300 400

174

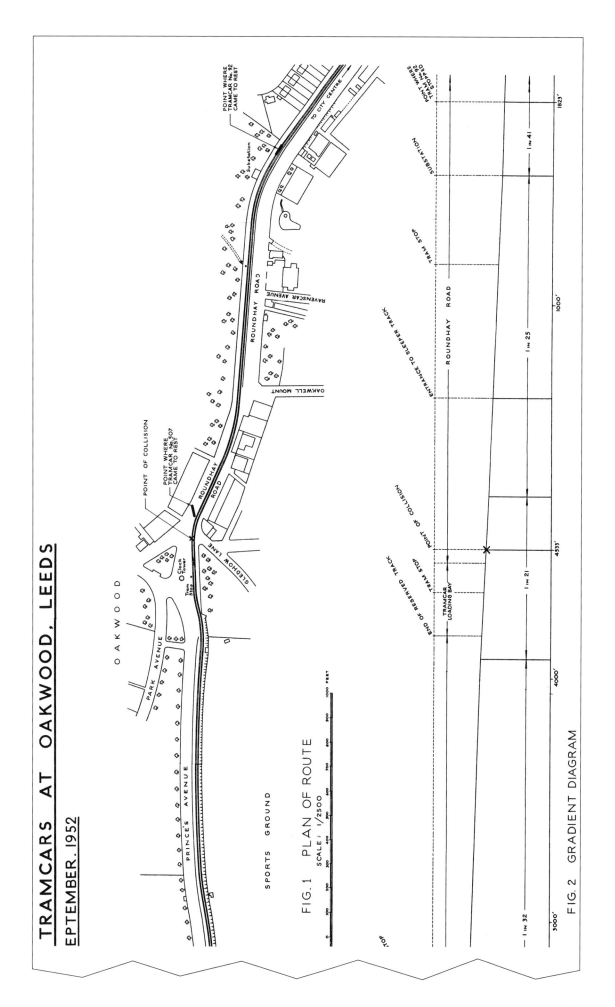

TRAMCARS AT OAKWOOD, LEEDS

EPTEMBER. 1952

FIG. 1 PLAN OF ROUTE
SCALE: 1/2500

FIG. 2 GRADIENT DIAGRAM

175

unconscious by the impact and lay collapsed upon his platform. The line continued to have a downward gradient. Only the presence of mind of a lower-saloon passenger, James Penwarden, who was travelling with his wife and son, prevented a further accident: an accident which could have caused much more serious consequences had the car reached the major traffic intersection at Easterly Road. Penwarden, although thrown to the floor and shaken, and somewhat alarmed by part of the floor being pushed up into the saloon as a result of the platform bearers being forced back, clambered over the recumbent motorman and manipulated the controls. He put the controller into what he thought was the "off" position and applied the hand brake. By doing so, he was able to bring the car to rest 600 yards from the point of impact.

Meanwhile, motorman Norris had waved down a passing motorist and got a lift to the scene of the collision at Oakwood. He went to the rear, undamaged, cab of no. 507, placed the air-brake handle,

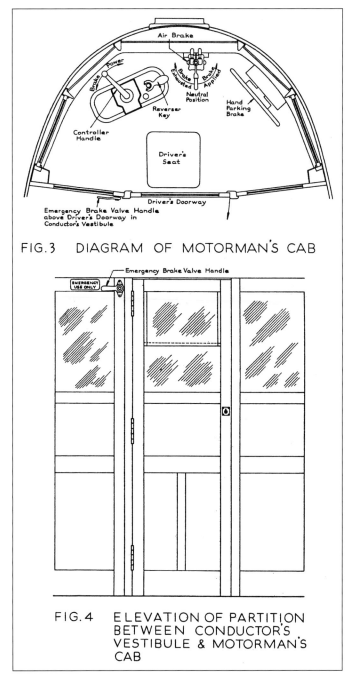

FIG.3   DIAGRAM OF MOTORMAN'S CAB

FIG.4   ELEVATION OF PARTITION BETWEEN CONDUCTOR'S VESTIBULE & MOTORMAN'S CAB

which he still had with him, in the "fully applied" position and ensured that the reverse handle in the same cab was in the "forward" position. These were the positions in which the tramway's senior technical staff found them on their arrival.

Leeds' tramway engineer, Victor Matterface, was very keen to establish the circumstances of the calamity and why no. 507 had started upon its fateful journey, particularly because there was a groundswell of opinion in Leeds that the Feltham cars, coming from London, were not suited to operation in Leeds. Following recovery of both cars to Kirkstall works, he paid close attention to the UCC car. The air pipes at the damaged end of the car were burred over and sealed, and the rest of the system was pressurised and found to work as it should. The brake cylinder pressure, after a normal application (40lb/sq in) and returning the brake handle to neutral, dropped down to a brake cylinder pressure of 18lb/sq inch after six minutes. With a full brake cylinder pressure of 80lb/sq inch, the pressure fell to 55lb/sq inch after six minutes.

These and other tests, involving resistance to motion, were sufficient to establish both the air and hand brakes were in full working order and were effective. The Inspector, Brigadier Langley[131], was very satisfied that this was so and noted that new brake blocks had been fitted to the car on 31 August. The brakes had been examined on the morning of the accident before the car left the depot, adjusted and the linkages lubricated. In this regard, the Brigadier's final paragraph of his report is worth quoting in full:

> *I am satisfied that the brakes, both air and hand, on the London U.C.C. type trams are thoroughly efficient, as was shown by the tests which were carried out at my request, and I am certain that if the brakes had been properly used on this occasion, the accident would never have happened.*

The Brigadier was less complimentary towards Norris and Cunningham, and the training and assessment of platform staff. Norris had failed properly to secure the car before he left it. Cunningham did not know how to use and apply the hand brake on UCC cars. Nor did he know of the position and function of the emergency brake valves on the car even though they were conspicuously marked as earlier described. The system of conductor instruction relating to brakes relied too much on verbal descriptions, without trainees having to perform the tasks and experience the effects on every class of car they were to expected to encounter.

The collision injured twelve passengers and three members of staff. Fortunately no one was killed. For his courageous action and presence of mind, James Penwarden was subsequently awarded the MBE. Both cars were later scrapped as a result of their encounter.

Operator: **Glasgow Corporation**
Location: **Commerce Street/Kingston Street, Glasgow**
Date: **30 March 1953**

Glasgow tramways feature in our last three accounts. This is not to be taken as indicating any particular shortcomings of that undertaking: Glasgow appears high on the list of accident inquiries, partly because of its considerable size, but largely because of its longevity, having survived for a greater period than virtually every other UK tramway. The first of these reports is yet another (the last) case of an overturning. It was also another case of driver error, although in this instance – uniquely in these reports – the driver was a woman. The accident occurred at the intersection of Commerce and Kingston Streets in the City of Glasgow, at 6.05pm on 30 March 1953. At that location, a double line of tramway extended north-south along Commerce Street, with a double junction taking tracks on an east-west alignment along Kingston Street.

The points at this junction were in the facing direction for cars travelling southwards from the city and were manually operated. The standard 5mph speed restriction through facing points applied. Normal services proceeded straight onwards at the junction, and the tracks along Kingston Street were normally used for depot purposes only (about 36 movements each day). The tramcar involved, no. 114, was operating on the Lambhill to

---

[131] Charles Ardagh Langley (1897-1987), Inspecting Officer 1946-58, Chief Inspecting Officer of Railways 1958-63.

Crookston service. However, instead of proceeding straight across the junction, as intended, it veered to the left because the points were set for Kingston Street. It derailed on the curve beyond the points and toppled over on its right-hand side.

All seats on the tram were occupied and in addition there were three or four standing passengers in the lower saloon. Altogether 54 passengers and two Corporation employees were injured and ten of them were detained in hospital. The rescue work was prompt and effective. The car was a double-deck, totally-enclosed vehicle of the standard class, mounted on a Brill four-wheel truck of eight feet wheelbase. The body was of timber, with a composite underframe, and a large number of window lights were broken as a result of the accident, but there was little structural damage. Unfortunately, owing to the restricted headroom in Kingston Street occasioned by the present of a bridge carrying railway lines serving Central station, a great deal more damage was caused during rerailment.

On inspection immediately after the accident, it had been found that the controller of the car was on the first notch of parallel with the reversing lever in the forward position: the circuit breaker was open. The brakes were on, but the air-brake handle had fallen off. The pressure in the brake cylinders and reservoir was 4lb/sq in.

The driver, Eileen McGibbon, of Possilpark depot, was aged 20. She had been a conductress for 12 months and had then volunteered to take a course in driving. She had begun this course as recently as 5 March and, at its conclusion on 25 March, was classed as "fair". She was placed on probation for one month and had nearly completed her fifth day of probationary driving when the accident occurred. During this period normal hours of duty were taken at driving, but for the first seven days the probationer had to be accompanied by a qualified driver acting as conductor.

Motorman instructor S Wilkin, who had supervised the girl's work when she was driving a service car under instruction, formed the view that she showed good road sense, observed speed restrictions and was a cautious driver. During her instruction, she had driven along Commerce Street every day and Wilkin had particularly pointed out the Kingston Street turning and reminded her that it was seldom used. On one occasion the track was set for Kingston Street, but McGibbon had stopped the car without any prompting and shifted the points.

On the day of the accident, inspector Wilson had supervised McGibbon's work for about half an hour between 4.0 and 5.0pm. She had driven perfectly and had controlled the car without any difficulty through some of the busiest streets in the city. He had noticed that there was no qualified motorman acting as conductor, but as the driver was coming off duty on completion of her next journey, he did not arrange to get another qualified conductor, though he said that he would have done so if he had known this earlier in the day. It transpired that McGibbon had volunteered for duty on the day, which was her rest day, and consequently no arrangements had been made by the Possilpark depot staff for a qualified driver to accompany her.

The Inspector taking the inquiry, Brigadier Langley, was satisfied that nothing in the condition of the car had contributed to the accident, which was due to the vehicle taking the Kingston Street curve at such high speed that it had overturned by centrifugal force. A bad mistake had been made by driver McGibbon who, in her anxiety to pass the intersection while traffic lights were in her favour, failed to notice that the points were set for the curve instead of for the straight track and who made no attempt to observe the 5mph speed restriction. The Inspector emphasisied the fact that the driver was a woman did not affect the case and the general manager had observed that in his experience women had been more meticulous in carrying out instructions than men of the same age.

The conductress, who was taking fares on the upper deck of the car at the time, was absolved from any blame, but the Brigadier said that had a motorman conductor been present, he might have noticed the tram was approaching the crossing at too high a speed and warned the driver accordingly. Failure to provide such a conductor was a serious omission on the part of the depot clerk in charge of traffic staff at Possilpark depot. He also recommended that the qualifying age for a driver should be raised to 21 years, which was the statutory minimum for drivers of public service vehicles. He went on to say:

> *A grave responsibility rests on the drivers of all passenger-carrying vehicles, whether trams, trolleybuses or oil-driven buses, since the safety of large numbers of the travelling public is in their hands. It is therefore essential that they should be persons selected for their high sense of responsibility and discipline, and they should not be allowed to take sole charge until they have acquired a thorough knowledge of the vehicles they have to drive and of the routes over which they have to operate.*

These comments took on a particular emphasis since a postscript to the report reveals that a further accident had occurred at the junction of St Andrew's Drive and Albert Drive (Glasgow) during the night of 8/9 July, when another tramcar had derailed and overturned.

Operator: **Glasgow Corporation**
Location: **Great Western Road/Byres Road, Glasgow**
Date: **11 July 1955**

The penultimate report is the first to be addressed to the Minister of Transport and Civil Aviation. It concerned a derailment at the junction of Great Western Road and Byres Road, which occurred at 7.17pm on 11 July 1955. Standard tramcar no. 292, which was travelling eastwards along Great Western Road on the no. 10 service from Hyndland station to London Road, had stopped at the traffic lights at the junction. On re-starting, the car was diverted incorrectly through a right-hand turnout leading into Byres Road. In doing so, it went into the face of oncoming motor traffic proceeding westwards. It struck the rear of a private motor car and then collided almost simultaneously with a bus and a motor-cycle and sidecar combination. At this point, the tram derailed to the left, carrying the motor-cycle combination before it until the tram stopped against the kerb on the opposite side of the road.

Motor-cycle combinations seem particularly vulnerable to damage in collisions and mercifully they are now rarely to be seen on British roads. To make matters worse, the vehicle on this occasion was carrying no fewer than six persons. Of these two were killed, two seriously injured and the other two received minor injuries. None of the passengers on the tram was injured, but the driver and conductress, who both either fell or jumped from the front platform of the car, were bruised and suffered from shock. The inquiry was conducted by Brigadier Langley and his report is additionally helpful in appending a drawing of the junction, of the features involved in automatic point operation and of the tramcar controller and brake equipment. In his report, the Inspector mentions that Great Western Road was a main traffic artery to the north and west, carrying heavy traffic of all descriptions. The tram service at peak times operated at a frequency of 47 cars per hour in both directions, with every third eastbound car turning into Byres Road.

For the first time since the Dublin accident of 1 February 1914, the Inspector had to explore the technicalities of point turners. At the time of the accident, the eastbound points were operated electrically by a Forest City automatic point turner. In order to set or maintain the points for the through route, power had to be "off" when the bow collector was passing under the contactor on the overhead wire and "on" to set or maintain the points to the right-hand turnout into Byres Road. The position of the bow relative to the contactor was indicated to the driver by a triangular stud and an arrow laid in the surface of the roadway and so placed that the bow would be under the contactor when the front of the tram was between the stud and the arrow[132]. A round stud indicated the point beyond which a following tram was not to pass until the leading vehicle had cleared the points, so as to ensure that they would not be changed inadvertently by the second tram. Sufficient space had been allowed between the studs to cater for the different types of car in use in Glasgow. As the effective length of the contactor was 2ft and the distance from a raised bow to the front of a standard car was 18ft 5in, it follows that in this case the bow would have been passing under the contactor when the front of the tram was between 18ft 4in and 16ft 4in from the white line laid slightly forward of the leading traffic light signal[133].

Car 292 was a venerable survivor, having entered service in 1909. As the drawing on page 182 shows, the controller was equipped with a magnetic brake, applied by turning the controller handle in an anti-clockwise direction. There was also an air brake, with an interlock between the two brakes to ensure that only one was applied at any one time. The air brake was applied by the motorman pulling towards him the separate brake handle mounted on the controller top, and released by pushing the handle away from him. This brake was exhausted whenever power was applied, but in an emergency it could be re-applied with power "on" by pulling more strongly on the handle and overcoming a second spring in the interlock gear.

The brakes were tested by engineering staff after the accident and were found to be in order. The controller was found to be in the first notch of parallel and the brakes were off. The motorman, N Stephenson, had no complaint with the equipment. He had qualified only six weeks previously, and had taken over the car at 3.30pm on that afternoon. He said that it was in good running order, the brakes were good and he was

---

[132] The use of an arrow was to indicate, by its alignment, the route direction for which it was required to select power.

[133] Most, if not all, of the Forest City point turners used by Glasgow at the time of the accident were of the delayed action variety. This design was developed to cater for occasions when a tramcar might come to rest with its bow collector in contact with the active portion of the detection contactor on the overhead wire. It was designed to overcome the problems with the original equipment design of overheating and burnout of the point-operating solenoids, and also flashover, burning and possible welding of direction-selection relay contacts when the car moved off the contactor. With the delayed action design, the points were not thrown until the instant the bow was leaving the 2ft-long active section of the contactor. Route selection depended on the action of the motorman, powering or coasting, at that precise point.

Glasgow, Great Western Road, accident dated 11 July 1955.

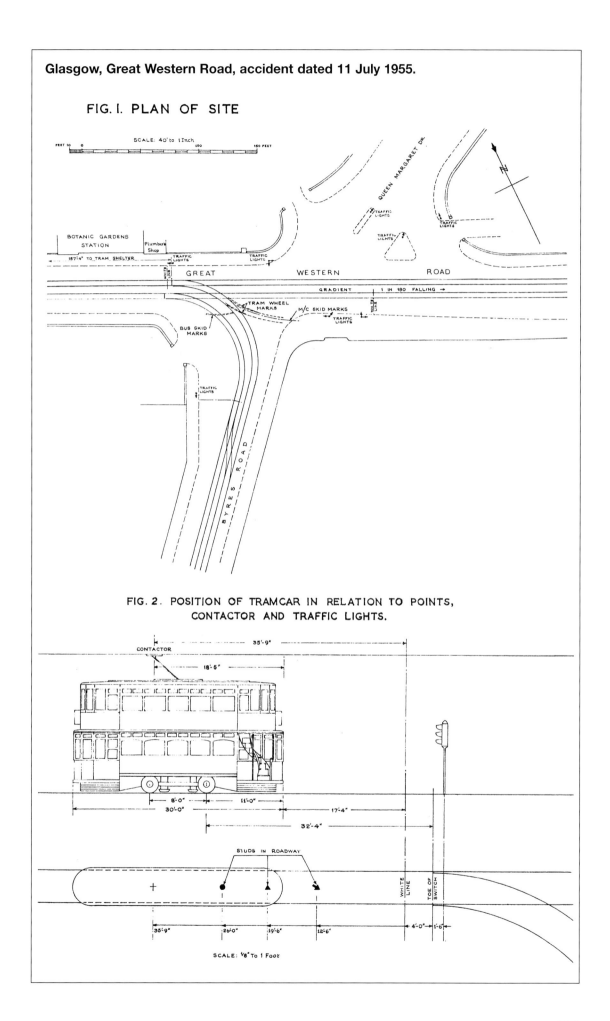

FIG. 1. PLAN OF SITE

SCALE: 40' to 1 Inch

FEET 10   0   100   150 FEET

QUEEN MARGARET DR.

BOTANIC GARDENS STATION
Plumbers Shop
157'4" TO TRAM SHELTER
TRAFFIC LIGHTS
TRAFFIC LIGHTS
WHITE LINE
GREAT   WESTERN   ROAD
GRADIENT   1 IN 180 FALLING →
TRAM WHEEL MARKS
M/C SKID MARKS
TRAFFIC LIGHTS
WHITE LINE
BUS SKID MARKS
TRAFFIC LIGHTS
TRAFFIC LIGHTS
TRAFFIC LIGHTS
B Y R E S   R O A D

FIG. 2. POSITION OF TRAMCAR IN RELATION TO POINTS,
CONTACTOR AND TRAFFIC LIGHTS.

35'-9"
CONTACTOR
18'-6"
8'-0"   11'-0"
30'-0"
17'-4"
32'-4"
STUDS IN ROADWAY
WHITE LINE
TOE OF SWITCH
35'-9"   26'-0"   19'-6"   12'-6"   4'-0"   1'-6"

SCALE: 1/8" To 1 Foot

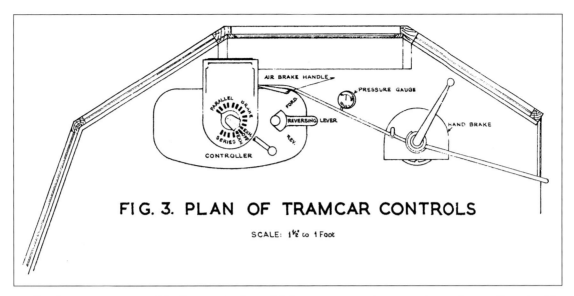

FIG. 3. PLAN OF TRAMCAR CONTROLS

SCALE: 1½" to 1 Foot

perfectly conversant with the controls, which were easy to operate.   According to his account, immediately prior to the accident, he had stopped at the Botannic Gardens' stop and had seen the tram ahead (on service no. 1) go straight over the crossing.   He knew therefore that the points were correctly set for him.   On leaving the stop, he gave the car one notch of power and had then shut off to coast down to the traffic lights, which were at red.   He stopped a short distance from them, and when they turned green he started again with one notch of power.   The tram, however, turned to the right at the points and, before he could take any action, the collision occurred.   Stephenson was quite sure that when he stopped at the traffic lights the points were set for the straight, and he could not account for their subsequent change.

The Brigadier, in his conclusions, said that he was satisfied that the points were in good order and were set for the straight when 292 approached them.   In his opinion the accident was entirely due to the irregular operation of the points by the driver, who must have applied power when the bow collector was on the contactor.   There were three ways in which this could have occurred: (1) after leaving the Botanic Gardens' stop, Stephenson may have shut power off too late, *i.e.* after the front of the tram had passed the triangular stud;   (2) he may have shut off power too soon and then re-applied it when the front of the tram was between this stud and the arrow;   or (3) he may have stopped sufficiently far short (over 16 feet) of the white line for the bow collector to be still on the contactor, and would thus have reversed the points when he applied power on seeing the traffic lights turn to green.

Both the driver and his conductress were inclined to think that they had stopped short of the white line, and since this view was corroborated by the evidence of a pedestrian witness, the Inspector felt that the hypothesis put forward at (3) above was the correct one and that Stephenson had notched up quickly for the straight road without looking at the points.   If he had been more alert, he would still have had time to make a brake application and if he had done so he might have avoided the collision or at least reduced speed very considerably.   Since the conductress fell or jumped from the front platform, the Inspector concluded that, despite her testimony to the contrary, she had been present either on the platform or in the saloon doorway and this might well have distracted the driver's attention at a critical moment.

In his final remarks, the Brigadier observed that tramway facing points, unlike railway points, were not positively locked either in the normal or reverse position. Particular care was always necessary since the close fitting of tramway points could not be guaranteed, and for this reason a 5mph restriction was always imposed. At the time of the accident, there were 71 sets of electrically-operated points on the system. Over the previous five years there had been 205 accidents involving this type of equipment and it was highly desirable that this accident rate should be reduced. In his view, this could be best achieved at locations where turnouts were little used in one direction by installing a contactor in the overhead of the lesser-used route which would reset the points after a car had negotiated the junction. Equipment of this nature had been installed at the London Road/Moir Street junction following an accident there earlier in the year. At the Inspector's request, similar equipment was being installed at the Great Western Road/Byres Road junction. If these arrangements proved to be satisfactory, there were 13 other places where the same arrangements could be put in place and the Inspector recommended the conversion of the points in those locations too. However, it has to be said that even if these arrangements had been in place at the time of the accident, it would appear that they would not have prevented the occurrence of the accident there.

Operator: Glasgow Corporation
Location: Shettleston Road, Glasgow
Date: 28 January 1959

If the British tram did not go out in a blaze of glory, so far as this list of woes is concerned, it went out in a blaze which killed three people and burned or otherwise injured 24 more, badly enough for them to be taken to hospital.

Rather too late to do them much good, tramways had bestirred themselves in getting away from the Victorian concepts and practices of carriage building and design. Nudged and jostled by omnibus competition, enterprising managements began to take advantage of the possibilities of welding, of light-weight metals and plastics. The "Coronation" cars of Glasgow Corporation (they took their name from the coronation of King George VI and Queen Elizabeth in the year of their origin, *viz.* 1937) were vehicles of this "new order". The skeleton or body frame was of steel angle sections, welded to a steel underframe, mounted on two equal-wheel bogies. The steel angles were faced with teak, to which panels of patent "alhambrinal" were secured, the same material being used for the ceiling of both saloons. Another sign of the times was the use of safety glass in all windows around the platforms[134].

For many years tramwaymen had been pleading to be provided with seats, but there was difficulty in so doing while they had to deal with tall controllers requiring fairly heavy physical effort, and needing to put their weight frequently to bear on revolving brake pillars for service stops. Now, with the application of relay-actuated contactors (an adaptation from electric railways), needing only a small easily-manipulated controller and power-brake handle, it became practicable for the driver to sit down. (This improvement was not, of course, confined to Glasgow cars, but wherever it applied, or still applies, a seated tram driver doesn't seem quite "right".) The

---

[134] A car of this type, no. 1173, is on display at the Museum of Transport, Kelvin Hall, Glasgow, and another car of the same type, no. 1282 (the official last car to operate in Glagow, at Clydebank), forms part of the collection of the National Tramway Museum, Crich, Derbyshire.

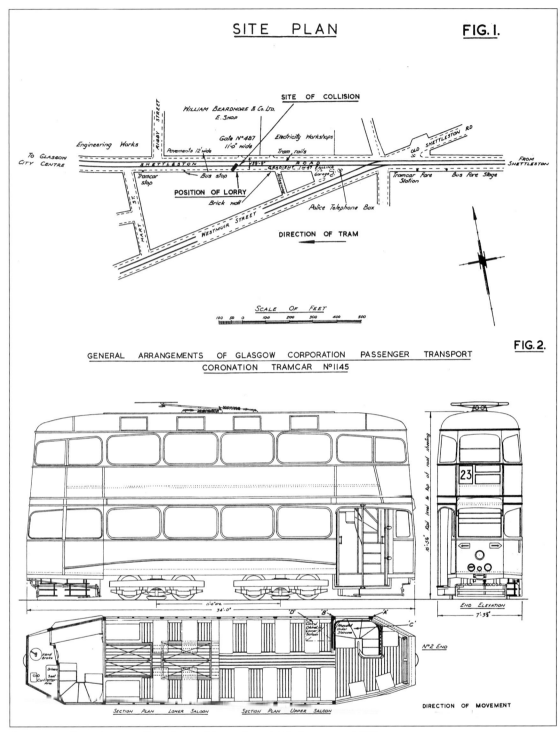

SITE PLAN   FIG.I.

SITE OF COLLISION

WILLIAM BEARDMORE & Co. Ltd.
E. SHOP

Engineering Works   Gate Nº487   Electricity Workshops
                           11'-0" wide
To Glasgow   Tram rails
City Centre   SHETTLESTON   ROAD
                                                        FROM
                                                        SHETTLESTON

Tramcar stop   Bus stop

POSITION OF LORRY   Tramcar Fare   Bus Fare Stage
                           Station
        Brick wall
                      Police Telephone Box

WESTMUIR STREET

DIRECTION OF TRAM

SCALE OF FEET

                                                      FIG.2.

GENERAL ARRANGEMENTS OF GLASGOW CORPORATION PASSENGER TRANSPORT
              CORONATION TRAMCAR Nº1145

END ELEVATION
7'-3⅝"

SECTION PLAN LOWER SALOON   SECTION PLAN UPPER SALOON   DIRECTION OF MOVEMENT

Glasgow, Shettleston Road, accident dated 28 January 1959.

accompanying drawing (Fig 3 on page 185) shows quite clearly at no. 2 end the
presence of the contactor cabinet in the corner of the lower saloon and the rheostat
underneath the staircase.   It should be noted also that the circuit breakers had forsaken
their traditional places on the canopy ceilings and had been relocated under the driver's
seat at each end.

Exactly what happened to Maryhill depot's car no. 1145 at 10.00am on 28 January 1959
in Shettleston will never be known, because the driver was killed in the inferno.   From
the evidence, it is fairly certain that the car was running at normal speed on that cold

184

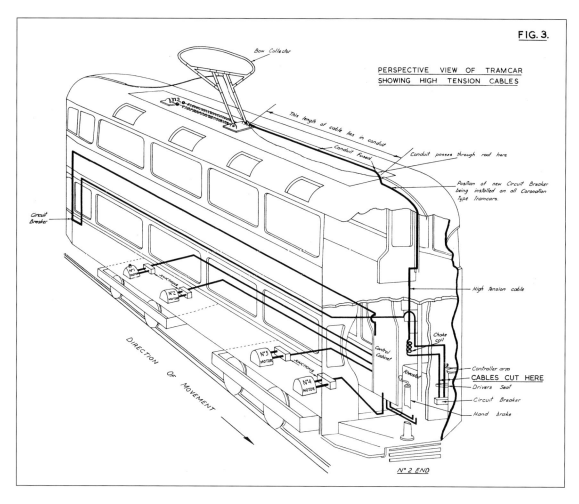

FIG. 3.

PERSPECTIVE VIEW OF TRAMCAR
SHOWING HIGH TENSION CABLES

misty morning, when the driver braked owing to the presence of a lorry foul of the track. He may have assumed that the lorry would get clear and left his brake application until too late, but for whatever reason, the tram failed to stop short of the lorry, but hit it at an angle and drove it into the wall to the left of the footpath. The lorry was a sort of wedge between tram and wall. The impact impaled the tram on to the lorry at the worst possible height, where the electrical vitals of the tram were centred.

The main cables direct from the bow collector were sliced through and the live end short-circuited to earth via the metal frame of the car and its wheels. The intense heat generated by the arc set fire to everything combustible, and exploded the accumulated dust in the control cabinet. Panelling, seats, cable insulations, the hair and clothing of people all caught alight in seconds in the searing heat. The power station recorded an upsurge in current of 1,600-2,000 amps at the time the collision took place. The voltage was 600, so it is easy to calculate that the heat of about 1,000 domestic single bar electric fires was unleashed in a matter of seconds, and passengers tumbled through the acrid smoke and flames to escape, some smashing windows to jump out.

The car was gutted, its glass fused and aluminium melted; the bow collector continuing to feed the arc until the roof collapsed and the bow collector fell. In a case such as this, many questions had to be asked. Why was the lorry there? Why did the tram not stop? Why was current not cut off immediately? Was the car dangerously flammable etc. etc.?

The lorry, a long heavy one, was delivering six scrap steel rollers to William Beardmore and Company's works and, as frequently happened, the driver misjudged the amount of

185

Two photos dramatically depicting Glasgow Coronation car 1145 gutted and still in flames after its collision with a lorry in Shettleston Road, Glasgow, on 28 January 1959. Little of the car body remains beyond the twisted frame, its panelling and window glass having melted and its interior fittings having been consumed. A cloud of black smoke overhangs the scene.   *Courtesy: Newsquest Media Group*

"lock" needed to back through the narrow gateway on the far side of the road. He had gone ahead again and was starting to reverse across the road for the second attempt when he saw the tram approaching. He changed into forward gear to pull clear to let the tram pass, but before he could straighten up, the tram hit the lorry forcing it across the path into the wall. He was out of his cab in a few seconds, but the tram was alight by the time he got to it.

Why did the tram, with all its mod cons in the way of brakes, not stop? It had track brakes applied by compressed air, wheel brakes also employing compressed air, the usual motor-energised magnetic brakes and a hand-operated wheel brake, but this last was intended as a "parking" brake only. There were also two interesting emergency arrangements *viz.* the conductor could apply the air brake, and the magnetic brake applied itself if the equipment in the control cabinet failed. The sanding gear was another unusual feature and was no doubt devised to remedy the shortcomings of the conventional arrangement which, it will be remembered, figured in some of the accidents discussed earlier. By placing the delivery pipes between the bogies, it ensured that, in whichever direction the car was travelling, sand would be dropped ahead of some of the wheels. On one side of the car, sand was blown on to the rail by twisting the air-brake handle – a hand movement like that of inconsiderate young men on motor bikes when they make needless noise revving up. Over the other rail, sand fell by gravity when released by a foot pedal. Both pipes ejected sand automatically from a heavy application of the magnetic brake, but all this galaxy of safeguards failed to stop the car in emergency. Nobody can now know the reason – it can only be conjectured.

It is patently clear that the driver was aware of the impending collision, for he had time to leave his cabin, enter the lower saloon and shout a warning to the passengers to "look out", or it may have been "get out". There is a curious parallel with the tragic crash of the airship R.101. There again, the "bridge" became aware of imminent disaster which they could not prevent as, going aft towards the crew's quarters, the Chief Coxswain said "We're down, lads". Neither he nor the tram driver knew that within seconds their vehicle would be a mass of flames, distorted angles and melting metal.

There would be no reason for the tram driver to anticipate fire and in fact there would have been none if the car had been the other way round, *i.e.* no. 1 end leading. In that event, short-circuiting would have blown the circuit breaker. As it unfortunately occurred at the vulnerable end, the severance of the cable shorted the power before it reached either breaker. Although the current was high – high enough to create an arc which singed the hair and clothing of people several feet away, it was not high enough to trip the breakers at the power station, where the equipment had to deal with the heavier loads needed to cope with the nearby Parkhead depot and the rush hour services through Parkhead Cross. It was a Corporation rule that in the event of fire the bow should be taken off the overhead wire – but how could the conductress, a young woman of 19, do it? Even if she had remembered the rule, this girl could not have climbed the stairs, opened the back window to get hold of the cord, with the upper saloon passengers rapidly bearing down in a heap to escape the inferno[135].

The subsequent inquiry was searching – cables, panelling, seating and dust all being subjected to flammability tests. Colonel McMullen's[136] report noted that these cars were all due to be scrapped within the following three years, so he hardly expected his recommendations to be adopted on all remaining trams in Glasgow, but it was agreed that all Coronations should have an additional circuit breaker in the roof where it was inconceivable that any collision could cause rupture of cables on the "live" side. For

---

[135] A cord attached to the bow collector, led across the roof and through a small window at the end of the upper deck, where it was secured to a hook. The purposes of the cord were to enable the bow to be removed from contact with the overhead wire and to assist in the reversal of the bow when the car changed its direction of travel. If this cord had been extended to the lower deck, as was the practice in other systems (*e.g.* Aberdeen, Leeds and Birmingham), the problem described in the text would not have arisen. This point was not addressed at the inquiry.

[136] Denis McMullen (1902-1973), Inspecting Officer 1948-63, Chief Inspecting Officer of Railways 1963-68.

emergencies, a button would be installed in the driving cabin for tripping the breaker[137].

So ends my story, or should I say, concatenation of stories. To me, it is apt that it finishes in Glasgow, the city where I made my final journey by British tram only a few days before the last withered limb of the atrophied remains of a wonderful tramway died. Writing all this has been a labour of love spread over many hours, and I shall feel satisfied if it gives hours of informative, as well as interesting, reading and that it is a worthwhile contribution to tramway literature.

Operator: Conwy County Borough Council
Location: Upper Passing Loop, Great Orme's Head
Date: 30 April 2000

(In the absence of a published report on this accident, this account has been compiled by J D Markham, who was the Railway Inspector who carried out the investigation into it. It is published with the kind permission of the Health & Safety Executive.)

This century-year old tramway has a technology which is unique in the British Isles. It has also managed to survive (along with the Blackpool system) from the first generation of tramways, despite the serious accident that occurred in 1932 (*qv*) which led to its closure for 20 months. The undertaking was acquired by Llandudno Urban District Council in 1948 and remains under municipal control, although the UDC has been absorbed into Conwy County Borough Council.

The line is cable-operated throughout and works in two distinct sections, known as upper and lower, of roughly equal length, with a winding house at a place appropriately called Halfway, forming the meeting, but separation, of the two sections. This separation is also one of technology, perhaps not appreciated by the casual observer, but it is of great importance and significance regarding safety of the operation. Braking of the tramcars, cable handling (by drum and pulley systems) and driving techniques (by the winding machine operator) are unique to each section, and problems on one section often do not necessarily impact on the other. Each section has a mid-point passing loop (known locally as a pass-by) where pairs of cars meet and pass, interlaced or single track being used elsewhere. All points have a toggle action.

Apart from the "sledge" brake on the lower section referred to in connection with the 1932 accident[138], both upper and lower sections have two other brakes which are part of the winding machinery. For general use the "service" brake is a manually-applied band brake, controlled by the winchman, which acts on a drum of similar diameter to the flanges of the cable spools, and is located between them. This brake is used to assist in controlling the speed of the cars, as a parking brake and as a means of ensuring a jerk-free start. It is applied by means of a screw mechanism.

To cater for the need for an immediate brake application, a "thruster" brake[139] is fitted between the electric driving motor and the gearbox, through which the power is taken mechanically to the cable drums. The brake works on the output shaft of the driving motor, which is fitted with a cylinder. The cylinder piston rod, when forced out, acts to apply the brake. The outward force is provided by a spring forming part of the cylinder

Car 5 of the Great Orme Tramway, Llandudno, on 14 March 2003, undergoing an annual brake test.   On the step is Dr Mervyn Thomas of HM Railway Inspectorate, with Neil Jones, the General Manager, on the platform.   *M C Crabtree*

assembly, which acts on the piston rod.   Release of the brake is achieved by electrical energisation of a solenoid coil within the cylinder, which drives the piston rod back in against the force of the spring.   It is fail safe: any fault which interrupts the current holding the piston rod back causes the brake to be applied with full force, arresting drum rotation and cable winding quickly.   Simultaneously power to the winding motor is shut off.   Facility is given to the winchman to initiate the thruster-brake action, but it is also triggered by an emergency signal from either car on the section.   Details as to how this signal has been transmitted are given in further paragraphs below.

When I first travelled on the line in 1953, the steam winding engines were still in use (they were converted to electricity later in the decade) and communication between trams and the winding house was by hand-cranked magneto telephones on each car: proof that car 'phones were introduced to North Wales in 1902, but only on tramcars!   The telephones were replaced by a private mobile radio system around 1990, and the previous emergency stop button on the "driver's" canopy replaced by a button-initiated coded signal sent over the radio link.   Different codes were used for the two sections of the line so that the correct winding machine could be stopped if necessary.   The radio system had

---

[137] The alterations were also made to cars of the later "Cunarder" class using equipment, suitably-modified, taken from scrapped standard cars.

[138] See footnote no. 117 *supra* for a description of this brake.

[139] The term "thruster" is derived from the motion of a piston associated with a cylinder assembly which governs the application of the brake in the manner described in the text.   This brake is also used as a parking brake after power to the driving motors has been shut off in normal operation.

its own problems, not all of which were apparent at inception, but these were later to show themselves[140].

It was the practice on both sections for the tramcar drivers (I use this term, rather than brakesmen) to announce progress of the journey to their respective winchman at significant points on the route, which in many cases were warning of approach to, and later successful passage past, particular hazards.   At busy times, when both sections of the line were running simultaneously, the two winchmen would be listening for reports which related to one or other of them coming over the radio.   On one occasion, a motor car obstructed passage of a downward car on the street part of the lower section and the driver asked that the speed be reduced with the possibility of a stop being required. Unfortunately, this request coincided with one of the regular announcements of progress on the upper section and this jammed his signal.   The descending car did not slow or stop as became necessary, and collided with the motor car, jamming it against a stone wall. This resulted in separate radio channels being introduced for the two sections.

We now come to the accident of 2000, which unlike that of 1932, occurred on the upper section of the tramway rather than the lower.   At the close of the preceding season, the inspecting engineer from the Council's insurance underwriter had drawn attention to the condition of the pointwork at the upper section pass-by.   He recommended that remedial action was required to address excessive looseness and the deteriorating condition of some of the sleepers.   The problems had not reached the stage of being hazardous to traffic, but he considered it would be prudent to undertake the work.

The Council took heed and, rather than carry out remedial work, which would have been of limited life, they decided to put out a contract for the points and trackwork in question to be relaid with new materials.   The contract went to a commercial track-laying company based in South Wales and a consultant engineering company which had local offices in nearby Colwyn Bay.   It is a very sad and disturbing reflection on British industry and engineering consultancy at the time that such a praiseworthy effort on the part of the Council in this regard was so grievously rewarded.

Ten days before the operating season was due to commence, it was found by two representatives of the insurance underwriters and, later the same day, by two HM Railway Inspectors (one of whom was myself) that the brand new track, and points in particular, had been laid in a manner totally incompatible with cable operation.   Yet the consultants had submitted a certificate of completion and declared the line ready for use.

Work to address the worst problems was put in hand immediately, but the results could only be described as barely tolerable when the tramway opened at the intended date, immediately before the Easter weekend.   The line then worked in this fashion for a few weeks, with problems being dealt with as they arose.   Towards the end of the week prior to the May Day bank holiday problems came to light with the points at the lower end of the pass-by.   Occasionally there was a tendency for them not to complete their throw, or even to revert to their previous position, after the passage of a descending car.

This was noticed by drivers, who accordingly made a special point of checking the indication given by a mechanical point indicator located in advance of the lower end of the pass-by, which displayed a flag to approaching trams proceeding in the upward direction.   The flag operated so as to display the number of the car for the direction for which the points were set (car 6 always taking the northern (seaward) track and car 7 always taking the southern (highway) track). Cars were stopped and the points properly set when there was doubt.

Whilst this was an inconvenience on the Saturday of the bank holiday, it was realised that it would be far less tolerable on the Sunday and Monday, when much heavier traffic was anticipated. It was accordingly decided that it would be beneficial to have a man stationed by the points to ensure that they were set correctly for uphill tramcars on these two days, after which contractor's staff could attend to make adjustments on the Tuesday. Since all tramway personnel were fully committed at this busy time, a man from the Highways Department's site security team was drafted in for this purpose. He was given a chair and taken to the troublesome points by one of the tramway technical team. There the features of the points and their "tumbler" mechanism were pointed out and it was explained to him what he was required to do.

So the tramway started running for the bank holiday Sunday. All went well throughout the morning, but went sadly wrong during the early afternoon. At that time car 6 was descending from the summit and car 7 had left the Halfway station and winding house. The driver of car 7 had just returned from his meal break and was making his first journey of the afternoon. As is usual, the descending car reached the points of the upper end of the pass-by some time before the ascending car reached those at the lower end. Car 6 was thus fully into its side of the pass-by (the north side) before car 7 entered the lower points. Car 7 also entered the north side of the pass-by and its driver did not realise anything was wrong until he noticed his haulage cable jumping off its pulleys ahead and increasingly to the left. (Unlike the lower section in street, which has the cable operating in conduit, the cable of the upper section is uncovered.) He then saw he was approaching car 6 on the same track!

Both drivers immediately radioed "emergency stop" to the winding house but, as before with the motor car incident on the lower section, they jammed each other's transmissions. The pass-by is in full view of the winch operator, but since his viewpoint is mainly side on, with little lateral perspective, he got no warning of the collision until cables suddenly became tight and began displacing "top-hat" pulleys from their mounts. By then 6 and 7 had been well and truly brought into abrupt contact.

It appears that the emergency stop signal did, at a late stage, shut off winding power and cause the thruster brake to bring the winding drums quickly to rest. But on the upper section of the line this action does not of itself stop the cars; indeed it is unlikely that it will do so immediately unless conditions are favourable as they are when the cars are arriving at the terminals. This perhaps surprising state of affairs arises from a combination of physical and dynamic factors not immediately apparent to the casual observer, but it has to be known and understood by the winchman and drivers of cars 6 and 7. It is crucial in the operation of the upper section that all three work as a team exercising skills of control unique to the section, and is the significant technical difference between upper and lower halves of the tramway.

---

[140] The previous system had employed an overhead wire, closely resembling an overhead electric conductor wire, and each car was equipped with two trolley poles to provide contact with the wire. With the adoption of the radio system, the overhead wire was gradually dismantled and the trolley poles, while remaining on the cars, were permanently stowed under retaining hooks at the canopy ends.

It should be noted that the winding machinery is installed at the lower end of the section and that there is a separate cable, with its own drum, from it to each car. But the two drums on which the cables are wound or unwound are on the same shaft and so rotate at the same rpm. At the start of a run the drum winding in is almost empty, whilst that for the car departing from Halfway station is very full, with several layers of cable. There is therefore a difference in the rate of paying out and winding in, resulting from the difference in diameter between empty and full spools. These differences in rate change during the run, as the layers of cable held on each drum change.

Two slack compensators are installed at the winding house, one for each cable, each comprising a heavy counterweight and multiple cable sheaves which fall and rise in a vertical pit shaft to absorb and release the resulting slack. The greatest slack absorbed by the counterweight system occurs at the mid-point of the wind as the tramcars are negotiating the pass-by. So while the haulage may cease, the dynamic effects resulting from gravity and relative gradient, relative passenger loadings and momentum do not. To add to the complexity, the relative gradients vary as the journey progresses. Once winding has stopped, both cars continue to run freely as the slack compensator starts to pay out and absorb, resulting in changing the total slack from one counterweight to the other, from uphill to downhill side. It may not have been obvious to the two drivers that winding had ceased and that they were running free as the cables ahead of them would have appeared to have been running normally. It would have taken very prompt action by the drivers of cars 6 and 7, each applying their wheel and track brakes, to have stood any chance of avoiding collision during this short free-running period. Time and distance were not on their side.

Ambulances and police were quickly called to the scene. All passengers and the crew were severely shaken. There were about 40 people on each car and 17 of them suffered injury. Fortunately, none was found to be seriously injured.

By one of those strange coincidences which sometimes happen, one of the local residents observed the dramatic scene in the wake of the accident, and telephoned the news to her daughter, who chanced to work in a secretarial capacity in the Manchester office of the Railway Inspectorate. The latter lady then immediately telephoned me, so that I became aware of the accident about two or three hours before being notified of it through formal channels. By arrangement with the tramway management and North Wales police, the two trams were secured at the scene until I, together with a colleague, could attend the following morning, which was of course the bank holiday Monday. At an early stage we were confronted by the local press, whose prime question was "How long will it be before the trams are running again?" I could only respond that it was far too early to hazard an estimate as to when this might be. I did, however, make the point that there was no reason why the lower section should not continue to operate normally since the accident could not be reproduced there because its cable slot system would prevent this.

The task then began to assemble the evidence to ascertain the cause of the accident. It will have been appreciated that car 7 had been mis-routed by the points at the lower end of the pass-by, but the question arose as to why this should have been so when there was an attendant present at the points, a point indicator, a driver on 7's leading platform and an approach speed of only 4mph.

The driver of car 7 gave evidence that as he approached the points they were set correctly for him, and he passed a radio message to say so. Evidence from the winchman confirmed that he had received the message from car 7's driver via the radio that the points were set correctly. The only other witness was the point attendant. His evidence was quite straightforward. He had been present at the points since the morning. He had not interfered with them on the occasion of car 7's previous passage through them. He could not explain how car 7 had taken the wrong route on this last occasion.

Faced with the fact that the evidence was unchallengable that there had been a wrong routing, it was clearly necessary to go more deeply into the reasons why those involved said, apparently independently and with reasonable conviction, all was well immediately prior to the mishap.

Evidence from the tramway's technical man, who had explained to the point attendant what he had to do, proved helpful. He had shown the attendant the points and their mechanism and had warned him of the danger of derailment which could occur if the appropriate moving blade was not held firmly in contact with its stock rail when trams went through in the facing direction. This danger was demonstrated by showing how the points could stick part way through the throw from one setting to the other, and if that were to happen it was the attendant's job to move the blade hard up against the stock rail. This he was sure the attendant understood, but there were no trams running when it was explained and the attendant was alone when the first car went through.

The attendant confirmed that he had had this instruction, which must have been effective since no derailment had occurred. But, on being asked how he knew which way the points were set as far as routing was concerned, he became less sure. He said he made no claim to have tramway or railway knowledge and knew only what he had been told to do. He could not read points, but did not have to be able to do so as the drivers did this and they knew from the indicating flag which way the points were set. His hand signal to a driver merely confirmed that the blade was home against the stock rail and not the setting of the points.

The driver of car 7 was almost as raw as the attendant. He had been taken on at the start of the season and, whilst he had been trained on both sections, he had spent most of his service time on the lower section. He knew the importance of checking points on the lower section as there was no point indicator there and only a short, narrow, single blade to look for. That had been his first day as a service driver on the upper section, where the track was open and the points were quite different: for one thing, they had the indicator flags which he always checked. He knew that there was some difficulty with the lower end points and that an attendant had been stationed there to supervise them and signal that all was well. This had been the case all the morning, when he had been driving car 6, up to the time that he had gone for his meal break. Asked if he had checked the setting of the point indicator flag on the fateful trip, he said that he was unable to see the flag because where the point attendant was stationed was in his line of sight of the flag. But he took the attendant's hand signal to mean that the points were as they should be and they looked all right to him. In fact they probably looked just the same as they had all morning – but he was now on car 7, not 6, which of course used the opposite side of the loop.

Whilst the sticking point mechanism contributed to the accident, the action of stationing a man by the points should have taken care of this. The root problem was one of staff training. Both the man at the points and the driver on board car 7 did not appreciate the subtleties of the tasks with which they were charged; and those who had trained and passed them had not appreciated this. In view of the seriousness of the accident to the two trams and the number of casualties, a prohibition notice was issued preventing further operation of the upper section of the line until the issue of staff training had been satisfactorily addressed. The notice was in due course lifted when the formal training and appraisal systems, together with the associated records, met the requirements of the relevant Regulations.

Since the accident much other refurbishment has taken place. Most noticeable has been the total rebuilding of the Halfway station and winding house. There is now undercover transfer for passengers (welcome on the more boisterous weather days on the Orme) with displays featuring the history and technical features of the line. There is also an innovative cable-management system to bring one of the lower section cars into the workshop at the end of the day. The private mobile radio system has been replaced by a leaky feeder system giving every car its own communication link with the winding house, so that signal jamming should now be a thing of the past. The line recently celebrated its centenary and is now well-equipped to face its second without any of its unique operational charm having been lost.

APPENDIX A

Accidents listed alphabetically by location, with corresponding details of operators, dates and fatality numbers

Location	*Operator*	*Date*	*No. of deaths*
Accrington	Rawtenstall Corporation	1911, 11 November	-
Barnsley	Barnsley & District E T Co	1914, 2 December	2
Bath	Bath Electric Tramways	1933, 3 July	2
Birmingham:			
Camp Hill	City of B'ham Tmys Co	1898, 2 February	-
Holyhead Road	South Staffordshire Tmys Co	1922, 10 December	-
Saltley Road	Birmingham Corporation	1935, 12 December	-
Warstone Lane	Birmingham Corporation	1907, 1 October	2
Bournemouth	Bournemouth Corporation	1908, 1 May	7
Blackburn	Darwen Corporation	1941, 20 September	-
Bradford:			
Allerton Road	Bradford Corporation	1918, 1 February	1
Church Bank	Bradford Corporation	1907, 31 July	-
Five Lane Ends	Bradford Corporation	1921, 3 February	-
Great Horton Road	Bradford Corporation	1898, 19 September	2
Burnley	Burnley Corporation	1919, 28 November	-
Burton-upon-Trent:			
Bearwood Hill	Midland Railway	1919, 8 October	2
Station Street	Burton-upon-Trent Corpn	1921, 3 November	-
Carshalton	Southmet	1907, 1 April	2
Chatham	Chatham & District Lt Ry Co	1902, 30 October	4
Dartford	Bexley Council	1919, 5 February	-
Darwen	Darwen Corporation	1926, 20 September	2
Devonport	Devonport & District T Co	1914, 27 November	3
Dewsbury	Yorkshire (WD) E Tmys Co	1904, 20 May	-
Dover	Dover Corporation	1917, 19 August	11
Dublin	Dublin United Tramways	1914, 1 February	1
Dudley	Dudley, Strbdge & D E T Co	1920, 29 November	-
Edinburgh	Edinburgh Corporation	1925, 26 February	-
Eltham – see London (Eltham)			
Enfield	MET	1929, 11 December	8
Glasgow:			
Great Western Road	Glasgow Corporation	1955, 11 July	2
High Street	Glasgow Corporation	1908, 3 January	2
Kingston Street	Glasgow Corporation	1953, 30 March	-
Queen's Drive	Glasgow Corporation	1917, 5 December	3
Renfield Street	Glasgow Corporation	1902, 6 September	-
Shettleston Road	Glasgow Corporation	1959, 28 January	3
Glyn Ceiriog	Glyn Valley Tramway Co	1874, 19 December	-

Location	Operator	Date	No. of deaths
Halifax:			
Bull Green	Halifax Corporation	1920, 23 November	1
Horton Street	Halifax Corporation	1904, 14 October	-
Lee Bridge	Halifax Corporation	1915, 22 May	-
North Bridge	Halifax Corporation	1906, 1 July	2
Pye Nest Road	Halifax Corporation	1907, 15 October	5
Huddersfield:			
Leech's Hill	Huddersfield Corporation	1938, 4 October	-
Somerset Road	Huddersfield Corporation	1902, 28 June,	3
Westgate	Huddersfield Corporation	1883, 3 July	7
Lancaster	Lancaster Corporation	1920, 27 September	1
Leeds:			
Churwell Hill	Leeds Corporation	1923, 12 May	7
Oakwood	Leeds Corporation	1952, 4 September	-
Liverpool:			
Leece Street	Liverpool Corporation	1906, 22 January	-
Paddington	Liverpool Corporation	1934, 3 January	3
Llandudno:			
Great Orme's Head	Conwy Council	2000, 30 April	-
Old Road	Great Orme Tramway Co	1932, 23 August	2
London:			
Archway	MET	1906, 23 June	3
Eltham	LPTB	1934, 25 March	-
Dog Kennel Hill	LCC	1925, 31 July	-
Highgate Hill	Highgate Hill Tramways Co	1884, 31 July	-
Highgate Hill	Highgate Hill Tramways Co	1885, 8 January	-
Pancras Road	LCC	1919, 16 August	1
Shardeloes Road	LCC	1911, 2 September	1
Maidstone	Maidstone Corporation	1939, 7 August	-
Manchester	Manchester Corporation	1914, 25 February	-
Millbrook:			
Ditchcroft Hill	SHMD	1904, 11 October	1
Ditchcroft Hill	SHMD	1911, 5 June	1
Morley – see Leeds (Churwell Hill)			
Mossley	SHMD	1911, 20 October	6
Newcastle-under-Lyme	Potteries Electric Traction Co	1922, 6 September	-
Newcastle upon Tyne	Newcastle Corporation	1913, 21 June	-
New Silksworth	Sunderland District El Twys	1907, 29 July	-
North Shields:			
Borough Road	Tynemouth & Dist.El Trmys	1919, 27 September	-
Borough Road	Tynemouth & Dist.El Trmys	1921, 31 July	5
Old Brompton – see Chatham			
Outlane – see Huddersfield (Leech's Hill)			
Pemberton – see Wigan			
Pontypridd	Pontypridd Council	1920, 22 March	-
Ramsgate:			
Belle Vue Road	Isle of Thanet El Ty & Lg Co	1903, 12 August	-
Madeira Hill	Isle of Thanet El Ty & Lg Co	1905, 3 August	-

Location	Operator	Date	No. of deaths
Rochdale	Rochdale Corporation	1914, 14 February	-
Rowley Regis	Birmingham & Midland Tys	1908, 20 February	2
Scarborough	Scarborough Tramways Co	1925, 16 September	-
Smethwick	Birmingham Corporation	1911, 1 October	1
Sowerby Bridge – see Halifax (Pye Nest Road)			
Spen Valley – see Dewsbury			
Stoke-on-Trent – see Newcastle-under-Lyme			
Swindon	Swindon Corporation	1906, 1 June	5
Tynemouth – see North Shields			
Wakefield	Yorkshire (WR) El Trmys Co	1920, 29 January	1
West Bromwich	South Staffordshire Tmys Co	1906, 5 May	1
Wigan	Wigan Tramways Co	1883, 29 December	

APPENDIX B

Brief details of noteworthy Railway Inspectorate inquiries not available from HSE sources and culled from trade journals

Date: 1895, 26 August
Location: Bushmills
Operator: Giant's Causeway, Portrush & Bush Valley Railway & Tramway Co
Nature: Cyclist electrocuted when falling on conductor rail
Inspector: Major Cardew
Deaths: 1
Source: *The Electrical Review* vol 37 p 541

Date: 1902, 21 February
Location: Albert Road, Devonport
Operator: Devonport & District Tramways Co
Nature: Runaway and derailment caused by absence of sand; car 18
Inspector: Major Pringle
Deaths: 0
Source: *The Electrician* vol XLVII p 474

Date: 1904, 19 January
Location: Thorncliffe Road/Track Road junction, Batley
Operator: Yorkshire (Woollen District) Electric Tramways Co
Nature: Excessive speed causing derailment; car 55
Inspector: Major Druitt
Deaths: 0
Source: *Light Railway and Tramway Journal* vol X p 142

Date: 1915, 3 September
Location: Alexandra Road South/Wilbraham Road junction, Manchester
Operator: Manchester Corporation Tramways
Nature: Car overturned owing to excessive speed in blackout
Inspector: Colonel von Donop
Deaths: 0
Source: *The Tramways and Light Railways Association Journal* 1915 p 1386

Date: 1915, 12 November
Location: Victoria Road/Lichfield Road junction, Aston, Birmingham
Operator: Birmingham Corporation Tramways
Nature: Car derailed after runaway owing to faulty application of brakes
Inspector: Major Druitt
Deaths: 3
Source: *The Electric Railway and Tramway Journal* vol XXXIII pp 270 and 309, vol XXXIV p 42

Date:	1917, 29 July
Location:	Ford Hill, Queensbury
Operator:	Halifax Corporation Tramways
Nature:	Runaway down hill, derailment and overturning; possible brake failure
Inspector:	Colonel Druitt
Deaths:	0
Source:	*The Electric Railway and Tramway Journal* vol XXXVII pp 29 and 30

APPENDIX C

A review by John D Markham of the causes of the accident at
Stamford Road, Mossley, on 20 October 1911

I FIRST heard of this disaster as a boy with a developing interest in tramways from my father who remembered the incident and the stir to which it gave rise in the local community. Over 30 years ago, while working as a control engineer for GEC Traction, I found reference at Trafford Park to the similar runaway accident in Bournemouth (*qv*) in notes about British Westinghouse type 90 controllers. Knowing that SHMD used type 90, or their 90M derivative, exclusively, I wondered if similar reasons for the incidents could have occurred.

On reading the BoT report concerning Mossley, I was pleased to see that exactly the same point had been identified by Lt-Colonel von Donop, the investigating Inspector (his report is copied at page 215). Indeed he states that in his opinion the most probable cause of the Mossley incident was a failure of the magnetic brake due to a fault in a controller. Due to the very extensive damage to equipment, including both controllers, it was said to be not possible to produce evidence to prove this point. But it had been possible to investigate further at Bournemouth, comments about which were in the notes at Trafford Park, the salient points of which have been in my mind since I read them.

The BoT investigation by Major Pringle into the runaway at Bournemouth, where the tramcar was not damaged so severely as that at Mossley, showed that the reverse drums in the rear controller were out of position. This, according to the Trafford Park notes, was identified as being because the mechanism was worn to the extent that the reverse barrel was not in its correct, central position when the reverse handle was removed. The reverse handle on type 90 controllers does not set the position of the reverser. It (quite literally) selects "forward" or "reverse" gear.

The reverser was found not in the neutral position, as it should have been, but was in reverse and so corresponded to the front controller for forward motoring, an effect not immediately apparent, as, when driven from the other end, the tram would be able to start quite normally. But in braking the result would have been catastrophic. The combined effect of the two reverser shafts being in opposition, when braking was called for, was the short-circuiting of both motor armatures preventing them from generating and exciting their fields. Electric braking could never become established in these circumstances. Had the failure been in the opposite sense, it would not have been possible to obtain traction – a "right-side" failure.

But an out-of-position reverse shaft in the rear controller was not the only fault which could have created no brake response. The same would have resulted if the reverse shaft in the front controller had not changed over fully when braking was required. Had it stuck in the centre ("off") position, the armatures would have been connected to nothing. Current would not have been produced and no retardation achieved. Colonel von

Donop's conclusion that electric brake failure was very likely caused by a fault with a controller is therefore most probably true. But many accidents occur, or are made worse, by the coincidence of more than one unrelated events.

With this in mind, let us now turn our attention to the hand brake and its failure to check the speed of the car. The evidence from the driver was that after starting away from Stamford Road, Brookbottom, he was never able to get retardation from the hand brake, and possibly thought that the wheels were picking up and sliding whenever he applied the brakes. He is reported to have repeatedly released the hand brake and re-applied it, with sand, all the way down the hill. Colonel von Donop's report states that in his view this may well have happened, and thought this was because the speed was too high when the driver started to use the hand brake, causing the wheels to skid. But there were no signs of flats found on the wheels. The Colonel appears to have accepted that the hand brake was functional, but applied inappropriately, lack of flats being explained by skidding of very short duration.

What other evidence exists nearly a hundred years after the event? At least two photographs of the recovery operation have been published. Reproduced here as photograph (1) is an illustration which appeared in *SHMD Board*[141], while the second, photograph (2) (which it is important to note is taken from the opposite direction from photograph (1)), appeared in the memoirs of A G Grundy[142], latterly general manager of SHMD Tramways/Transport. Both pictures show the truck upside down on the railway track, the second clearly taken after the winching and slewing operation underway in the first had been completed. But there is one significant difference between the state of the truck as illustrated in the photographs. In photograph (1), the braking equipment can clearly be seen, whereas in photograph (2), *the entire brake equipment is missing*. Why should this be? The equipment would not have been in the way of the recovery process up to that stage. I have seen no reference to its removal as part of the recovery process in any text on the subject. But its removal would have ensured that the good Colonel would not have been able to see it in its true accident configuration.

The time from the moment of derailment to coming to rest on the railway track with the body totally destroyed can only have been a matter of seconds. I would estimate five or less. As an example, the leading lifeguard is likely to have been one of the first casualties by the effect of its hitting the kerb and the lower course of stones in the railway boundary wall. At the estimated speed attained by the runaway, 60mph, the whole lifeguard would have been destroyed in about one fifth of a second. In the time taken to read this paragraph the entire tram would have been demolished.

From photograph (1), it can be seen that an intact lifeguard tray still existed on the end of the car nearest the camera. No traces of lifeguard are visible at the far end. The end with the tray remaining must thus have been at the rear of the car because the leading lifeguard would have been smashed to pieces on its impact at high speed with the kerb and the lower course of stones in the wall of the railway. The tram cannot therefore have

[141] *British Bus, Tram & Trolleybus Systems number 12: Stalybridge, Hyde, Mossley & Dukinfield Tramways & Electricity Board*, by W G S Hyde and Eric Ogden, published by Transport Publishing Co Ltd, Glossop, 1990, at p 27.
[142] *My Fifty Years in Transport*, by Anthony George Grundy, republished by Adam Gordon, Chetwode, 1997, at p 31.

(1) The upturned truck from SHMD car 24 on the railway track at Mossley station. The area of particular interest for the purposes of the text has been shown outlined.

Courtesy: W G S Hyde

"somersaulted" (end over end) as has been stated by Grundy, but rolled to its left down the side of the cutting.

There is a very curious feature illustrated in photograph (1). So much so that one of the men at the distant end is pointing to it whilst in discussion with others nearby. The subject of discussion appears to be the brake beam operating lever at the leading end of the truck, which is protruding in a way which would not have been expected. It looks as though it may have been bent so as to be pointing almost vertically upwards. Again, why should this have been the case and how could it have come about?

On most 4-wheel trucks, the hand-brake operating lever normally lies laterally across the car from the centre of the brake beams, where it is pivoted in two places and secured, towards the right side where the local hand-brake staff is situated. The action of applying the hand brake is to pull on this lever, which typically then moves through an angle of about 10° to 25° to apply the wheel brakes. It is still dominantly transverse to the car. On hitting an obstruction, one would have expected it to have been pushed back towards the release position. This is not compatible with the scene depicted by the photograph. Compare this scene with the rear-end brake beams, where I think the lever can just be seen below the brake rod, neatly tucked in and parallel to the brake beams. It certainly does not protrude. This, incidentally, strongly suggests that the hand brake was not applied at the rear of the car, and confirms Colonel von Donop's conclusion on this point.

The presumption derived from all this is that one or other of the brake beam lever pivot pins at the leading end of the car was missing or broken, and allowed the brake lever to swing forward ineffectively when pulled by the hand-brake staff chain. In this position,

(2) This photograph, at the same scene, was taken after the previous one and views the truck from the opposite direction.

Courtesy: W G S Hyde

it might well have been aligned so that it would dig in as the car hit the side of the cutting. It could thus get bent downwards into the ground as the kinetic energy of the tram continued to propel it forward. The truck would then have turned over, and downwards would have become upwards. Even if the lever is still in the horizontal plane in photograph (1), its orientation is quite abnormal for brakes in proper adjustment. It has to be borne in mind that bending the lever downwards would be bending it "on the flat" but for forward would require it to have been bent on the edge. The latter occurrence would have been unlikely in the course of the accident.

The accident occurred at about 5.30am on 20 October and although the BoT order to Colonel von Donop to carry out the investigation was issued on the same day, even if he had been able to leave London immediately, it is highly unlikely that he would have been able to reach Mossley from London in less than six hours. It is highly improbable, therefore, that the Colonel was able to visit the scene before the wreckage had been moved. Almost certainly there would have been sufficient time for the debris to have been moved off the railway and the railway service reopened. The Joint Board would clearly have wished to minimise the time that the tram was obstructing the railway so as to minimise the amount of any claims for compensation by the LNWR. The Colonel's investigations would thus be dependent on statements made to him by witnesses and their answers to any questions which he might have posed. His report lays stress on "so little evidence available". Could more, vital, evidence have existed which was withheld from him? Would any individual have a motive for doing this?

There is a reasonable probability that Colonel von Donop suspected that such evidence had been concealed from him, but without proof, he could only report the facts of his findings. That withholding of evidence, or even false witness, did occur in accident investigations is illustrated by the case of a derailment of an express train at Witham in 1905. In that case, the investigating officer was also Colonel von Donop.

Let us return to the matter of the hand brake. For it to have been ineffective, loss or breakage of the brake lever pivot pin must have occurred near the beginning of the journey down Stamford Road. In either eventuality, it is likely that the pin, or part of the pin, fell into the roadway in that vicinity. Let us postulate that night foreman Parry, at the adjacent Mossley tram shed and substation, was alerted at an early stage to the occurrence of the runaway and agreed to attend the scene. Knowing that he himself had adjusted the brakes on car 24 overnight, as noted in the BoT report, it is quite possible that before going down to the railway station he went first to Brookbottom, searching the track in the process. Human nature being what it is, suggests that he would want to take possession of any evidence that could implicate him of possible negligence. Were there a pin, or part of a pin, on the track, then it is likely that Parry would have found it, not necessarily being aware of its relevance at that time.

In attendance at Mossley Station with the Chief Engineer was A G Grundy, since 1907 Superintendent of SHMD's Park Road depot and workshop, Stalybridge, and the person in overall charge of the rolling stock. He would no doubt have been concerned as no. 24 had undergone a thorough overhaul in the works only two months' prior to the incident, where the entire braking system "had been rebuilt as good as a new car". In these circumstances, one would not be surprised for new pivot pins to have been installed. In photograph (1), it is believed to be Grundy himself who stands with his right foot on the rail. It is perhaps Parry who is doing the pointing.

What if any new pins fitted were not of the correct material? Mountain & Gibson, who built the trucks, had gone out of business. The SHMD tramways were consistently losing money, which suggests they may have been looking for ways of cutting costs. It is possible that pins were obtained which were of the wrong composition, and whose heat treatment (if any) had not produced the correct combination of ductility, hardness, toughness and resistance to shear required for their duty. BS5750 regarding quality control systems was many decades in the future. It is a great pity that the Inspector does not appear to have recorded any enquiries in these directions.

As stated above, in the short time between the taking of photograph (1) and photograph (2), the brake equipment had been removed. Furthermore, how convenient it was for the equipment to have been "too badly damaged in the accident to prevent a test being carried out on its effectiveness". One can be reasonably confident that when the components had been straightened out and reassembled on the truck (doubtless with any missing components carefully replaced) it would work as it should. Grundy's memoirs, published in 1944, says that after the BoT inquiry "the service hand brake was afterwards found to be in good order"[143], a point on which the Colonel's report is conspicuously silent.

With the passage of time, any information tucked away in people's minds will have been carried with them to the grave, but they then would be answerable elsewhere, and to a judge who had all the evidence. As a churchgoer, Grundy should have known this.

---

[143] *Op cit* at p 32.

APPENDIX D

Commentary by John D Markham on Lieutenant-Colonel Edward Druitt's report on the accident at Rawtenstall on 11 November 1911

THE true extent of the problems that existed in connection with this accident does not appear to have been established by the report (which is reproduced on page 212). There are a number of factors which do not seem to have been taken into account.

In accordance with the then standard BoT rules for tramcar equipment, there should have been "an emergency switch provided for the driver by which he may cut off the current in the event of failure of the controller". No reference is made to this in the report, nor to the lack of its use by the driver (Cuff) or the inspector (Slattery). This could point to a possible weakness in the training of tramway staff by both Rawtenstall and Accrington Corporations.

Colonel Druitt does not appear to have appreciated the difference between a shunt coil and a shunt winding. He uses the term "coil" when "winding" is implied by the text of his report. There would be four coils in series, one per pole, forming the winding. The failure would have been at one of the coil connections, of which there would have been several in series per motor. I have doubts that all of them (or indeed any) could have been seen adequately by the form of inspection that the fitter (Thompson) undertook. He could truthfully say that he had not seen a fault when he examined the motor. But a question such as "Can you say for sure that all shunt coil connections were in good order?" might have been much more difficult for him to have answered.

The presence of two motors meant that there would have been twice as many internal shunt coil connections per car equipment, which across the country as a whole could have brought the total to several hundred. Up to the time of the Rawtenstall incident, these, by implication, had survived without a problem. Perhaps other cases had occurred elsewhere, but none of these had resulted in disaster, nor had the potential for disaster been realised. The importance of the analysis of near-miss incidents cannot be over-emphasised.

It is interesting to note that the first sign of the incident took place just as car 14 entered the single line. This raises the question whether the sudden jerk at that location, perhaps caused by negotiation of the points, contributed to the final break of the shunt field connection to the motor concerned. It must be a possibility, although I accept that the connection must already have been weak: a classic case of fatigue failure. Were any shunt coils loose on their poles?

Colonel Druitt was clearly a humane person, perhaps covertly anxious that neither Cuff nor Thompson should be dismissed over the incident, for which he may deserve some credit. Certainly he probed the incident sufficiently deeply to establish that he had a route to put the cause down simply to a failure in equipment – which by then would have been well out of warranty.

Colonel Druitt's opinion about the unsuitability of regenerative equipment for hilly routes is, I feel, unfair and far too sweeping. If the Johnson-Lundell Company (with whose regenerative braking system, according to Robert Rush, about half of Rawtenstall's fleet was equipped[144]) had still been active, they could have seriously challenged his statement. With their system, it was always possible for the driver to return his controller to "off" without causing the car to decelerate – simply by not selecting to use the regenerative braking function. The Raworth company's challenge to the Inspector's statement would have been that their system, where the driver did not have this option, was bound to be used every time. They may even have applied this argument during the promotional phase of regenerative equipment in earlier years.

Colonel Druitt's remarks about the unsuitability of Raworth equipment on down gradients could be questioned. A car with this equipment could coast down a hill under the control of the slipper brake by simply allowing the car to start by gravity on the falling gradient and leaving the controller in the "off" position. In this particular case, there would have been no loss to the Rawtenstall electrical system. The saving benefit from the regenerative equipment would have accrued to Accrington, the car being on their electrical system at the time of the accident.

In an Appendix to the report, by Mr A P Trotter, there are a number of references of interest and significance. His first sentence – "The termination of a shunt winding in a fine wire is a defect of construction" – would have given every purchaser of Raworth equipment an immediate claim against that company, even though trading by the company was, by that time, somewhat in the doldrums. Sensing liabilities which it might well not have been able to meet, may well have prompted the company's liquidation, if Trotter's remarks were intended to apply to all units. Was it a design defect or one of quality control? The question does not appear to have been explored.

Trotter's comments in relation to corrosion ("The wire is likely to corrode where it leaves the magnet, and may have sparked on breaking and may thus have shown signs of fusion") suggests that he thought that any chemical flux used when making a soldered connection between the coil termination and its winding wire may not have been thoroughly cleaned off after the joint had cooled. Evidence of similar corrosion can sometimes be seen today on copper pipework which has soldered joints in the form a green patina near the joint.

Rawtenstall would clearly have been involved in substantial cost in making good the damage resulting from the collision, and claims arising from injuries.

---

[144] Robert W Rush, *The Tramways of Accrington 1886-1932*, published by the Light Railway Transport League, London, 1961, at p 79.

206

APPENDIX E

Instructions to Conductors as to how to act when a car is out of control and the Motorman is in difficulties issued by the Tynemouth & District Electric Traction Company subsequent to the accident which occurred in Borough Road, Tynemouth, on 27 September 1919

How to know when the car wheels are skidding:
By the sliding motion of the car, or by the "sissing" noise of the wheels. When skidding is observed conductors must note as to whether the motorman is in difficulties or not.

Car out of control going down hill:
As soon as the conductor realises that the car is getting out of control going down hill, he will apply the track brake as tight as it will go. Under these circumstances, DON'T apply the hand wheel brake. DON'T knock the canopy switch off. DON'T pull the trolley off. When travelling in this direction it would be useless to apply sand at the rear platform.

Car running back down hill:
As soon as the car commences to run back, the conductor must apply the track brake as tight as it will go. He will then insert the sand pin and work it briskly so as to get a good flow of sand to the rail. Again, under these circumstances DON'T apply the hand wheel brake. DON'T knock the canopy switch off. DON'T pull the trolley off. Should the automatic switch blow out above the conductor's platform, he will replace it at the direction of the motorman. Should the motorman require the conductor to apply the hand wheel brake at the rear end he will give the three bells signal.

Should anything happen to the motorman causing him to be unable to operate the handles, and the car is in motion with the power on:
It is most important that the conductor should promptly observe if the car is travelling on a level road, or whether it is going up hill or down hill, and then to act according to the following instructions, whichever is the most applicable –

(1) Should the car be going up hill, the conductor will smartly proceed to the front platform and allow the power to remain on until the car reaches a point of safety on the level, then shut off the power, and apply the hand wheel brake.

(2) Should the car be going down hill or along a level road, and the conductor is on the upper deck at the time, he will smartly proceed to the front platform and first see that the power is off, and apply the track brake as tight as it will go, and then put on the hand wheel brake as well.

If the conductor is inside the car, or on the rear platform, he will apply the rear track brake as tight as it will go, and then put on the hand wheel brake as well.

APPENDIX F

Facsimile copies of Railway Inspectorate reports of significant tramway accidents in Dover, Rawtenstall and Mossley.

RAILWAY DEPARTMENT,

BOARD OF TRADE,

WHITEHALL,

LONDON, S.W.1.,

13th September 1917.

19/5/17

DOVER CORPORATION TRAMWAYS.

SIR,

I HAVE the honour to report for the information of the Board of Trade, in compliance with the instructions contained in your Minute of the 20th August, 1917, the result of my Inquiry into the circumstances attending the very serious accident which occurred on the Dover and River Light Railway at about 3.25 p.m. on the 19th August.

In this case Car No. 20 got out of control as it was descending Crabble Hill. The speed rapidly increased, and the car left the rails on a curve at the foot of the hill. In crossing the road to the right it overturned ; and, in falling, struck the front wall of Crabble Paper Mills premises. I regret to report that the conductress and 10 passengers were either killed or died subsequently from injury ; and that all the remaining passengers (59) suffered more or less seriously from injury or shock. The driver, A. J. Bissenden, jumped from the platform half way down the hill, and escaped unhurt.

The gauge of the Dover Corporation Tramways, of which this route is a section, is 3 feet 6 ins. Car No. 20 was a double-deck, single-truck car. It contained seating accommodation for 22 inside and 26 outside passengers. The principal dimensions were as follows :—

Length over all	...	...	...	...	27 feet 1 in.
Length over body	...	...	...	...	16 feet 3 ins.
Width over all	...	...	...	...	6 feet 0 in.
Wheel base	...	...	...	...	6 feet 0 in.

it was equipped with :—

    (a) Hand brake working cast-iron blocks on all four wheels by means of a handle, vertical spindle and chain.

    (b) Electric Rheostat brake.

    (c) Track brake, consisting of two oak-shod shoes, one between each pair of wheels, actuated by hand wheel from each platform.

The section of tramway concerned (Dover and River Light Railway No. 1) commences in London Road at the old Buckland terminus, and has a total length of 4 furlongs 2 chains. Double track is laid throughout. The first 3 furlongs are in London Road, and the remainder in Crabble Hill Road. In the northward direction the gradients along London Road rise continuously to the junction with Crabble Hill Road. The inclination near the summit is about 1 in 21·5 for a length of 200 yards. From the summit (X) the gradients fall as follows : —

200 ft.	...	...	...	average	1 in 24·5
90 „	...	...	...	„	1 „ 10·4
100 „	...	...	...	„	1 „ 11·5
180 „	...	...	...	„	1 „ 12·8
120 „	...	...	...	„	1 „ 33·0

There is a left-hand curve (radius 90 ft.) about 215 ft. from the point X, and a second left-hand curve (radius 180 ft.) about 560 ft. from X. The superelevation on these two curves is 1·03 and 0·9 ins. respectively. Crabble Hill Road is crossed by an arch carrying the South Eastern and Chatham Railway at a point 415 ft. from X.

The route was inspected in September, 1905, and opened to traffic shortly afterwards. There has been no previous case of a car getting out of control.

(13554—14.) Wt. 33—9526. 200. 10/17. D & S. G. 4.

The Board of Trade Regulations for traffic are as follows :—

(1) Speed is limited (*a*) to 12 miles an hour in London Road between Old Park Road and the junction with Crabble Hill ; (*b*) to 4 miles an hour from Crabble Hill Road at its junction with London Road to the Crabble Paper Mills.

(2) The track brake has to be applied to all cars before leaving the junction of Crabble Road and London Road on the downward or northward journey.

(3) All cars have to be brought to a standstill before reaching the junction of London Road and Crabble Road on the northward journey.

Driver A. J. Bissenden was formerly in the Army (Army Ordnance Department). He returned to England in February, 1917, after 15 months service in Egypt, suffering from nervous breakdown due to heat and overwork. He was discharged from the Army as unfit for further military service on the 1st June, 1917. He applied for employment on the Dover Tramways on the 21st July, 1917. The manager (Mr. Carden) judged he was likely to prove suitable for the position of motorman, and put him for instruction under driver Brett, who had over 10 years' service on the Dover Tramways. He was under tuition for nine days. During this time he was kept under observation, and, after examination by Electrician Bond he was finally put on the list as regular motorman on the 1st of August. Between the 1st and the 15th August inclusive he drove a car daily on the level portion of the tramway system between Buckland and the Pier. On the 16th August he drove a service car for the first time on the River section. Prior to the accident he had driven down Crabble Hill on service on 8 or 10 occasions.

On the 19th August he came on duty at 10.40 a.m. and drove on the Buckland-Pier route until 1.38 p.m. After dinner he relieved, at 2.40 p.m., another driver on Car No. 20 to work the River route service. He proceeded first to the Pier, and there turned to run to the River terminus at Minnis Lane. Before reaching Buckland, the conductress (Lottie Scrase) told him that the car was full, so as to avoid stopping at traffic points to pick up other passengers. Bissenden stopped the car at the foot of the hill near the Buckland tramway shed by using the hand brake, which was then working efficiently. He then proceeded up the incline in London Road, and, passing the summit, threw over his controller, and tried to stop the car at the compulsory stopping-place with the hand brake. The actual spot where the cars are accustomed to stop is about 100 ft. below the actual summit. He found the brake would not stop the car—the brake handle turning round as if something was wrong with the spindle and chain. He then tried to screw down the slipper brake, but the car was making speed so rapidly that the blocks would not hold. He then tried to apply the rheostatic brake, but could not get the small reversing handle to move into the right position. As he could do nothing more, he jumped off the front platform before the car reached the railway arch.

Other witnesses relate that a soldier (Trooper Gunner) and a gentleman (Naval Pensioner Miller) went on the front platform after the driver had jumped off it. It is not clear whether these men attempted to work the brakes or not. The impression given by the evidence of other passengers inside the car is that they appeared to be using their right hands. In any case, no retardation of speed was effected. A passenger on the top deck states that the jolt, when the car passed over the first curve, was so severe that a number of passengers who were standing on the top deck were nearly thrown off it. Passing under the railway arch the trolley pole left the conductor wire and swung loose. The conductress was on the top deck during the rush of the car down hill, and no one was observed to attempt to apply the hand or slipper brake from the rear platform.

About 140 feet below the railway arch, with speed further accelerated by the decline, the car entered the second curve and left the rails. There are clear marks on the setts of two wheels leaving the right-hand rail, but no corresponding marks of the left-hand wheels. The wheel marks cross the road diagonally to the right for a distance of about 39 ft., and then disappear. It is evident that on this short distance the car was overturning to the right, with the left-hand wheels in the air. In falling over, first the trolley pole or standard came into contact with the wall of the Crabble Paper Mill, and then the front portion of the top railing of the upper deck. The blow broke down the wall and, as the side of the car came down to road level, the momentum carried the car forward on its side, whilst the rear end swung round to the left, so that, finally, when the car came to rest, it lay on its right side at right angles to and across the roadway.

I examined the condition of the car after it had been moved to one side of the roadway. The two oak shoes of the track brake showed considerable signs of wear, but they were still in thoroughly serviceable condition. They were out of adjustment as the result of the accident, but could still be operated by the hand-wheel at each end of the car. The cast-iron wheel blocks were also adequate for service purposes. Those at the rear were tight on the wheels, with the chain taut. On the front wheels the blocks and chain were loose. It was still possible to work the hand lever operating the wheel blocks on both platforms. The controller contacts and fingers were in fair order, and there was no difficulty in moving either the controller or power handles in any of the proper directions. Generally speaking. all the brake equipment was in adequate working order, allowing for damage caused by the accident. There was also a supply of sand in the four boxes, and no evidence of choking in the sand pipes. The track is in good condition for speeds considerably in excess of that authorised.

Bissenden states that after the accident he found the front brake chain, which is wound round the spindle to bring the blocks to bear on the wheels, unhooked from the rod operating the levers. He claims that this disconnection was the cause of the failure of the hand brake to stop the car at the Board of Trade stopping-place. On the other hand, the brake was in working order, by his own account, when he stopped the car at Buckland tramway shed. Moreover he denies that it was his practice to allow any more slack on the brake chain than was sufficient to ease the blocks off the wheels. I do not, therefore, think it was possible for the chain to become unhooked, whilst the car was travelling a distance of about 700 yards from the tramway shed to the top of Crabble Hill. Possibly, after Bissenden jumped off the car, either Trooper Gunner or Mr. Miller, if they worked the hand brake handle, turned it in the wrong direction and thereby caused the chain to slacken considerably off the spindle and hang loose. If this was done, it is arguable that the dog was not in the rachet, and the hand brake not applied when Bissenden jumped off the car. In the evidence at the coroner's inquest, Driver Pay, whose attention after the accident was called by Bissenden to the condition of the front brake, states that the chain was slack and loose, but not unhooked.

The evidence given by driver Cook and mechanic Knott, who were the first to observe the position of and remove the controller handles, is to the effect that the small handle was in the "ahead," and the large in the "last power" (full parallel) position. I agree with these witnesses that no jolting or jarring during the overturning of the car is likely to have thrown both the handles into these positions, and they bear no marks of having been struck by any object.

Bissenden's own statement that he was unable to move the controller (small) handle into the emergency brake position confirms, in my opinion, the view that power was applied as the car came down the hill. The interlocking of the two handles makes it impossible to move the small handle unless the large (power) handle is in the "off" position. I proved for myself after the accident that there was no difficulty in moving the controller handle from "ahead" to "astern" or "emergency" with the power handle in the "off" position.

I come, therefore, to the conclusion that this lamentable accident was caused by driver Bissenden failing to cut off power as he approached the compulsory stopping-place on the summit of Crabble Hill, and by his further failure to utilise properly the sand and brake equipment. Power was not, I think, cut off until the trolley left the conductor at the railway bridge, when the speed attained by the car probably already exceeded 20 miles an hour. It is evident that Bissenden completely lost his head at the critical moment.

I have to draw attention to three important points in connection with this accident :—

(1) Nerve and experience are necessary qualifications for tramway drivers, especially when traffic has to be conducted over severe gradients and in crowded centres. Men discharged as unfit for military duties on account of nervous breakdown are unlikely to prove suitable, two months later, as drivers on difficult routes. At all events, medical opinion should be sought before a candidate of this description is accepted. I doubt whether Local or County Appeal Tribunals are aware of the difficulties which tramway managers nowadays encounter in finding suitable substitutes 'to fill the places of experienced drivers taken for military service, or attracted by higher-paid employment. Possibly also they do not recognise the risk that is incurred by the public when insufficiently trained men are employed.

At my request the Manager of the Dover Corporation Tramways has furnished me with information regarding the length of service, etc., of tramway drivers on the system. At the outbreak of war 24 men were employed. Of these, 16 had 5 or more years' service, and only 4 had less than 1 year's service. None of them were under 23 years of age. At the present moment the staff has been reduced to 18. Of these, five only have 5 or more years' service, nine have less than 2 months, two less than 4 months, one less than 8 months, and one under 15 months service. Six of those now employed are under

18 years of age. During the war 22 drivers have enlisted, or been claimed for military service, and 19 have left for better-paid employment. These figures speak for themselves. I do not think that the accident would have occurred had it been possible to maintain a staff of experienced drivers, such as was in existence in August, 1914. The fact must be faced, that the war has materially reduced safe working conditions on tramways. It is better policy to close a route of this description, if the number of experienced drivers is insufficient to work it, than to employ men who have not, as a general rule, a year's experience to their credit.

(2) A longer training (especially with regard to the use of the rheostatic brake) and experience than that possessed by driver Bissenden are necessary to qualify a driver to work traffic on such a section as the River route. It is evident that Bissenden's lack of familiarity with the rheostatic brake was a contributory cause of this accident. He had only used it once previously on service.

(3) Overcrowding, when a car gets out of control on a steep gradient, causes a serious list of casualties. If that can be avoided, the list in an accident of this sort is likely to be comparatively small. The liability to overturn on the narrow (3 ft. 6 in.) gauge is considerably greater than on the ordinary (4 ft. 8½ in.) gauge. The determining factors in overturning, outside the gauge, actual speed, curvature, superelevation, &c., are the height of the centre of gravity of the car and the nature of the load—*i.e.*, fixed or shifting. The more passengers on the top deck, the higher becomes the centre of the gravity. Standing passengers add to the shifting character of a load of human beings, and increase the instability.

From the casualty list, there appear to have been 68 passengers in the car—20 more than the seating accommodation. How many were on the upper deck is uncertain ; but there must have been, from passengers' accounts, 30 or more. It was, I think, this heavy load on the upper deck, which had already been jolted violently out of position when the car passed round the first curve, which eventually caused it to overturn when it left the rails at the lower curve with a further violent jolt in the same direction.

My recommendations in the case are :—

(*a*) That only motor drivers of considerable experience (say, 12 months) be permitted to work the traffic on Crabble Hill ;

(*b*) That the men be familiarised with the rheostatic break by being instructed to use it more frequently ;

(*c*) That either single-deck cars be used for traffic on Crabble Hill, or no passengers be permitted to travel on the Hill on the upper deck.

I have, &c.,

J. W. PRINGLE,

Colonel.

RAWTENSTALL CORPORATION TRAMWAYS.

RAILWAY DEPARTMENT,
BOARD OF TRADE,
8, Richmond Terrace,
Whitehall, London, S.W.,
22nd November, 1911.

SIR,

I HAVE the honour to report for the information of the Board of Trade, in compliance with your Order of the 13th November, the result of my inquiry into the circumstances under which a collision occurred between two cars belonging to the Rawtenstall Corporation, in Manchester Road, Accrington.

In this case as car No. 14 was coming down Manchester Road between Sunnyside loop just beyond Laund Road and the next crossing loop at Harcourt Road, it got out of control of the driver and, jumping the facing points of the latter loop, came into collision with car No. 11, which was waiting in the loop for car No. 14 to pass.

There were 16 passengers on No. 14 car and 29 on No. 11 car, and 20, including the conductor of No. 11 car, were injured.

The seating capacity of each car was 22 inside and 29 outside.

Car No. 14 was a four-wheeled double-decked car with a top deck cover, 6 ft. 6 in. wheelbase, weight when empty 11½ tons, including 22 cwt. for the top cover.

It was fitted with Raworth's Regenerative Control System, and had in addition a slipper brake on each side of the car applied by a hand wheel and wheel brakes applied in the ordinary way by a revolving handle.

Car No. 11 was similar in all respects.

The accident occurred at 11 p.m. on a frosty night, and the rails were in a very greasy condition.

Description.

The tramway line in the part of Manchester Road, Accrington, concerned in this case is a single one with passing places ; gauge, 4 ft.

Sunnyside loop, where the car No. 14 came last to a stand, is on a gradient of 1 in 20·3 falling for the direction in which the car was going, and the distance between the trailing points of this loop and the facing points of the next loop by Harcourt Road, near the Victoria Hotel, is 356 yards.

The falling gradients of this piece of track are as follows, viz. :—

1 in 23·2	for a distance of	15	yards.
1 in 20	,,	100	,,
1 in 17·3	,,	136	,,
1 in 24·3	,,	12	,,
1 in 29·2	,,	80	,,
1 in 45·2	,,	13	,,
Total	... ...	356	yards.

The loop at Harcourt Road, near the Victoria Hotel, is on the 1 in 45·2 gradient.
No. 11 car was waiting just inside the loop.
The radius of the points of the turn-out is 200 feet.

Conclusion.

The circumstances attending this collision were fully explained in the evidence of the motorman on car No. 14, F. Cuff, and of Mr. C. L. E. Stewart, the electrical engineer to the Rawtenstall Corporation and also tramway manager.

The car had been in service all day, and was taken over by driver Cuff at 1.10 p.m. and he drove it until the mishap, which occurred at about 11 p.m.

Cuff states that the car worked all right and he had taken it over the same route five times that day, and on the final trip everything went as usual until he stopped in what is known as the Sunnyside passing place. When he started he was on a falling gradient of about 1 in 20, and he states he fed up the controller handle normally until he reached the 13th notch when the motors would be in full parallel and the car should have gone at about 10 miles an hour. But just as he had cleared the loop points the car shot away at a high speed, and although he dropped sand all the time, and after first trying the electrical brake, and lastly the wheel brakes and slipper brakes, he was unable to regain control of the car, which after running 356 yards on a falling gradient varying from 1 in 17 to 1 in 29, reached the facing points of the next loop and owing to its high speed jumped them, with the result that the right hand corner of the car collided with the right hand corner of car No. 11 which was waiting in the loop for car No. 14 before proceeding up the hill.

Both cars were considerably damaged at the parts mentioned, and the top deck cover of No. 14 was torn off and fell in the roadway. Car No. 11 was derailed and driven back a short distance. Car No. 14 ran on some little distance beyond No. 11, crossing to the right hand side of the road and came to a stand against an electric light standard in the footpath.

As soon as car No. 14 began to exceed the normal speed inspector Slattery, of the Accrington Corporation Tramways, who was in the car, getting no response from the driver when he signalled to him, applied the mechanical slipper brake, but by the time he got it hard on the speed of the car was evidently too high for any braking effect to result.

Inspector Slattery also states that when he noticed the car was going too quickly he missed the usual humming sound made by the motors on these cars when regenerating.

The failure of the braking effect resulting from the motors of the car ceasing to regenerate current and transmit it back into the trolley wire is explained in the evidence of Mr. C. L. E. Stewart, the electrical engineer and tramways manager of the Rawtenstall Corporation, the cause being the fuzing of the shunt coil of No. 1 motor, that is the motor which would take the current from the trolley wire first.

The result of this fuzing of the shunt coil was stated by Mr. Stewart to be that the car instead of being driven steadily at a speed of about 10 miles an hour was driven forward by a powerful current, and as the gradient was a rather steep falling one, the car gained at once a very high speed.

Driver Cuff states he thought the car was skidding on the greasy rails, so at first tried to steady it by using sand only, and he says he tried this for quite half the time between the car shooting forward and the collision, before moving his controller handle back to the 6th notch and finally to the emergency or full brake notch. It was impossible for driver Cuff to even suspect what had really happened, and he is not to blame in any way for the mishap.

The car appears to have been regularly examined, and the fitter, A. Thompson, whose duty it is to inspect the motor equipment, states that he had examined the motor in question on the previous day, and that then there was no sign of fuzing in connection with the shunt coil.

It appears that even with the most careful examination of a car fitted with this system of control before being put into service, a similar failure might occur, and so to prevent a repetition of a runaway either cars so fitted should not be run on any but quite level routes, or else some further precautions must be taken to prevent the fuzing or breaking of the shunt coils.

I would suggest therefore that if the latter course be decided on the Rawtenstall Corporation be asked to send their proposals in the matter as soon as possible to the Board of Trade.

Personally, I do not consider cars fitted with regenerative control are so suitable as ordinary cars for steep gradients, as it is not possible to coast down a gradient with the former by means of the application of the slipper brake and wheel brakes, as the current cannot be cut off by the controller handle being brought into the off position, until all the electric braking effect has been brought into play, and the car thereby brought almost to a standstill.

It will be seen from the time sheet of driver Cuff's duties for the week, appended to this report, that he had worked very long hours on the day of the accident, though he had only worked 60 hours in the week ending that day, for which number of hours he is guaranteed payment.

It will be further observed from the explanation with the time sheet that the extra tours on the 11th were due to another man failing to take his proper turn of duty. But the short period of rest of only 6 hours between going off duty at 11.20 p.m. after 10 hours' duty and coming on duty again at 5.30 a.m. is quite insufficient, and steps should be taken to prevent a repetition of such hours.

I have, &c.,

E. DRUITT,
Lieut.-Colonel.

APPENDIX.

TIME SHEET.

Name.—Driver F. Cuff.   *Rank.*—Motorman.

Week ending Saturday, 11th November, 1911.

					On.	Off.		h.	m.			h.	m.
Sunday	...	...	...	... Off.									
					On.	Off.		h.	m.			h.	m.
Monday	...	...			5.30 a.m.	6.30 a.m.	=	1	0	}	=	11	5
					1.15 p.m.	11.20 p.m.	=	10	5				
Tuesday	...	...			5.30 a.m.	6.30 a.m.	=	1	0		=	1	0
Wednesday	...	...			5.30 a.m.	6.30 a.m.	=	1	0	}	=	11	5
					1.15 p.m.	11.20 p.m.	=	10	5				
Thursday	...	...			5.30 a.m.	6.30 a.m.	=	1	0	}	=	11	5
					1.15 p.m.	11.20 p.m.	=	10	5				
Friday	...	...			5.30 a.m.	6.30 a.m.	=	1	0	}	=	11	5
					1.15 p.m.	11.20 p.m.	=	10	5				
Saturday	...	...			5.30 a.m.	6.35 a.m.	=	1	5	}	=	14	55
					7.40 a.m.	10.45 a.m.	=	3	5				
					1.10 p.m.	11.55 p.m.	=	10	45				
												60	15

It is the rule for a shedman to run the early morning car shown on the above time sheet, but he left the service at a moment's notice, and driver Cuff was brought in until the Corporation could replace the shedman who had left their employ.

NOTE

BY THE ELECTRICAL ADVISER TO THE BOARD OF TRADE (MR. A. P. TROTTER).

The termination of a shunt winding in a fine wire is a defect of construction. Both at the inner and at the outer end of the fine wire a stout wire strong enough to stand handling and cleaning should be carefully jointed. This stout wire should be wound three or four times round the magnet before bringing out.

It is not likely that the shunt wire was fused, unless part of the shunt winding was short-circuited or unless very high voltage had been produced by regeneration. The wire is likely to corrode where it leaves the magnet, and may have sparked on breaking and may thus have shown signs of fusion.

A. P. T.

November 22nd, 1911.

STALYBRIDGE, HYDE, MOSSLEY AND DUKINFIELD TRAMWAYS.

Railway Department, Board of Trade,
8, Richmond Terrace, Whitehall, London, S.W.
12th January, 1912.

Sir,

I have the honour to report for the information of the Board of Trade, in compliance with the Order of the 20th October, the result of my Inquiry into the circumstances under which an accident occurred at about 5.30 a.m. on the 20th October in Stamford Road, Mossley, on the Stalybridge, Hyde, Mossley and Dukinfield Electric Tramways.

In this case, as a tramcar was descending Stamford Road, the driver lost control of it, and it ran away on a falling gradient for a distance of about half a mile ; by the time that it arrived at the bottom of the hill it had attained a very high rate of speed, and on reaching the commencement of a left-hand curve, which carries the tramlines by means of an overbridge over the London and North Western Railway, it ran off the rails to the outside of the curve and, breaking through a wall and gateway, ran on to the embankment, from which it fell over on to the railway, fouling both up and down lines.

It is believed that there were 14 passengers riding in the car at the time ; four of these were killed instantaneously, and the conductor of the car and one other passenger died shortly afterwards ; the driver and two passengers had to be taken to hospital, and six other passengers were severely injured, though not sufficiently to prevent their returning to their own homes. The driver was not in a fit condition to give evidence till eight weeks after the accident.

The car in its fall down the embankment turned completely over, and the truck was found lying across the rails with its wheels uppermost ; the whole of the body and upper portion of the car was reduced to matchwood, and the lower part was also considerably damaged. A train was approaching at the moment, but fortunately the signals were put to danger in time for it to be brought to a stand before reaching the scene of the accident.

The car was a four wheeled, single truck, single decked car ; its principal dimensions were as follows :—

Length over all ... 27 feet 6 inches.	Diameter of wheels... 2 feet 6 inches.
Width over all ... 6 „ 9 „	Seating capacity ... 30 passengers.
Fixed wheel base 5 „ 6 „	Weight unloaded ... 9 tons.

The car was fitted with a hand brake, working one cast-iron block on each of the four steel-tyred wheels, and with the Westinghouse magnetic brake which by one action applied a track brake on each rail and at the same time worked the brake blocks on the wheels. The application of the Westinghouse brake also acted similarly to the ordinary rheostatic brake, in causing retardation of the motors. The car was provided with two sanding arrangements at each end.

The controllers and the magnetic brake gear were supplied by the British Westinghouse Company, and the controllers were of the pattern which is known as No. 90.

Description.

Tramway No. 3, on which this accident occurred, commences from a dead-end at the south end of Stamford Street, and it runs as a double line along that street in a northerly direction for about 100 yards ; there is then a length of 39 yards of single line, leading up to the point at the northern end of Stamford Street where the line bifurcates, one single line running in a north-easterly direction along the Stockport Road to Haddens, and another single line running in an easterly direction along Stamford Road. The car to which this accident occurred had travelled from Haddens to Stamford Street, and it was after it had reversed and when it was running from Stamford Street down the Stamford Road that the driver lost control of it. It is not customary for cars which have to reverse in Stamford Street to make use of the double line at all ; they come to a stand on the single line portion at the north end of that street, and it is there that the driver and conductor change ends and the trolley is shifted to the other end of the car. The portion of Mossley in which Stamford Street is situated is usually known as Brookbottom.

Stamford Road, which thus commences at its northern end by a junction with Stamford Street, terminates by an overbridge carrying the road across the London and North Western Railway ; the distance between these two points is almost exactly half a

mile. The tramway line down Stamford Road is a single one, but there are two passing
loops, the first of which is situated 150 yards from Stamford Street, and the second
250 yards further on.   Starting from Stamford Street, Stamford Road runs in an easterly
direction for its first 150 yards ; it then inclines to the right by a curve of about 4 chains
radius, after which it runs almost straight in a southerly direction, and parallel to the
railway line, for about 650 yards, before reaching the overbridge ; at that point the road
makes a sharp turn to the left, crossing the railway line at right angles.

The car to which this accident occurred appears to have got out of the driver's control
almost immediately after leaving Stamford Street, and it left the rails at the commencement of the curve leading to the overbridge.

The gradient in Stamford Street from the dead-end to its junction with Stamford
Road is a falling one of 1 in 21·5. The gradients in Stamford Road, after leaving Stamford
Street, are all falling ones, and they are as follows :—

| 1 in 21·5 for a distance of 44 yards. | 1 in 18·1 for a distance of 396 yards. |
| 1 in 16·1   ,,   ,,   198 ,, | 1 in 15·8   ,,   ,,   242   ,, |

It was on the last-named gradient that the car was running when it left the rails.

Speed when running down Stamford Road is restricted to 6 miles an hour, and there
are two Board of Trade compulsory stopping places in it ; one of these is at the Town
Hall gates, situated 160 yards before reaching the bottom of the hill, and the other is at
the bottom of the hill at the commencement of the left-hand curve leading to the overbridge.   There are also in Stamford Road seven traffic stopping places, that is, points at
which cars stop by request, in order to pick up or set down passengers ; the first of these is
situated 90 yards from the junction with Stamford Street, and the second is at the
junction with Egerton Street, 115 yards further down the hill. The rails were in
fairly good order, and with the exception of their being in a somewhat slippery condition
there was nothing about them which contributed in any way to cause this accident.

There were marks on the rail at the commencement of the curve leading to the
overbridge, shewing clearly where the car had left the rails, and the curvature at that
point was of about 150 feet radius ; there were wheel marks at intervals on the pavement
between that point and the portion of the wall and gateway which were carried away by
the car.   The only other marks on the line which call for note were at the second of the
two loops or passing places described above.   Near what would have been the facing
point to a descending car, there were wheel marks, shewing that one pair of wheels had
left the rails when passing through the points, and had run for about 15 yards on the
roadway at a short distance to the right of the line ; there were then further wheel marks
on the rails, shewing that this pair of wheels had again rejoined the rails near the further
end of the loop.

Evidence.

There is a tramway depôt on the west side of Stamford Road, situated 190 yards
from its junction with Stamford Street, and car No. 24 had been stabled in this
shed during the night previous to the accident.   Driver Houchin and conductor Nield
took charge of this car about 5 a.m. on the 20th October, and they left the depôt with
it a few minutes later, in order to take it to Haddens, from which point it was due to
start for Stalybridge at 5.15 a.m. as a workmen's car.   There were no passengers
on the car during its journey to Haddens ; the car had, however, to be stopped twice
after leaving the depôt, once outside the depôt, and once at Brookbottom, where the
driver and conductor had to change ends ; it also ran through four loops at which the
speed had to be checked.   Houchin states that he used his hand brake on all these
occasions, and that it acted quite well.   Houchin states further that, when entering the
last loop at Haddens, he made use of the magnetic brake, in order to test it ; it acted well
and stopped the car, so Houchin started back thoroughly satisfied with the condition of
both his brakes.   It should be noted, however, that the gradient on which the magnetic
brake was tested was a falling one of only 1 in 108, so the test was by no means a
conclusive one.   There are in fact no severe gradients in the Stockport Road, the steepest
being 1 in 39.

The car started back from Haddens at 5.15 a.m., and on its way to Brookbottom it
was stopped on four occasions to pick up passengers ; on each of these occasions it was
brought to a stand by means of the hand brake, which is again stated to have acted well.
Houchin states that, when running through the last loop before reaching Brookbottom,
he applied the magnetic brake in order to again test it, and that it again worked
satisfactorily.   He brought the car to a stand on the single line at Brookbottom just
beyond the " George Hotel," which is the usual place at which the driver and conductor

change ends. Houchin states that, before leaving the end from which he had been driving, he applied the hand brake tightly, but without overstraining himself, and he is positive that he took both the controller and the reversing handles with him, leaving both the controller and the reverser in the off position. Passengers who were on the car during the journey from Haddens to Brookbottom state that the speed of the car was the same as usual, and it seems clear that the car was at that time well under control.

As soon as the car came to a stand at Brookbottom, Houchin walked through the car to the other end and fixed his two handles, placing the reversing handle in the forward position and the controller handle on the fourth braking notch. Meanwhile the conductor first shifted the movable points through which they had just run, setting them for the Stamford Road in lieu of the Stockport Road, and then shifted the trolley pole round to the rear end of the car. He then, whilst still standing on the ground, gave Houchin a whistle signal to start. In the first instance, it was only desired that the car should run forward a short distance and then be brought to a stand immediately past the points so that the conductor might shift the trolley on to the Stamford Road wire. Houchin states that, on receiving the conductor's signal, he applied one notch of power, that the car at once commenced to move forward, that he stopped the car by means of the hand brake as soon as it had moved forward about its own length, and he then at once applied the magnetic brake again at the fourth notch.

The car stopped on this second occasion only long enough for the conductor to shift the trolley, and Houchin then received a bell signal from the conductor to start again.

Houchin's account of what then occurred is as follows :—On receiving the bell signal from the conductor to start, he released his hand brake and the car at once started forward without power being applied at all ; the controller handle was at this time on the fourth brake notch, so he thought that after the car had moved forward a yard or so the magnetic brake would come into action ; when, however, the car had moved two or three yards he found that the brake was not acting, and from the noise made by the wheels, and from the speed at which the car started, he formed the conclusion that the wheels were skidding ; he at once applied sand, and moved the controller handle up and down amongst the various brake notches, but without any effect at any of them. The speed was meanwhile increasing, and by the time that the car reached the entrance to the depot it was so great that he thought the car would not get round the curve in safety. At this point he tried applying the hand brake, but its application seemed only to make the car go faster ; and he also at this time made signs to the conductor to see whether the hand brake was released at the rear end of the car. It is evident therefore that Houchin had at that time a doubt in his mind whether the hand brake had ever been released at that end. The car ran round the curve without leaving the rails, but whilst doing so the lights went out, showing that the trolley had left the wire. Houchin continued applying and releasing both brakes, but neither appeared to have any effect. On reaching the second loop he thinks that his car was derailed on running through it, but that it subsequently re-railed itself. At this time also he tried short circuiting his motors, but that also had no effect. From this second loop down to the bottom of the hill the line is perfectly straight for a distance of about 400 yards, and throughout this length Houchin continued applying and releasing his brakes and sanding the rails, but with no effect. The car consequently attained to a very high rate of speed by the time that it reached the bottom of the hill, and its derailment at the commencement of the curve was practically inevitable. Houchin remembers the car reaching the bottom of the hill, but after that he remembers nothing more. He is strongly of opinion that his wheels were skidding the whole way down the hill, though he admits that he bases that opinion mainly on the fact that the magnetic brake did not act.

The evidence of the passengers and of some eye-witnesses of the accident practically corroborates Houchin's evidence as to the speed of the car. According to their statements, the car started away quicker than usual ; on reaching Manchester House, situated about 50 yards from the end of Stamford Street, the car was going very fast, and the driver was seen to be working his brakes, without any result as regards checking the speed ; it was at this point that the passengers appear to have first become alarmed. At the traffic stopping place at Egerton Street the speed was very high, and the driver was heard shouting to people to keep clear of the line. When going round the first curve the car rocked considerably, and the lights in it went out. From this point all the way down the straight portion of the hill the speed of the car increased, and was never checked at all, though the driver was seen to be working at his hand brake wheel and at the sand pedal. The speed by the time the car reached the bottom of the hill is stated to have been equal to that of an express train, and under those circumstances its derailment was inevitable when it reached the commencement of the curve.

A 2

None of the passengers or eye-witnesses can give any evidence as to whether the wheels were skidding or not. The only evidence which the passengers can give as regards the action of conductor Nield is that at the time at which the car commenced running away he was seen to be attending to the trolley rope; subsequently he was seen to be trying to get inside the car for the purpose, it was thought, of obtaining some sand. It is clear that he was still on the car when the derailment took place, and he died from his injuries almost immediately after it.

Car No. 24, to which this accident occurred, was purchased by the Stalybridge Joint Board in 1904; in August, 1911, it underwent a thorough overhaul, and as far as its brake equipment was concerned it was made into a brand new car, though it was not fitted with new controllers; it was then taken into use again, and had been regularly at work up to the 20th October. On September 21st it had been fitted with new brake blocks, and these were on the car at the time of this accident. On the previous day, viz., the 19th October, the car had been at work under the charge of three different drivers, viz., driver Sherratt from 4.47 a.m. till 2 p.m., driver Cowan from 2 p.m. till 11.15 p.m., and driver Charnley from 11.15 p.m. till 11.45 p.m. Sherratt took the car about six times down the Stamford Road, and had no difficulty whatever in controlling it; Cowan did not take the car down Stamford Road at all, but he took it nine times down the Ditchcroft Hill, which is a severer gradient, and he too had no difficulty in keeping it under control; Charnley took it once down the Ditchcroft Hill with the same result. These three men all assert that both brakes were in good working order, and when Charnley handed in the car at the depôt at 11.45 p.m. he signed the Car Equipment Report Book without entering any defect in it. Charnley states that he was quite satisfied that at that time there were no defects in the brakes of the car. It should further be added that during the three weeks previous to this accident there had been practically no complaints regarding this car recorded in the Car Equipment Report Book.

Foreman Parry, who is employed as night-foreman at the Mossley Car Shed, examined the car at about 3.0 a.m. on the 20th October; he states that he found everything in good order, but that he adjusted the whole set of brake blocks slightly; he could not, however, make any practical trial of either of the brakes. As far however as he is aware, the car was in good order when it left the shed, and when driver Houchin took it out he made no representations to him about it. Everything points, therefore, to the car having been in good order when it left the shed at 5.0 a.m., and no defect was detected in it during the run to Haddens and back to Stamford Street, a distance of over one-and-a-half miles. There appears also to have been an ample supply of sand on the car.

Driver Houchin joined the Board's service in January 1908, previous to which he had been employed for about 14 years with the St. Helens Tramway Co., who had given him the character of being sober, industrious, and attentive. Houchin was passed as a "hilly route" driver on the 29th March 1908; he had been driving regularly on those routes ever since, and there has been no previous instance of his letting a car get out of his control. He was thoroughly acquainted with Stamford Road, having been working cars on it three or four days a week for three and a half years. He certainly appears to have been a thoroughly efficient driver.

Conductor Nield had been in the Board's service since August 1904, and had been employed as a conductor ever since. The Board gives him a very good character, and states that he was a very efficient conductor. Both these men appear therefore to have been thoroughly qualified to carry out their duties.

The car was examined after the accident, but, owing to its wrecked condition, there were several important details on which it was not possible to obtain any reliable information. The wheels, however, were not much injured, and, though these have been examined most critically, not the slightest trace of flats can be found on them. From this therefore it would appear that the wheels were revolving whilst the car was running down the hill. Both the hand brake and the magnetic brake fittings were too much damaged for any practical test to be made of their condition. The hand brake blocks were partly worn, but were still in thoroughly serviceable order; at one end of the car the blocks were in their proper places fitting lightly against the wheels, but at the other end they were entirely out of position, owing to the brake beam being considerably bent. The surfaces of the slipper shoes appeared bright looking as if they had been in contact with the rails when running down the hill, and the springs supporting them were in good condition. The leads connecting the magnets to the motors and to earth were intact, and these were tested and found correct. The controllers had, however, suffered considerable damage; they were found to have been torn away from their platforms and to be hanging by their leads: the arc shields and covers had been wrenched off them, and the fingers, which had thereby become exposed, were broken and bent; the motor barrels shewed signs of having experienced very rough treatment. Under these circumstances no reliable test could be made as regards the condition of the controllers and their connections.

Conclusion.

There is no doubt that this accident was due to the fact that driver Houchin lost control of his car immediately after starting down the hill and that he never gained control over it again. This loss of control may have been due either to mismanagement on the part of driver Houchin or to some defect in the controlling mechanism of the car, and on both these points the evidence available is unfortunately very limited.

As regards Houchin's manipulation of his power and brakes when starting down the hill : the conductor is dead, and the passengers cannot speak definitely on the matter, so the only direct evidence available is that of Houchin himself. According to his own evidence, Houchin carried out the instructions for starting a car from rest down an incline quite correctly ; it must be remembered, however, that Houchin had been unconscious for five days after the accident, and that on account of his injuries his evidence could not be taken until eight weeks subsequent to it. Under these conditions it is very unlikely that Houchin can remember accurately all the details of his action ; without therefore in any way questioning his good faith, I do not think that his evidence can be regarded as absolutely reliable, and it must, I consider, be recognized that his loss of control may possibly have been due to some mismanagement or error of judgment on his part.

As regards the action of the magnetic brake, though it is doubtful whether this brake had been effectively tested on the morning of the 20th, it had certainly been in good working order up till 11.0 p.m. on the previous day. After the accident the leads and connections were tested as far as was practicable, and all that was tested was found correct. But the brake gear and the controllers were far too much damaged for any practical test to be made of them. The fact of there being no trace of any flats on the wheels proves almost conclusively that they were revolving whilst the car was running away ; under these circumstances the motors must also have been revolving, and current should have been generated thereby which would have brought both the magnetic brake and the rheostatic brake into action. If Houchin's evidence is correct both these brakes absolutely failed to act, and the question arises whether from any cause the motors, though revolving, were not generating current. The accident which occurred at Bournemouth in 1908 was in many respects very similar to this one, and in both cases the controllers were practically of a similar type. After the accident at Bournemouth an examination of the controllers revealed the fact that owing to the reversing barrel of the controller at the conductor's end of the car having been in the wrong position, the armatures of the motors were short circuited when the car was being driven from the other end ; consequently no current was generated by the revolution of the motors and neither brake was actuated. From the description given above of the condition in which the controllers of the car at Mossley were found, it can be readily understood that it was impossible, after the accident, to ascertain whether there was any similar defect in them or not. But there is no doubt that a similar defect may have existed in this case also, and if so, it would entirely account for the brakes not coming into action. A defect in the controller must therefore, in my opinion, be regarded as a very possible cause of this accident.

As regards the hand brake, this had been well tested when running to Haddens and back, and the fact of its release causing the car to start forward down Stamford Road shews also that until its release it had been holding the car ; there appears no doubt therefore that that brake was at that time acting effectively. Houchin states however that it was just before reaching the points of the loop opposite the depôt that he first tried applying his hand brake, and that its only effect appeared to be to make the car go faster. The points of this loop were distant just 150 yards from where the car started, and for nearly the whole of this length the gradient was a falling one of 1 in 16.1 ; by the time therefore that the car reached the points, it would have undoubtedly acquired a very high rate of speed, and the evidence of the driver and the passengers shews conclusively that that was the case. Under those conditions the hand brake would be incapable of stopping the forward motion of the car ; all it could do would be to stop the revolution of the wheels and cause them to skid, and it was doubtless this skidding which made Houchin think that the speed of the car was increased. Houchin states that during the rest of the journey down the hill he kept on applying the hand brake and taking it off again ; this will account for there being no flats on the wheels, as it was only for a short distance each time that the wheels were skidding. There is therefore no reason for thinking that there was any defect in the hand brake, and had Houchin made use of it before the car gained such a high rate of speed, he would probably have regained control over it.

The suggestion has been made that at the time that the car commenced the descent the hand brake had not been released by the conductor at the rear end of the car. No one actually saw conductor Nield release the brake, though that is by no means conclusive evidence that he did not do so ; but at one time whilst the car was running away, driver Houchin clearly had a suspicion that the hand brakes might be still applied from the rear end. In this connection it should be pointed out that, on arrival at Brookbottom from Haddens, Houchin stopped the car on a gradient of 1 in 21, and before changing ends he applied the hand brake "tight," though, as he says, "without overstraining himself." This brake clearly held the car securely on that gradient. When the conductor gave Houchin the first signal by whistle to start he (the conductor), was still standing on the ground, and I think that it is not only possible, but probable, that at that time he had not gone to the rear end of the car and had not released the hand brake. Houchin, however, on this occasion applied power to start the car ; it moved forward accordingly, and Houchin was able to stop it by tightening up the hand brake from his end. But on the second occasion on which the conductor gave the signal to start, the signal was given by bell, so it is almost certain that by that time the conductor had mounted the rear platform. On this occasion Houchin did not apply power to start the car, but he merely released the hand brake, and that caused the car to start off forthwith. The gradient on which the car was then standing was practically the same as on the first occasion, so, if the brakes had been still applied from the rear end they would still have held the car and would not have allowed it to move forward when they were released from the front end. For this reason therefore I do not consider it likely that the hand brakes were still applied at the rear end of the car when it finally started down the incline, and it is probable that the conductor released them at the same time that he gave the second signal to start from the rear platform.

It is very unfortunate that in the case of such a serious accident there should be so little evidence available on which to form an opinion as to the cause of it. The Staly-bridge Joint Board has afforded me all possible assistance in holding this inquiry, but the circumstances do not allow of any additional evidence being produced. The driver clearly lost control over the car, and, as previously stated, this may have been due either to mismanagement on his part, or to some defect in the mechanism of the car. A defect in the controller, which cannot now be detected, is in my opinion the most probable cause of the accident, as it accounts for what occurred more fully than any other explanation, but it cannot be conclusively proved that such a defect did exist.

The Stalybridge Joint Board inform me that with the view of preventing a recurrence of this accident, they are arranging to fit all the cars which are used on their hilly routes with the Huddersfield form of Mechanical Slipper brake ; the action of this brake is entirely independent of the rotation of the wheels of the car, and it can be applied before a car commences to descend a steep gradient. They are also arranging to close the Mossley Car Shed and to stable all their cars at night at Stalybridge, which will ensure that drivers will always obtain some suitable inclines on which to test their brakes before reaching any severe gradients. Both these alterations should, I consider, tend to safety.

Two other points in my opinion call for notice :—

(1) It appears to me that Tramway Authorities do not always sufficiently recognise the possibility of the existence of a defect or a faulty connection in the interior of a controller ; such defects do undoubtedly at times exist, and very careful examination and supervision of controllers by skilled mechanics is therefore called for.

(2) The officials of the Stalybridge Joint Board inform me that it is not customary on their lines to use the magnetic brake for ordinary stops, but to reserve it for emergency stops and for descending steep gradients. It has been previously pointed out in Board of Trade reports that under these circumstances there will always be a risk that drivers, owing to want of practice, will apply this brake wrongly, or that some defect in it will not be detected until its use is urgently needed. Drivers should, I consider, be instructed to habitually use their most powerful brake, and not to treat it as one to be only used on an emergency.

I have, &c.,

P. G. von DONOP,
Lt.-Col. R.E.

APPENDIX G

Miscellaneous photographs of tramway accidents not the subject of Railway Inspectorate reports appearing in the text.

Chatham & District Light Railways: 15 July 1908. A runaway car at Brompton, which derailed and crashed into the dockyard wall. *Courtesy: Alan Brotchie*

Dewsbury & Ossett Tramways: 12 October 1915. Car no. 3 embedded in the wall of a boot shop in Dewsbury Market Place after a runaway. Shortly after this view the boot shop and the Scarboro Hotel above it collapsed on to the tram. *Courtesy: F. Hartley*

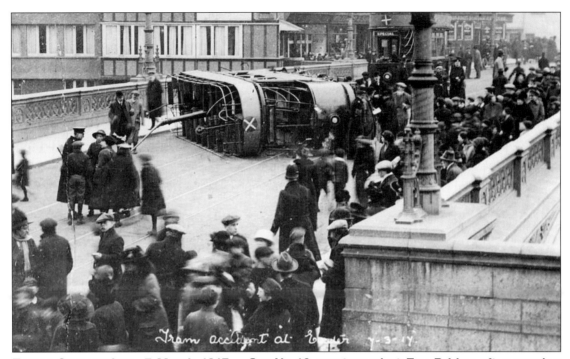

Exeter Corporation: 7 March 1917. Car No.12 overturned at Exe Bridge after running away down Fore Street hill. *Courtesy: Alan Brotchie*

Huddersfield Corporation: 22 April 1905. A view of car no. 24 in a garden after it had overshot the terminus at Bradley.

Huddersfield Corporation: 6 June 1905. Car no. 67 shown in a field after leaving the rails in Holly Bank Road, Lindley, following a runaway. *Courtesy: J E Thorpe*

Huddersfield Corporation Tramways: 3 March 1906. Car no. 26 on the left after its derailment in Newsome Road following a runaway. The accompanying car no. 35 was not involved in the accident.

Isle of Thanet Tramways: 26 May 1905.   Car no. 47 in a runaway down the hill to the Plains of Waterloo, Ramsgate, ending up in a grocer's shop.   *Courtesy: J H Price*

Leamington and Warwick Tramways: 3 January 1916.   Car no. 7 damaged beyond repair after crashing into the Castle Arms Hotel, Warwick.   *Courtesy: Alan Brotchie*

Luton Tramways: 28 December 1916. Problems with a derailment on the system at that time operated by Balfour, Beatty & Co. *Courtesy: Alan Brotchie*

ADAM GORDON BOOKS

TRANSPORT BOOKS

The Life of Isambard Kingdom Brunel
by his son, reprint of the 1870 edition, s/b, 604pp, £20

The Cable System of Tramway Traction
reprint of 1896 publication, 56pp, s/b, £10

The Definitive Guide to Trams (including Funiculars) in the British Isles
3rd edition; D. Voice, s/b, A5, 248pp, £20

Double-Deck Trams of the World, Beyond the British Isles
B. Patton, A4 s/b, 180pp, £18

Double-Deck Trolleybuses of the World, Beyond the British Isles
B. Patton, A4, s/b, 96pp, £16

The Douglas Horse Tramway
K. Pearson, softback, 96 pp, £14.50

Edinburgh Street Tramways Co Rules & Regulations
reprint of 1883 publication, s/b, 56 pp, £8

Edinburgh's Transport, vol. 2
1919-1975, D. Hunter, 192pp, s/b, £20

The Feltham Car of the Metropolitan Electric and London United Tramways
reprint of 1931 publication, s/b, 18pp, £5

Glasgow Subway Album
G. Watson, A4 s/b, all colour, 64pp, £10

How to Go Tram and Tramway Modelling
third edition, D. Voice, B4, 152pp, completely rewritten, s/b, £20

London County Council Tramways, map and guide to car services, February 1915,
reprint, c.12" x 17", folding into 12 sections, £8

Metropolitan Electric, London United and South Metropolitan Electric Tramways
routes map and guide, summer 1925, reprint, c.14" x 17", folding into 15 sections, £8

Modern Tramway, reprint of volumes 1 & 2, 1938-1939
c.A4 cloth hardback, £38

My 50 Years in Transport
A.G. Grundy, 54 pp, s/b, 1997, £10

Next Stop Seaton! – Golden Jubilee history of Modern Electric Tramways Ltd.
David Jay & David Voice, B5 softback, 136pp, covers coloured on both sides, £17

Omnibuses & Cabs, Their Origin and History
H.C. Moore, h/b reprint with d/w, 282pp, £25

The Overhaul of Tramcars
reprint of LT publication of 1935, 26pp, s/b, £6

Source Book of Literature relating to Tramways in East Anglia
A5 s/b, 28pp, £4

Source Book of Literature relating to Tramways in the East Midlands
A5 s/b, 36pp, £4

Source Book of Literature relating to Tramways in Merseyside & Cheshire
A5 s/b, 36pp, £4

Source Book of Literature relating to Tramways in the North East of England
A5 s/b, 28pp, £4

Source Book of Literature relating to Tramways in N. Lancashire & Cumbria
A5 s/b, 39pp, £4

Source Book of Literature relating to Tramways in Scotland
A5 s/b, 48pp, £5

Source Book of Literature relating to Tramways in South Central England
A5 s/b, 26pp, £4

Source Book of Literature relating to Tramways in South-West England
A5 s/b, 36pp, £4

Source Book of Literature relating to Welsh Tramways
A5 s/b, 28pp, £4

Source Book of Literature relating to Yorkshire Tramways
A5 s/b, 52pp, £5.50

The History of the Steam Tram
H. Whitcombe, h/b, over 60pp, £12

The History and Development of Steam Locomotion on Common Roads
W. Fletcher, reprint of 1891 edition, 332pp, £18

A History of the British Steam Tram
volume 1, David Gladwin, case bound, coloured covers, 176pp, 312 x 237mm, profusely illustrated, £40

Volume 2 of **A History of the British Steam Tram**
D. Gladwin, hardback, 256pp, £40

Street Railways, their construction, operation and maintenance
by C.B. Fairchild, reprint of 1892 publication, 496pp, hardback, profusely illustrated, £40

Toy and Model Trams of the World – Volume 1: Toys, die casts and souvenirs
Gottfried Kuře and David Voice, A4 s/b, all colour, 128pp, £25

Toy and Model Trams of the World – Volume 2: Plastic, white metal and brass models and kits
Gottfried Kuře and David Voice, A4 s/b all colour, 188pp, £30

George Francis Train's Banquet
report of 1860 on the opening of the Birkenhead tramway, reprint, s/b, 118pp, £10

My Life in Many States and in Foreign Lands
G.F. Train, reprint of his autobiography, over 350pp, s/b, £12

Trams, Trolleybuses and Buses and the Law before De-regulation
M. Yelton, B4, s/b, 108pp, £15

Tramway Review, reprint of issues 1-16, 1950-1954
A5 cloth hardback, £23

Tramways – Their Construction & Working
D. Kinnear Clark, reprint of the 1894 edition, softback, 812pp. £28

Tramways and Electric Railways in the Nineteenth Century
reprint of Electric Railway Number of Cassier's Magazine, 1899, cloth h/b, over 250pp, £23

Life of Richard Trevithick, two volumes in one, reprint of 1872 edition
softback, 830pp, £25

The Twilight Years of the trams in Aberdeen & Dundee
all colour, A4 s/b, introduction and captions by A.Brotchie, 120pp, £25

The Twilight Years of the Edinburgh Tram
> 112pp, A4 s/b, includes 152 coloured pics, £25

The Twilight Years of the Glasgow Tram
> over 250 coloured views, A4, s/b, 144 pp, £25

The Wantage Tramway
> S.H. Pearce Higgins, with Introduction by John Betjeman, h/b reprint with d/w, over 158pp, £28

The Wearing of the Green
> being reminiscences of the Glasgow trams, W. Tollan, s/b, 96pp, £12

NON-TRANSPORT PUBLICATIONS

From Death Into Life
> W. Haslam, 250pp, s/b, £8. Autobiography of a clergyman converted by, or at least during, his own sermon!

The Chateau Story
> Elizabeth Varley, 64pp, s/b, £10. An animal "fairy-tale" set in France in the reign of a King Louis, described as "a children's story for grown-ups, or a grown-up's story for children" – so ideal for any age!

TERMS

RETAIL UK – for post and packing please add 10% of the value of the order up to £4.90 maximum, apart from the Brunel biography and Street Railways, which because of their weight, please add £3, and £5 respectively. Orders £50 and over post and packing free. I regret that I am not yet equipped to deal with credit/debit cards.

RETAIL OVERSEAS – postage will be charged at printed paper rate via surface mail, unless otherwise requested. Payment please by sterling cash or cheque, UK sterling postage stamps, or direct bank-to-bank by arrangement.

SOCIETIES, CHARITIES, etc. relating to tramways, buses and railways – a special 50% discount for any quantity of purchases is given **provided my postal charges are paid**.

WHOLESALE (TRADE) DISCOUNTS FOR MULTIPLE COPIES OF THE SAME TITLE, UK post free:

1-15 copies – 35%; 16-30 copies – 40%; 31-45 copies – 45%; 46 & over – 50%

Apart from being a publisher of tramway titles I buy and sell second-hand literature. I issue lists 4 times a year which contain a variety of books, periodicals, timetables, postcards, tickets and "special/unusual material"; postage is charged at cost and there is no charge for packing. Please send a stamped addressed envelope for the latest list, or if resident abroad, an international reply coupon or UK postage stamps.

I also provide an approval service of black and white plain backed postcards of trams, as well as commercials, and hold a stock of over 25,000. Prices of most of the plain backed ones vary between .50p & £2, and my only requirements are that customers pay my outward postage and return unwanted cards within a reasonable time (otherwise I don't know if they have got lost in the post!).

Bus tickets are also sent out on approval, and I have large quantities priced from .05p to £1. Some tram tickets are also available but at higher prices.

ADAM GORDON

Kintradwell Farmhouse, Brora, Sutherland, KW9 6LU

Tel: 01408 622660

Email: adam@adamgordon.freewire.co.uk

228